ADVERSITY AND GRACE

ESSAYS IN DIVINITY

JERALD C. BRAUER, GENERAL EDITOR

Vol. I: The History of Religions
Vol. II: The Impact of the Church upon Its Culture
Vol. III: The Dialogue between Theology and Psychology
Vol. IV: Adversity and Grace

Adversity and Grace

Studies in Recent American Literature

BY PRESTON M. BROWNING, JR., GILES B. GUNN

DAVID HESLA, JOHN W. HUNT, MAYNARD KAUFMAN

JAMES T. LIVINGSTON, HENRY RAGO

NATHAN A. SCOTT, JR., GUNNAR URANG

Edited by NATHAN A. SCOTT, JR.

THE UNIVERSITY OF CHICAGO PRESS
CHICAGO AND LONDON

Standard Book Number: 226-74283-0

Library of Congress Catalog Card Number: 68-16717

THE UNIVERSITY OF CHICAGO PRESS
CHICAGO 60637

The University of Chicago Press, Ltd., London

© 1968 by The University of Chicago
All rights reserved. Published 1968

Second Impression 1969

Printed in the United States of America

General Editor's Preface

The present volume is the fourth in a series of eight books being published under the general title "Essays in Divinity." This does not appear, at first glance, as a particularly auspicious moment for such a formidable enterprise. At the very moment the so-called radical theologians announce that "God is dead," an eight-volume series investigating various dimensions of the study of religion or of theology is published. Is this not an ill-timed venture?

In point of fact, however, in America the discipline of theology was never in a healthier state. To be sure, there are no giants such as Tillich or Niebuhr on the scene, but there are many new and exciting factors in the picture. The very presence of the "God is dead" movement is evidence of a new vitality and ferment among the younger theologians. In no sense does such a movement herald the end of systematic theology or the impossibility of using God-language. It is but one of many significant attempts being made now at basic reconstruction and reinterpretation of Christian theology.

One primary fact marks this new age — the pre-eminence of dialogue in all aspects of divinity. Basic conversation between Roman Catholicism, Protestantism, and Judaism is just beginning, and its full effect on theological construction lies ahead. At the time systematic theology entered the preliminary phase of dialogue, Paul Tillich's last lecture pointed to the future of this discipline in relation to the world's religions. Dialogue is not to be understood as the "in" movement in religion today; it is to be viewed as providing a new base that will profoundly affect not only the systematic study of doc-

trines and beliefs but every dimension of religious studies.

Another mark of the vitality of religious studies today is their dialogic relationship to other disciplines. Studies in divinity have never been carried on in complete isolation from other areas of human knowledge, but in some periods the relationship has been more fully explored than in others. The contemporary scene is marked by the increasing tempo of creative interchange and mutual stimulation between divinity and other disciplines. Several new theological disciplines have emerged recently to demonstrate this fact. The interplay between theology and literature, between theology and the psychological sciences, and between theology and the social sciences promises to reshape the traditional study of religion, as our major theological faculties are beginning rapidly to realize.

The emergence and increasing role of the History of Religions is a case in point. Until recently it has been a stepchild in the theological curriculum. Today it is developing a methodology that probably will prove influential in all areas of theological study. History of Religions also appears to be the way that most state universities will introduce the serious and disciplined study of religion into strictly secular curriculums.

These are but a few of the factors that demonstrate the present vitality of the study of religion today. It makes both possible and necessary a series of books such as this. The particular occasion for the publication of "Essays in Divinity" is supplied by the one hundredth anniversary of the Divinity School of The University of Chicago and by the University's seventy-fifth anniversary.

The editor of this series proposed that this event be celebrated by the Divinity School faculty and alumni by holding seven conferences, each of which was focused on the work of one of the seven academic fields of the School. Out of these conferences have come eight volumes which will, it is hoped, mark the progress in the various disciplines of theological study and point to the ongoing tradition of scholarship in the University's Divinity School.

Though something may have been lost in thus limiting the

roster of contributors to these books, this very limitation may have the effect of marking the distinctive genius of one theological center long noted for its production of scholar-teachers in American theology. Also, it will enable an observer to determine the extent to which several generations have been shaped by, and have shaped, a particular institution. It will be possible to note the variations of approach and concern that mark respective generations of that institution. Furthermore, it will help to assess the particular genius, if any, that a given institution possesses. It will demonstrate to what extent its graduates and professors are in the midst of contemporary theological scholarship. It is to be hoped that the series will provide both a bench mark for today's scholarly discussions and research in religion and a record from which future generations can assess the contributions of an institution at the turn of its first century.

None of these volumes pretends to be definitive in its area; it is hoped, however, that each will make a useful contribution to its area of specialization and that the entire series will suggestively illuminate the basic tendencies of religious scholarship at the present moment. The intent has been to devote each volume to a particular issue or area of inquiry that is of special significance for scholarly religious research today, and thus to keep each volume from being simply a disconnected series of essays. It is hoped that these books will be found to have, each in its own terms, a genuine unity and that the reader will note a cumulative effect, as he moves from essay to essay in each volume.

This volume is probably the most unusual in the entire series of eight. Occasionally, professors have offered individual courses in the area of correlating theology and literature, but until the Divinity School of the University of Chicago formed an independent field for that discipline, it was at best an avocation of certain systematic theologians in only a few schools. Theology and Literature represents the dialogue between Christian faith and culture in a special and almost unique way. On the one hand, the interrelation between the two disciplines appears obvious. On the other hand, that interrelationship is precisely not what theologians usually have made of it. Because the dialogue is not along the lines traditionally understood by Christian piety, this field of theological analysis provides a convincing demonstration of the possibility for a new kind of understanding and mutual enrichment between religion and culture. In the brief time the discipline has had an independent existence, it has produced a group of competent young scholars who are living proof of the necessity of this discipline for the continuing creativity and relevance of divinity studies today.

JERALD C. BRAUER, *General Editor*

CONTENTS

NATHAN A. SCOTT, JR.   1
Introduction: *Theology and the Literary*
Imagination

NATHAN A. SCOTT, JR.   27
1. Sola Gratia — *The Principle of Bellow's Fiction*

GILES B. GUNN   59
2. *Bernard Malamud and the High Cost of Living*

JOHN W. HUNT   87
3. *Comic Escape and Anti-Vision: The Novels of*
Joseph Heller and Thomas Pynchon

JAMES T. LIVINGSTON   113
4. *J. D. Salinger: The Artist's Struggle to Stand on*
Holy Ground

PRESTON M. BROWNING, JR.   133
5. *Flannery O'Connor and the Grotesque Recovery*
of the Holy

MAYNARD KAUFMAN   163
6. *J. F. Powers and Secularity*

GUNNAR URANG   183
7. *The Voices of Tragedy in the Novels of William*
Styron

DAVID HESLA   211
8. *The Two Roles of Norman Mailer*

HENRY RAGO   239
9. *Epilogue: Faith and the Literary Imagination — The*
Vocation of Poetry

ix

CONTENTS

Biographical Notes   261

Acknowledgments   263

Index   267

Introduction: *Theology and the Literary Imagination*
NATHAN A. SCOTT, JR.

The essays here collected constitute one of a series of books
being published under the auspices of the Divinity School of
the University of Chicago, whose observances of the University's seventy-fifth anniversary took the form of a number
of conferences arranged by the Divinity faculty's various
Fields. This series is a consequence of these colloquia, the
present volume having been prepared by those attached —
either as faculty or former doctoral students — to the Divinity
School's Theology and Literature Field.

It will doubtless seem a little odd to some that a university
faculty of theology should provide in its curriculum for the
systematic study of imaginative literature. A visitor from
another academic department entering a hall of divinity
might naturally expect to find scholars at work on the canoni-
cal texts of the Church, on the many complicated strands of
the history of the Church, and on the rich and various tradition of its theological formulations. Indeed, this visitor might
also expect a divinity faculty whose orientation is basically
Christian to give large place to the phenomenology of the
religious impulse in its various great expressions outside the
world of Christendom. Yet he may be entitled to a certain
astonishment, when he finds not only these and related enter-
prises under way but finds also theologians seriously studying
drama and fiction and poetry — and not merely, or even principally, in those special phases where formally Christian
motifs are explicitly present. And this visitor, if he brings
some antecedent skepticism about the validity of any en-
franchisement at all for theological pursuits in the university,
may even suspect that, in a theological faculty, a department
of study in which a Rimbaud or a Brecht or a Faulkner is at

the fore does itself simply attest to a basic insecurity infecting the total enterprise of theology in our time.

In 1961 Professor Ernest Sirluck of the University of Toronto (then, of the University of Chicago), in a review published in *Modern Philology*, turned his splendid gift for polemic on the not invulnerable target presented by a book that had appeared in the previous year, on Milton and Bunyan — "and," as its title stated, "the Great Theologians." Though written by a professional scholar, it is a book without any real urbanity of scholarship or grace of style, and Professor Sirluck could therefore, and did, swiftly expose its shortcomings (most especially in the simplistic account given of Milton's religious position). But, despite what he found to be stale and bland and gauche in this essay, the book struck him as having a certain lively interest, since it stood for him as an expression of "the New Apologetic" — whereby the contemporary Christian apologist (for what Professor Sirluck's tone leads one to feel is in his view an essentially bankrupt tradition) attempts to shore up a crumbling edifice by attaching it to prestigious cultural forms — whose "attitudes, insights, presuppositions, and principles [he analyzes] and relates . . . to, corrects . . . by, and reinforces . . . with religion. . . . From the human work, thus enhanced, he then deduces validation for the religion, or some aspect of the religion, he teaches." Thus, says Professor Sirluck, the New Apologetic proceeds — "aided by the multiplication of eleemosynary foundations for the support of religion in higher education, religion in art, religion in literature, etc., and by the consequent proliferation of university and seminary programs and courses built upon this interest . . ."

Now it is such a response as this that can most assuredly be expected from certain quarters, when the actuality of the curriculum in the major centers of American theological education is discovered to be the complex interdisciplinary undertaking that it has come to be. For what the visitor from some other department of the academic community will find there is not only a vigorous enterprise of research and teaching in the traditional areas of biblical study and theology and church history but also a lively enterprise of research into the various modes of mutual involvement between Christian tradition and the general culture. He will find, for example, strict attention being paid to traditional and modern philosophy, and he will discover that, on the contemporary scene, a Wittgenstein or a Merleau-Ponty is studied as rigorously as a Barth or a Rahner. It will be apparent that the most careful stock is being taken of the sciences of man, both social and psychological; Weber and Lévi-Strauss, Freud and Erikson are being scanned as closely as are Bultmann and Tillich. And the full gamut of the intellectual situation engaging Christianity today will be seen to claim a very large place in the forum of a university faculty of theology.

It was a social scientist, the historian Donald Meyer, who noticed a few years ago with a good deal of surprise how carefully the theological community today is often to be found addressing itself also to the literary imagination and to the whole spectrum of the arts. Towards the close of a book devoted to an analysis of political thought in American Protestantism since the War of 1918,[1] Professor Meyer remarks the extent to which, starting in the early 1950's, the great themes of the artistic culture of our period began to compete with the issues of politics for the attention of American theology. And here, too, is an area of man's self-interpretation that has often seemed to be raising essentially theological questions about human existence, so brilliantly and powerfully as to invite the most considered response from those whose business it is formally to articulate and interpret the Christian sense of reality. So the inquiry of academic theology into the total transaction to be negotiated between Christianity and its present cultural environment has increasingly emphasized the aesthetic realm, especially as it involves the literary imagination and its rendering of modern experience.

Now it is an interesting fact of our cultural life that those for whom the issues of religion are of no real importance at all can be counted on to have the strictest notions of what reli-

[1] *Vide* Donald B. Meyer, *The Protestant Search for Political Realism* (Berkeley and Los Angeles: University of California Press, 1960).

gion ought to be and do. Their preference seems normally to be for a religion that is anti-intellectualist and hostile to cultural enterprise, and, when its appeal is to some form of the *credo quia absurdum*, they can then comfortably utter the conventional expressions of bemusement and dismay at the terrible *sacrificium intellectus* which it exacts. But when they confront a religion which is affirmative of the vitalities of culture and which looks toward some reciprocity between itself and those vitalities, they indignantly declare it to be a fraud: tears are shed over its misguided rejection of its native substance and uniqueness; and there is much condescending talk about a New Apologetic which, it is implied, simply betokens a loss of self-confidence and the consequent desire of the strategists of religious thought to become fellow travelers of whatever is modish and *au courant* in the hope that their position may thereby win some slight strengthening.

In fact, however, the kind of close attention given the modern cultural scene in the great centers of theological education in this country today — at Yale, Chicago, Harvard, Union Seminary — is not at all prompted by any frivolous fascination with what is approved and *recherché*. It stems rather from a profound reconstitution in Christian theology of its own self-understanding — which in our time follows upon a very radical repossession of the biblical message and, consequently, a drastically changed conception of the cultural stance to which the Christian enterprise is committed by that message.

Here, the decisive development — prepared for by a long line of distinguished modern research into the mentality of the biblical people — is the discovery, gradually shaping over the past thirty years, that the sovereign intention of biblical faith (and hence of Christian theology) is that of addressing itself not to questions of metaphysics and ontology but to questions concerning the meaning of man's historical existence. The biblical people do not, of course, suppose that man dwells in an absolutely finite province of meaning or that the human reality is self-contained and without transcendent reference; and any such histor*icism* is surely alien to the real ethos of Christian thought, for (as Ronald Gregor Smith re-

4

minds us) it is always the intention of Christian theology to address itself to what men "are not themselves": it has to do with

. . . what they do not and never can possess at all, as part of their self-equipment or as material for their self-mastery . . . with what comes to them all the time from beyond themselves.[2]

Yet biblical faith is not, as we have come to see, slanted towards ontology or metaphysics — but towards the dynamism of historical existence: as the late Carl Michalson remarked, ". . . it is an *answer* to the question of the meaning of history where the answer is given within history *as* history and not at the horizon of history as being."[3] Though the Bible contains many statements about the cosmos, they are almost always subservient to the basic intention of interpreting and commenting on the actualities of historical experience, on the immediacies of the life-world, for this is what the Bible wants basically to do — to publish, to declare, to interpret "a series of events, an *oikonomia*, an *ordo salutis*."[4]

The Dutch philosopher-theologian, Cornelis van Peursen, is recalling in one of his recent essays the passage of the people of Israel over the Red Sea, how the east wind parted the waters and enabled them to cross over and escape their Egyptian pursuers, and how their sense of reality not only led them in effect to say, "It is the east wind. . . ." but also led them to say, "It is *He*. . . ."[5] This incident from the Exodus-narrative suggests very nicely what is most striking in the biblical mentality, for, in the context of Israel's experience, God is not so much *a* Thing, *a* Being, to be inferred from events or to be

[2] Ronald Gregor Smith, "A Theological Perspective of the Secular," *Christian Scholar*, 43, no. 1 (March, 1960):15.

[3] Carl Michalson, "Theology as Ontology and as History," in *The Later Heidegger and Theology* (vol. 1 of *New Frontiers in Theology*), ed. James M. Robinson and John B. Cobb, Jr. (New York: Harper & Row, 1963), p. 147.

[4] Théo Preiss, *Life in Christ*, Studies in Biblical Theology, no. 13, trans. Harold Knight (London: S.C.M. Press, 1954), p. 66.

[5] *Vide* Cornelis A. van Peursen, "Man and Reality — The History of Human Thought," *Student World*, 56, no. 1 (First Quarter, 1963):20.

resorted to as a principle of explanation for events that would otherwise be inexplicable. He is, rather — the "I am who I am" — the name given the deepest meanings that the inspired imagination of the people locates in the events themselves, in the concrete situations of their own lives. Their historical experience is not one thing, and God another: on the contrary, the two are but obverse sides of one reality. And though the children of Abraham are a people who have a great responsiveness to the *mysterium tremendum et fascinosum*, the Glory and the Majesty belong to a Presence to be encountered only in the concrete blessings and defeats, only in the actual victories and calamities, that make up the living reality of the people's sojourn on this earth.

So faith — that radical kind of faith which enables a man to endure all the shocks and vicissitudes of life with an ultimate nonchalance and cheerfulness and hope — for the biblical community, does not belong to a sphere above or outside the realm of time and history: for them it is not (as Gerhard Ebeling puts it) "a kind of speculative soaring into transcendence. But it determines existence as existence in this world, and thus it is not something alongside all that I do and suffer, hope and experience, but something that is concretely present in it all, that is, it determines all my doing and suffering, hoping and experiencing." [6] In the biblical perspective, the *material of faith* (in Dr. Ebeling's phrase) is simply this actual world — there where a man must hold out against this and take a stand against that and resist whatever threatens to stain or contradict or blaspheme the Glory. The sphere of faith, in other words, is the shifting, conditioned, ambiguous site of history itself.

Thus the Bible does not accord ultimate validity to any distinction between the Sacred and the Profane, though such a distinction occasionally bids for Israel's suffrage. It never manages to prevail, however, for the One in whose gracious fidelity Israel finds the hinge of her history solicits from the people of the Covenant, above all else, a true steadfastness in

[6] Gerhard Ebeling, *The Nature of Faith*, trans. Ronald Gregor Smith (Philadelphia: Fortress Press, 1961), pp. 159–60.

historical responsibility, acts of justice and charity and compassion, not any sort of abdication from the precincts of the world for the sake of attaining the security afforded by some pure and holy realm outside the historical continuum. So it is that the central thrust of Hebraic faith is generally defined in our time by the great interpreters of biblical experience, by Gerhard von Rad and Walther Eichrodt, Otto Procksch and Martin Buber, Abraham Heschel and numerous others.

Nor does the New Testament present an essentially different orientation. Though it may, in the occasional rigorism of its eschatology and apocalypticism, appear to be moving towards an otherworldly spirituality, the ultimate norm it invokes is by no means a transcendent datum lying beyond time and historical existence. Indeed, in one of the most stunningly brilliant essays of our generation in biblical theology, the professor of New Testament studies at Basel, Oscar Cullmann, argues with great power — in his book of 1946, *Christus und die Zeit* (*Christ and Time*) — that the very distinction between time and eternity is something essentially alien to the deepest commitments of primitive Christianity: this characteristically Hellenic scheme, he maintains, is displaced in biblical thought by the polarity between this present age and the age to come, and "eternity" in the New Testament is nothing more than "the endless succession of the ages." Not even the advent of Christ breaches the consistent temporalism of the biblical community. It is redeemed, of course, from a purely futurist orientation to time, for the center of history is now brought out of the future and into the present age: the decisive deed of God is now descried in Jesus of Nazareth. But even in Christ time is not felt to have been invaded by something that is not time: no, says Cullmann, in Christ time, for the primitive Christian imagination, has simply reached its "mid-point" — which is to say that the ultimate norm of the New Testament is an historical norm, namely, the single fact of Jesus Christ and the temporally connected series of events constituting the history of the biblical people which finds its "center" in Christ. And it is in something like Cullmann's direction that many of those constituting the avant-

7

garde in New Testament studies today seem to be moving. In the bluntness of his denial that otherworldliness is an *essential* ingredient of New Testament faith, he seems to be charting the general route being taken *in one way or another* by many scholars (most radically perhaps, and controversially, by the German, Herbert Braun) amongst that large corps that has responded to the *Entmythologisierung* program of Rudolf Bultmann, though he is not himself a Bultmannian.

Now this whole drift in the recent study of biblical thought has encouraged theology to disavow those interpretations of the Christian faith that have the effect of converting it into a supernaturalistic system of metaphysical doctrine — whose cultural role then becomes simply that of still another heteronomy standing over against its competitors in the forum of contending *Weltanschauungen*, with a whip and a sword. What is bequeathed to systematic theology by the radical biblical scholarship of our period, and its drastic reconceptualization of the biblical mentality, is not (as some young theologians have misguidedly concluded) any sort of scheme for having, as it were, the Gospel without God. It is, rather, the suggestion that any theology that wants, even in the slightest degree, to remain faithful to the traditionally ultimate norm of *sola scriptura* will forswear, in its explication of the Christian message, every version of the old "metaphysic of distinction between the place of God and the place of man" [7] as profoundly untrue to the essential logic of biblical faith. To be sure, this is not a faith for which belief in a transcendent God is a dispensable excrescence; but what the ablest scholars of Hebraic thought in our day have been perceiving ever more clearly over many years is that, for the people of Israel, the transcendence is always, and inseparably, related to their experience of their own history: as Gregor Smith says, it is not

. . . an addendum to this history, it is not excogitated from the events in such a way as to leave the events be-

[7] Ronald Gregor Smith, *The New Man: Christianity and Man's Coming of Age* (New York: Harper & Bros., 1956), p. 108.

hind; nor is it imposed upon the events in such a way as to exalt the transcendence at the expense of the reality of the events. But the two are woven together in an inextricable web which is itself the one single reality for Israel. Their history is their relation with God; and God is their history.[8]

It is appropriate, in other words, to speak of that ultimate reality under which Israel and the primitive Christian community stand as the will of God, but it is for them a reality discoverable only in the concrete political and cultural situations of their lives, and, as Walther Eichrodt says, it drives them ever more deeply "into the midst of history with all its insecurity and unforeknowable possibilities. . . ."[9]

The radical implications of this biblical legacy for theological reconstruction in our period have been very sensitively perceived by many of the central strategists of Christian thought at the present time — by the late Paul Tillich and Friedrich Gogarten, Rudolf Bultmann and Gerhard Ebeling, Ernst Fuchs, and numerous others. But our generation seems more and more to feel that none has grasped the issue with such acuteness and passion as did the gifted young German theologian Dietrich Bonhoeffer, who was martyred by Himmler's henchmen in the Bavarian forest on the tenth of April, 1945. The crucial document is, of course, that fragmentary collection of *obiter dicta* comprising a remarkable set of notes and letters to friends — *Letters and Papers from Prison* — nearly all written in Tegel Prison in Berlin between the spring of 1943 and the autumn of 1944. Here it was, amidst the bleakness of a Gestapo prison cell, that this young scholar boldly undertook a fresh assessment of the whole problem of faith in relation to modern experience. What seems most to have borne in upon him, with a strange new kind of compelling force, was the realization that indeed the very essence of "religion" is profoundly incompatible with any biblically

[8] *Ibid.*, pp. 28–29.
[9] Walther Eichrodt, *Man in the Old Testament*, Studies in Biblical Theology, no. 4, trans. K. and R. Gregor Smith (Chicago: Henry Regnery Co., 1951), pp. 25–26.

9

grounded faith. For the basic premise of "religion" is the old "metaphysic of distinction between the place of God and the place of man": "religion," that is, invites man to conceive of himself as a point of intersection between two spheres, the natural and the supernatural, the temporal and the eternal: "the religious premise" (as Bonhoeffer called it) postulates a *terra incognita* "above" or "beyond" the place occupied by man, and it rests upon the notion of a *Deus ex machina* to whose "existence" that of all other beings is subordinate. But the course his meditations took during the last months of his life led Bonhoeffer to realize how impossible it has become for any man breathing the cultural atmosphere of the modern world to think of reality as an affair of *two* realms. For "the linchpin" of the whole structure is gone: the *Deus ex machina* is simply no longer comprehensible by the modern imagination. "We are proceeding towards a time of no religion at all: men as they are now simply cannot be religious any more," [10] for they have "come of age," and, living in a world characterized by the regularities described by empirical science, they can no longer find any good reason for resorting to a God of the stop-gap, for supposing that the public world of normal experience is somehow completed and given a final coherence by a supernatural order.

In short, his meditation on the full meaning of the whole cultural enterprise initiated by the Renaissance and the Enlightenment led Bonhoeffer to the conclusion that the time for "religion" is gone, that — in the world of modern physics and biology and psychology — "the religious premise" is reduced to an irreparable débris, and man is no longer the *homo religiosus*. So, if God is still to be spoken of at all, it must be, he decided, in a "non-religious" way.

But — and here is what is really decisive — "non-religious interpretation" is not merely an apologetic maneuver required by the modern situation: it is, far more fundamentally, in Bonhoeffer's sense of things, a stratagem required by the

[10] Dietrich Bonhoeffer, *Letters and Papers from Prison*, trans. Reginald Fuller and ed. Eberhard Bethge (London: William Collins Sons, "Fontana Books," 1959), p. 91.

very nature of biblical faith itself, and by the inherent logic of Christian theology. For Christian faith is not itself "religion." Indeed, one might imagine the formula *religio est negatio Christi* as the motto for Bonhoeffer's whole message, since, in his lexicon, religion means a system of supernaturalism, the doctrine of the two realms, the God of the stop-gap, the interpretation of transcendence in metaphysical terms, the spatialization of the Divine, the projection into the skies of a heavenly *Pantokrator*, the "forcing [of] God out of the world" — and a biblically grounded faith stands as the fundamental opposite of all this. The man who finds his basic fulcrum in such a faith will not even be too fascinated with the Transcendent; certainly he will not cogitate upon "the plans and accomplishments of a self-existent Supreme Being" [11] for the sake of building a *system* of doctrine with which to assault that which is presumably opposed to this Being — namely, the world. For so to proceed would be to set askew the truly biblical reality which is constituted by the presence (in Bonhoeffer's phrase) of "the 'beyond' in the midst of our life" [12] — the "beyond" which is the creative ground and meaning of all our most significant social and political and cultural experiences: this is where, for the biblical people, the deep things of God are to be found. And such a procedure would be a *negatio Christi*, since Christ's great vocation was not that of promoting a new religion — "neither circumcision nor uncircumcision" — but, rather, of calling men to a radical solicitude for, and openness to, the world. Hence, for Bonhoeffer, the vocation of the Christian man is not primarily to be "religious" in any particular way but to live "a 'worldly' life," a life of the deepest engagement with the full human and cultural reality of the particular moment to which history commits him — and a life grounded in the confidence that the Holy and the Sacred are to be encountered in the true depth of that historical reality. Bonhoeffer recognized, of course, that the Bible message and the Christian faith have for countless ages

[11] Helmut Gollwitzer, *The Existence of God as Confessed by Faith,* trans. James Leitch (Philadelphia: Westminster Press, 1965), p. 88.
[12] Bonhoeffer, *Letters,* p. 93.

worn the "garment" of religion, but he felt that the great positive advantage brought by our secular age is the spur it provides the Christian faith to cast off inessentials and to strip itself of a garment which no longer has any vitally functional validity.

So faith, in his view — that is, genuinely Christian faith — is not a matter of acceding to difficult metaphysical propositions about spooky realities: it is, rather — insofar as its posture is in conformity with Christ's — an affirmative orientation toward one's neighbor and, in our time, toward a world come of age (in the sense of no longer needing "religion"). Thus the Christian community, if it truly understands the meaning of the biblical message and its present historical situation, will not be found prancing into the forums of our cultural life today with any "metaphysical" or "religious" baggage that has the effect of shutting it off from the characteristic intellectual vitalities of the modern period. It will instead be zealous in offering the world a "religionless" interpretation of its faith, an interpretation forswearing the old "metaphysic of distinction between the place of God and the place of man" and giving itself wholly to an inquiry into how the human future can be responsibly faced, with confidence and prophetic hope.

This is the testimony bequeathed us from Bonhoeffer's cell, during the last months of his life, in Tegel Prison. And there is, of course, much that is cryptic and obscure in the *Letters and Papers from Prison*. What precisely is the nature of the hermeneutic that is to govern a non-religious interpretation of biblical concepts and theological categories? How can a religionless Christianity be expected to preserve the real genius of the Gospel and not convert itself into simply another form of Ethical Culture? What really defines the doctrine of God on which a religionless Christianity rests? These and numerous other questions are raised but remain unanswered by the tantalizing fragments that came out of Bonhoeffer's jail between the fourteenth of April, 1943, and the twenty-eighth of December, 1944. For all their gnomic tenuity, however, they have more profoundly fascinated the theological imagination of our period than any other single body of utterance. And, despite the continuing prestige of Barth and Bultmann and Tillich and the Niebuhrs, it is the Bonhoeffer of the *Prison* letters (and to some extent of the *Ethics* — written between 1940 and 1945, but unfinished, and posthumously published in 1949) who is the great weather vane of contemporary theology. This is not to say, of course, that the *Letters and Papers from Prison* affords a simple index of a prevailing consensus, for it is itself too problematical to have established a basic program of work for theology — and what there is in it of real consistency has by no means, in all its detail, elicited anything like universal approval. Nevertheless, no other single document of our period seems so nicely to express the *temper* of mind that is today most pervasively characteristic of Christian theology. In his way of responding both to the received biblical message and to the modern situation Bonhoeffer may be considered, in relation to the general effort of theology in our time, as enacting a large exemplary role. For the best theological intelligence today has long since given up being aghast at the autonomy claimed by modern cultural enterprise and has become convinced that the Incarnation is best honored not by derogating an autonomous secularity or by attempting to bully it into submission to some presumably sacrosanct authority of the Church's *kerygma* but, rather, by allowing the world to be itself, most especially when that world, by the sophistication of its intellectual pursuits, has won access to great maturity and has (as Bonhoeffer liked to say) "come of age." The Word of God begins to be heard not only in the scripture and proclamation and sacraments of the community of faith but also in all those intellectual and cultural forms which, as they arise out of man's deepest encounter with his world and his own humanity, are stamped by a self-authenticating genuineness and relevance.

What begins, in other words, to be most repugnant to the newly emerging Christian sensibility is any doctrine of two realms, of a sphere to which the truth of faith belongs and, standing over against it, a sphere to which "the world" belongs. The supposition that the Christian man is related to

13

NATHAN A. SCOTT, JR.

two realms has become profoundly alien to the new ethos of
theological thought, primarily as a result of the repossession
of what Karl Barth many years ago called "the strange new
world within the Bible." What is more and more insisted
upon is that "the obedient devotion of the human spirit to
the objects of Christian revelation is not complete without
the recognition of the freedom of the human spirit" [13] in relation to all the realities and possibilities of its own history.
The world, in short, is *one*, and the only significant difference established in the case of the Christian man concerns
his faith as to whence it is from which come the great gifts
of courage and creativity and peace: but his role, it is felt,
is surely not, as I have elsewhere remarked,

> . . . to bully the world into granting its suffrage to some
> special system of propositions of his own invention. For
> he does not come into this world from another world like
> a *deus ex machina*, with a marvelous formula that can un-
> lock all the entanglements of human culture. No, he
> lives in the historical order like all his fellows; the re-
> source on which he relies is simply that particular hope
> and confidence to which he is given access in this world
> by reason of what he knows God to have done for this
> world. And, having this resource, his single vocation is
> to live, as did Jesus the Lord, in solicitude for, and in
> openness to, the men to whom he is related by the par-
> ticular moment in history in which he happens to stand.
> The Christian scholar faces the same world that is faced
> by all other men; and . . . it is outrageous arrogance for
> him to assume that his faith provides him with some sort
> of privileged perspective by means of which he can inte-
> grate internally the various fields of culture and then
> assign to each its proper place in some tidily compre-
> hensive arrangement that will be a Christian map of the
> modern mind.[14]

[13] R. G. Smith, *New Man*, p. 58.
[14] Nathan A. Scott, Jr., *The Broken Center: Studies in the Theological
Horizon of Modern Literature* (New Haven: Yale University Press,
1966), pp. 198–99.

Something like this forms the general basis on which theology is today undertaking to reconceive its own identity and its relation to culture at large, and what is most notable is its increasing loss of interest in elaborating — in any systematic and sharply separatist way — a distinctive *speculum mentis* for the Christian man.

This, then, is why today any characteristically contemporary attempt of theology at performing the act of self-definition tends to be the occasion for a kind of metaphoric exercise based on some version of the "I-Thou" figure of Martin Buber. Theology, it is more and more being said, *is* a form of "dialogue": the language of "divinity," we are being reminded, *is* a form of "conversation" — or at least the *effort* to initiate a fruitful conversation between those who speak within and on behalf of the Church of Christ and those who represent the significant intellectual and cultural disciplines whereby man's self-interpretation is undertaken, in the deepest dimensions of his encounter with reality. That is, the theological act occurs in the act whereby the truth of distinctively Christian faith is set forth and clarified, but occurs also, and perhaps in certain ways even more critically, in the moment when this particular faith is required to define and understand itself in relation to the general fund of human wisdom about what is important in man's life on this earth. The assumption faith wants to make is that, "if Christ is truly the *Logos*, then He is witnessed to in all apprehensions of truth, whether they occur within a framework of Christian concern or not,"[15] and the confession solicited from the Christian man, in a glad and joyous spirit, is that which was anciently enunciated, nearly two hundred years before Christ, by the Roman playwright Terence — *Homo sum; humani nil a me alienum puto.*

So the scrupulous attention now given in the major centers of theological education to the humanistic and social sciences — to philosophy and psychology, to politics and sociology, even to economics and anthropology — and to the issues

[15] *Ibid.*, p. 200.

15

they pose for Christian theology is not at all prompted by any unprincipled whoring after what is momentarily prestigious in the cultural Establishment, as a certain kind of smugly hostile secular observer may suppose. It springs, rather, from a profound recovery of the real intention of biblical faith and from a consequent change in theology's estimate of what ought generally to be the response of the Christian imagination to the cultural life of our time. It springs from a deep conviction that, by its own inner logic, Christian faith is required not only "to turn inward upon itself, asking what is authentically and ultimately its own kind of truth" but is also required "to move out into . . . 'a lover's quarrel with the world.'"[16] Athens, in short, is seen now to have a good deal to do with Jerusalem.

Certainly one must turn to this whole range of considerations to account for the decision of the Divinity faculty of the University of Chicago in 1950 to establish as one of its basic Fields a department devoted to the study of the great forms and expressions of the literary imagination, with special emphasis given to the literature of the modern period. Paramount in its thinking was the realization that the great literature of our time — the canon established by such artists as Baudelaire, Dostoievski, Yeats, Kafka, Eliot, Rilke, Mann, Joyce, Faulkner, Stevens, Brecht — constitutes one of the most powerful expressions of modern intelligence, and a body of writing whose special genius it is to focalize in a remarkably vivid and startling way many of the issues that must be very much at the center of any comprehensive theological anthropology. Indeed, many of the writers most influential in the shaping of modern sensibility can be called "spiritual writers," in a sense very close to the meaning given this term in Catholic theology, for the drama being enacted in such texts as *The Notebooks of Malte Laurids Brigge* and *The Waste Land* and *The Castle* and *The Sound and the Fury* and *Doctor Faustus* and the *Pisan Cantos* is essentially that of the soul's journey in search of God. So a fine opportunity

[16] Roger Hazelton, *New Accents in Contemporary Theology* (New York: Harper & Bros., 1960), pp. 11–12.

16

seemed to be beckoning, for theology to venture into those chambers of imagery where the human spirit today, often unassisted by any of the supports of traditional faith, is radically probing anew into issues of ultimate import with which it is also perennially the office of religion to deal, and doing so in a way so spirited and original as to have frequently the effect of helping faith toward a deeper apprehension at once of itself and of the larger scene in our age to which it wants to speak. Thus the Divinity School was persuaded, in the autumn of 1950, to create a program of study in theology and literature leading to the M.A. and the Ph.D.

In terms of curriculum, the establishment of this program was and remains one of the most significant innovations in American theological education, virtually without parallel. Important work is no doubt being done in this general area in other theological faculties, but nowhere else is so elaborately designed a program of interdisciplinary work in theology and criticism being conducted at the doctoral level. The various dimensions which are naturally a part of the total enterprise necessarily make a doctorate in the field an exceedingly arduous degree, for not only must the candidate acquire the linguistic competence that is usually a prerequisite for the Ph.D. and (in the Divinity School's system) survive a battery of stiff comprehensive examinations in the basic theological disciplines (biblical studies, church history, systematic and historical theology, etc.), but he must also, before undertaking his research, sit for rather gruelling Field Examinations (both written and oral) in literary history and criticism and aesthetics and theology of culture — and he must in these examinations demonstrate that he is able, with real urbanity and sophistication, to think about the fundamental issues of literary scholarship *as a theologian.* So, given the extensive work that must be done at once in the Divinity School and in the University's Division of the Humanities (in the various departments of literature), it is a rather expensive degree and, consequently, no great flood of alumni has been released into the academic marketplace. Ten men, to date, have taken the doctorate; another fifteen or more have nearly completed

their studies, and a much larger number are at a less advanced stage; nearly fifty M.A.'s have been awarded; and
many of these persons — only a small number of whom it was
possible to engage in the preparation of this book — are beginning already to have bright and productive careers as publishing scholars and teachers (in both theological and literary
faculties), and are beginning to provide helpful leader-
ship in the theological community at large as it attempts more
deeply to encounter what is prophetic in the great literature
of our time.

But now, apart from all that may be said about how theological perspectives may illumine the issues of criticism, it
should be noted that the customary definition of how theology itself may be fecundated by literary study, though it has
an undoubted validity, does tend to leave certain things out
of account. What is usually said is that the literary imagination offers a peculiarly direct access to those deep interiorities
of feeling that constitute a people's basic life-world; that it
is a kind of barometer registering the deep currents of sensibility which give to a culture its distinctive tone and style;
that it brings to light what is inaccessible to the procedures
of empirical study; and that it mirrors the age, in the subtlest
nuances of its fears and aspirations, of its dreams and myths,
of its hopes and nightmares. Thus, it is argued, the Christian
enterprise, as it seeks the living reality of its human environment, may find in literary art a most helpful resource. Art is
viewed, in other words, in its capacity to document the Time-
spirit, and, in this way, it is thought to offer churchmen an
indispensable index to the actual world to which the Christian
Evangel is to be addressed. Such an estimate of art's cultural
function — which descends from the German Romantics of
the eighteenth century, from Herder and the Schlegels, with
whom *Geistesgeschichte* theory has its real beginning —
though for various reasons it is today sometimes questioned,
has still a certain utility, in the degree to which it encourages
alertness to the integral relationship between the arts and the
generality of human experience. Goethe's *Werther*, for example, undoubtedly attests to a deep inflammation of sensibility

that at a certain point overtook that phase of the European mind which, in following the lines of Rousseau's rebellion against eighteenth-century rationalism and in tending to make a virtual religion of feeling, found its feelings after a time to be riotously exacerbated and tyrannical and intolerably raw. Or Tennyson's *In Memoriam* surely gives, in part, a poignant expression to the astonished sense many of the most sensitive Victorian people had — as a result of the inrush of the new biology and the new Higher Criticism — that all the traditional supports and consolations of Christian belief had suddenly been converted into a huge, nagging question mark. Or, again — in an age that has experienced the obscenity of Auschwitz and the hell of modern global warfare and the new *anomie* bred by the mechanisms of social life in an advanced technocratic culture — the profound dispiritedness and *apatheia* of the protagonist in Camus' *The Stranger* probably express a sentiment recurrently epidemic in our time. And, undoubtedly, a theology uninformed by that rendering the literary imagination gives of what we call the Human Condition is not likely to speak with power and cogency, or with any real brilliance of perception.

I should like to suggest in conclusion, however, that this customary rationale for the transaction between theology and literature does to some extent fail of the necessary completeness. For what needs to be kept in view is that the literary imagination may not only help theology to take a closer reading of cultural reality than it might achieve without such assistance, but it can also perform an important propaedeutic function in the quest of Christian theology for deepening of its own self-knowledge.

T. S. Eliot, it is true, bluntly denied many years ago that the imaginative writer does anything that could be called *thinking*. "I can see no reason," said he in his famous essay of 1927 on "Shakespeare and the Stoicism of Seneca," "for believing that either Dante or Shakespeare did any thinking on his own. The people who think that Shakespeare thought, are always people who are not engaged in writing poetry, but who are engaged in thinking, and we all like to think that great men were like ourselves." [17] And this is, I believe, a dictum which, if rigorously parsed, will yield some bit of foolishness. For to deny any "thought" to the kind of reflection that went into the making of Valéry's *Monsieur Teste* or Mann's *The Magic Mountain* or Stevens' *Harmonium* or Eliot's own *Quartets* is surely, to an absurd extent, to suppose in effect that "thinking" must necessarily entail nothing more than a purely logical operation — and this is to deliver thought over into "the rationalist trap from which it is likely to emerge as a cripple, full of animosity against that other deformed creature, mutilated in the same operation: the Romantic emotion." [18] But the real intent of Eliot's tartness on this occasion was, I take it, to assert, if somewhat obliquely, that the modalities of literary art are not, characteristically, distinguished by the systematic discursiveness belonging to formal dialectical discourse. And indeed they are not: for, drenched in "ideas" as such a poem as "Burnt Norton" manifestly is, it yet cannot be merely reduced to a doctrinal statement, because the poem *is* a collaboration *between* certain ideas and rhythms and dramatic gestures. The poem *qua* poem, in other words, is a structure of song and statement, of rhythm and vision, that cannot be rendered, exhaustively and without remainder, in the terms of any simple argument of a univocal sort — and far more must this be acknowledged as true of those forms of literature in which systematic ideas do not play so large a role in the poetic economy as in Eliot's own poetry. So, given the intransigently "non-discursive" quality of literary art, how, it may be wondered, can it be conceived as capable of helping a technical science such as theology towards a larger measure of inner clarity?

Here, the answer is, I think, to be found in the fact — if I may employ an ugly neologism invented by the English philosopher R. M. Hare — that no important work of literary art is without its *blik*. This is a term which Mr. Hare has contrived

[17] T. S. Eliot, *Selected Essays: 1917–1932* (New York: Harcourt, Brace & Co., 1932), p. 116.
[18] Erich Heller, *The Disinherited Mind* (Philadelphia: Dufour & Saifer, 1952), p. 121.

for the sake of specifying what it is that theological discourse is "about." Like most contemporary philosophers, he is unwilling to grant that theological propositions might be about any existing "state of affairs"; yet he does not want to conclude that they are, therefore, meaningless: no, he says, despite their empirical unverifiability, they may be adjudged meaningful, insofar as they express or affirm a *blik* — that is, a fundamental attitude or orientation toward the world, a basic presupposition about the meaning of experience that is not itself a consequence of empirical inquiry but which affords a standpoint from which experience may be ordered and interpreted.[19] Now, without judging the soundness of this notion in the field of theological semantics — though my inclination is to feel that, there, in the use he makes of it, Mr. Hare is quite wrongheaded — I should like to apply it to the field of literary theory, for in this region, certainly, much of what gives interest to the individual poem or novel is an affair of the *blik* that is being expressed. Here, of course, there is no abstract doctrinal scheme involved: there is the same resistance to discursive translation that Mr. Hare claims to find in the *blik* of religious faith — and *all* depends on the vivaciousness with which a given perspective is fleshed out and dramatized through a vibrant pattern of living images, on the extent to which (as Henry James liked to say) it is fully *rendered*. Nevertheless, the poem — by which I mean the work of verbal art — is, as Cleanth Brooks puts it, "a portion of reality as viewed and valued by a human being. It is rendered coherent through a perspective of valuing."[20] This perspective is not, of course, systematically elaborated or analyzed, for the poem seeks to convey what it *feels* like to hold a given perspective, and what the existential consequences are in which the holding of it eventuates. Thus Northrop Frye suggests, very acutely, that literature bears

[19] *Vide* R. M. Hare, "Theology and Falsification," in *New Essays in Philosophical Theology*, ed. Antony Flew and Alasdair MacIntyre (London: S.C.M. Press Ltd., 1955), pp. 99–103.

[20] Cleanth Brooks, "Implications of an Organic Theory of Poetry," in *Literature and Belief*, ed. M. H. Abrams (New York: Columbia University Press, 1958), p. 68.

something of the same relationship to theology that mathematics bears to the physical sciences. "The pure mathematician," he says, "proceeds by making postulates and assumptions and seeing what comes out of them, and what the poet or novelist does is rather similar."[21] Just as "pure mathematics enters into and gives form to the physical sciences," so the literary imagination vitalizes meditation on matters of ultimate concern by making concrete before the immediate gaze of the mind the real cost of a given life-orientation. It does not "line up arguments facing each other like football teams,"[22] but, rather — in the terms of drama and symbolic action — it *dances-out* (as Kenneth Burke would say) the real entailments of "religiousness A" and "religiousness B," and thus it can be considered perhaps a radically *experimental* theology, dwelling (like pure mathematics) on the postulatory side of what formal theology (like the physical sciences) addresses itself to in its existential dimension.

The great danger always is, of course, that formal theology will become something merely formal, and thus humanly superficial and irrelevant, that it (like any science of human existence) will fall into some version of what Whitehead called the Fallacy of Misplaced Concreteness, reifying its categories into a stiff sort of punctilio without any genuine relevance to the living actualities of human existence. So its own health very greatly requires the quickening and enrichment that come from the kind of *experimental* theology that literature can be, for the novelist and the dramatist and the poet can help the theological imagination to *see* how this or that particular faith or life-orientation really *looks*, under the full stress of experience. Apart from such "experimental" knowledge — which the artist is uniquely empowered to convey — the work of the theologian is likely to become an arid business of syllogism and logic-chopping, and theology is likely not to win that sharp awareness of its own variousness

[21] Northrop Frye, *The Educated Imagination* (Bloomington: Indiana University Press, 1964), p. 127.
[22] *Ibid.*, p. 126.

and breadth of possibility which imaginative literature can give.

It is, then, against this whole background that the enterprise to which this book is committed requires to be understood, in relation to the total program of the Divinity School of the University of Chicago and in relation to the general life and work of theology in our time.

The subject which has engaged the young critics joining me in these pages is, of course, that body of writing which is bidding for a position of honor today in the recent literature of American fiction. It is, to be sure, only a portion of the material needing to be considered in this connection which is touched in the following essays. Each of the contributors was asked to treat but one novelist, and this a figure whom he had found of particular interest; so, given the limited number of those involved in the project and the importance of keeping the book as a whole within a relatively modest scope, it was inevitable that many significant talents of the present time should appear to go unheeded. Among these, however, I do not have in mind Vladimir Nabokov, whose extraordinary genius has lately prompted numerous commentators on current American fiction (no doubt partly out of a nativist desire to push up our national stock) to include his novels of the past twenty years in the American accomplishment, by dint of his residence in this country during the forties and fifties. Were this a right calculation, our literature could indeed be thought to be graced by a most remarkable adornment, for *Pnin* and *Lolita* and *Pale Fire* are amongst the most impressive works of art of our time. But, trenchant as Nabokov's vision of American life often is, the plain fact is that he is a European whose mind and sensibility have their deep sources in a tradition which became an affair of Diaspora in 1917. So, not being truly "one of us," his exclusion from this book need not occasion any special regret.

There is, however, a large number of highly gifted novelists who have entered American literary life in the years since World War II, and who, though deserving careful notice in any comprehensive review of our recent fiction, go unconsidered in this present symposium. Each of our readers can, of course, make up his own list, and such names as James Baldwin, William Burroughs, Herbert Gold, Frederick Buechner, John Barth, Harvey Swados, Richard Stern, and Philip Roth would surely be among those to be taken into account. But the most serious omission, by my own estimate, is Ralph Ellison. He has, it is true, produced only one novel, and at a remove now of fifteen years; but, in the general consensus, *Invisible Man* is the most distinguished single performance of our period, and the installments of the "work in progress" appearing in recent years suggest that this fine artist, in mid-career, suffers no diminution of energy or craft. His work presses in upon us today most strenuously, and I think it is a pity that we have not dealt with it in this volume. Again, though the books of John Hawkes and James Purdy may not grab at us with quite the same measure of power that we feel in *Invisible Man*, I think it unfortunate that these two brilliant artists have had to be neglected.

But, for all the omissions, a good deal of what carries "the tone of the center" in the American novel today is being considered in the essays making up this collection. And it is by no means surprising that critics with theological interests should be drawn to artists such as Bellow and Malamud and Styron and the various other writers discussed here, for this is a generation of novelists whose work is ever more emphatically expressing that special sort of "piety" which Santayana called "the conscience of literature — by which, as he said, he meant the sense expressed in certain modes of literary art that the primary obligation of literature is to serve "a burdened and perplexed creature."[23]

American fiction of the immediate present does not, however, serve the "burdened and perplexed" people of our time by taking anything resembling the course proposed by the T. S. Eliot of forty years ago, when he announced his allegiance to classicism in literature and royalism in politics and Anglo-Catholicism in religion. For the imagination at work in

[23] George Santayana, *The Life of Reason*, vol. 4: *Reason in Art* (New York: Charles Scribner's Sons, 1905), p. 84.

our native literature today is a radically protestant imagination, wanting not to invoke old values and to honor old sacraments, finding no stable center in the funded deposits of cultural memory, but wanting to search out undepleted orders of meaning in "the tradition of the new." Thus the literature of our new fiction is rooted, characteristically, in sensibilities representing a considerable recalcitrance before Christian valuation, so that the kind of example presented here by the late Flannery O'Connor marks a rather startling deviation from the established norm. Yet, resolutely as many of our younger novelists appear to elect the role of Explorer in preference to that of Pilgrim and however much they may seem disinclined to render the human adventure in the terms of what Faulkner called "the Passion Week of the Heart," their way of plotting the story of how we live now does sometimes have the effect, strangely, of reminding us of older stories and rhetorics. And, thus clotted, the resonance of their music takes on even greater poignancy and richness of implication.

Indeed, a lively native tradition has grown up since the mid-1940's. Though there are not many signs and promises in contemporary American fiction of any large sort of greatness, the novel in this country today is, nevertheless, very much alive and kicking — and kicking with the kind of unignorable force belonging to a literature that wants to serve creatures burdened and perplexed. So we have a fiction that requires — and repays — close and serious study, and it is most essentially this which those who have contributed to this book want to affirm.

In the conference out of which this book comes one of the addresses was delivered by Henry Rago, who holds a joint appointment at the University of Chicago as professor of theology and literature in the Divinity School and in the College. And though, on that occasion, he was scanning the present scene in poetry, he did, nevertheless, explore so suggestively the interrelationship between faith and the literary imagination that it was decided (despite our general focus here on recent prose fiction) to include his essay in this book; and so it is carried here, in the form of an Epilogue.

25

1

Sola Gratia—*The Principle of Bellow's Fiction*
NATHAN A. SCOTT, JR.

In January of 1956, under the auspices of the Gertrude Clarke Whittall Fund, the late R. P. Blackmur delivered four lectures at the Library of Congress on the literature of the twentieth century. And, as one reads the printed text of these addresses, it tickles the imagination a little to think how baffled Mr. Blackmur's audience of housewives and students and government clerks must have been by the flailings and thrashings about of the strange language to which he gave himself in his last years. The little booklet comprising these lectures which the Library published in 1956[1] affords many sad examples of how great a hardship the attempt at communication had come to be for this distinguished critic in the late phase of his career. These addresses are all "great general blobs," such as Blackmur claimed to find in much of Whitman's poetry, and an odd sort of vatic delirium in the style makes everything nearly impenetrable. Yet, here and there, the darkness is lit up by flashes of the wit and brilliance of perception that made Blackmur over a long period one of the great princelings of modern criticism. The first of these is to be found in the title itself which he gave to these lectures, *Anni Mirabiles*, for this is how he assessed the early twenties — as marvelous years, a time of great harvest in the history of the modern movement. And so indeed the period was: it was a time of glory, a time of wonders, a time which saw the appearance in 1921 of Pirandello's *Sei personaggi* and

[1] *Vide* R. P. Blackmur, *Anni Mirabiles; 1921–1925: Reason in the Madness of Letters* (Washington, D.C.: Reference Department of the Library of Congress, 1956).

NATHAN A. SCOTT, JR.

some of Pound's most characteristic *Cantos*, in 1922 of Eliot's *The Waste Land* and Joyce's *Ulysses*, in 1923 of Wallace Stevens' *Harmonium* and Rilke's *Duino Elegies*, in 1924 of Mann's *Der Zauberberg*, in 1925 of Valéry's *M. Teste* and Kafka's *Der Prozess*. And so things went throughout the remainder of the decade — which saw, particularly on the American scene, a great efflorescence of remarkable creativity: Dreiser's *An American Tragedy* and Fitzgerald's *The Great Gatsby* in 1925, Hemingway's *The Sun Also Rises* in 1926, Wolfe's *Look Homeward, Angel* and Faulkner's *The Sound and the Fury* in 1929: wonderful years indeed.

Now it has been a habit of American critics lately to submit the achievement of our writers in this country since World War II to various kinds of stocktaking and fretfully to speculate on the possibility of regarding the years just gone by as having also been *anni mirabiles*. The twenties and early thirties are a golden time in American literary life which it is exhilarating to recall; but they are also years that weigh heavily upon us as a challenge, and as a challenge that constantly threatens to become a diminishing reproach, if there cannot be descried in our uncertain present the signs of a stature comparable to that splendid insurgency of forty years ago. So we are often taking polls and making tallies, most especially about our fiction; and when the tabulations prove sometimes to be unfavorable, the resulting dejection turns us suddenly into crestfallen obituarists of the novel. But then new polls will be taken and more tallies made, and the hope will revive of finding the present time to be as fruitful as that of Fitzgerald and Hemingway and Faulkner.

Yet, underneath the fervent encomia frequently offered the contemporary scene by the hucksters of *Tendenz*, there is a certain nettling mistrust, and a nagging intuition that, certainly in the novel, the postwar period has not augmented, has not *added* anything to the furniture of the imagination in the way a truly great literature does. It makes little sense, however, to launch out into windy pontifications about the death of the novel, for a national literature only rarely finds writers so gifted as the Fitzgerald of *Gatsby* and the Heming-

28

way of *The Sun Also Rises* and the Faulkner of *The Sound and the Fury* handling the same genre within a single generation. And surely it would be silly to postulate the death of a medium whose most characteristic practitioners today are people so talented as John Barth, Bernard Malamud, William Styron, John Hawkes, Norman Mailer, and Thomas Pynchon. But what counts most heavily against the alarmism of those who pronounce the novel to be dead is the simple fact that, at least on the American scene, we have, in Ralph Ellison's novel of 1952, *Invisible Man*, one indubitably great book and that, in the fiction of Saul Bellow, we have a body of work whose richness in both form and idea, already while he is only in mid-career, promises that his will eventually become one of the great careers in the literary life of this second half of the century.

In Mr. Bellow's case, however – and Mr. Ellison's is not dissimilar – critical assessment has tended frequently to miss its mark to an astonishing extent. When Maxwell Geismar, for example, is not searching out the "psychobiological [questions] . . . at the base of [his] work," he is undertaking to affiliate Mr. Bellow with "social realism," proposing that in a book such as *The Victim* he is doing, in terms of lower-middle-class Jewish life in New York City, the general sort of thing Orwell was doing in relation to the dinginess of the *petit bourgeois* London world of *Keep the Aspidistra Flying.* Or Mr. Geismar is proposing that a text such as *Seize the Day* presents, in relation to the drab gloom of the upper West Side of New York, essentially the same *kind* of account presented by a John O'Hara or a John P. Marquand (!) in relation to other areas of American life. Mr. Bellow's métier, we are told, is that of "the social realism school of Dreiser . . . and of such later figures as Ira Wolfert, James T. Farrell, and Nelson Algren."[2] It is an amazing verdict, but not unlike that delivered by other critics less committed in principle than Mr. Geismar to the issues of sociology and "psychobiology."

[2] *Vide* Maxwell Geismar, "Saul Bellow: Novelist of the Intellectuals," in *American Moderns: From Rebellion to Conformity* (New York: Hill & Wang, 1958), pp. 210–24.

A younger and more perceptive man, Marcus Klein, in a book generally marked by a very fine intelligence, has told us more recently, for example, that the problems faced by all of Mr. Bellow's characters "are reducible to a single problem: to meet with a strong sense of self the sacrifice of self demanded by social circumstance."[3] And a similar circle of definition has been awkwardly flung about his work in much of the critical discussion it has prompted in the last few years.

What is wrong, of course, in this version of things is not that Mr. Bellow's fiction is uninfluenced by any dialectical sense of the individual's relation to society: on the contrary, his books consistently reveal that the question of how the individual needs to respond to the requirements levied by "social circumstance" is one of his most absorbing preoccupations as a novelist. Yet social circumstance never defines the ultimate dimension of selfhood in the world of *Augie March* and *Henderson* and *Herzog*: the human individual is in no way shown here to be merely an epiphenomenon of social process; personality is not imagined in ways that suggest it to be wholly immersed in a social continuum and reaching only towards a social destiny. In fact, one of the more striking features of the fiction is that the central moments in the experience of Mr. Bellow's characters are always moments of *Existenz* in which a man, transcending the immediate pressures of his external environment and the limiting conditions of the social matrix, asks himself some fundamental question about the nature of his own humanity. Thus the contemporary line to which Mr. Bellow belongs is not that tag end of American naturalists — John O'Hara, Nelson Algren, Irwin Shaw — who are committed to a dreary automatism of social reportage and who are, to be sure, convinced that there is some "sacrifice of self demanded by social circumstances." It is, rather, a line reaching from Penn Warren and Faulkner back into the American past towards Mark Twain and Melville and Hawthorne, and towards the European tradition of Dostoievski and Kafka and Svevo and Sartre — the line, in other words, of

[3] Marcus Klein, *After Alienation: American Novels in Mid-Century* (Cleveland and New York: World Publishing Co., 1964), p. 34.

modern fiction whose principal area of inquiry is the phenomenology of selfhood.

Nor do I stretch language too greatly when I speak of Saul Bellow's novels as entailing an enterprise of phenomenology, for his fiction is in fact, one feels, stirred into life, fundamentally, by a certain sort of philosophical endeavor.

There comes a time, it will be recalled, in *The Adventures of Augie March* when, after having just barely escaped the nets flung at him by all sorts of people wanting to organize and control his life, Augie finds himself dealing with still another "Machiavellian." Having signed with the Merchant Marine after the outbreak of the War in 1941, he ships out from Boston, two days after his marriage to Stella. But on the fifteenth day out, the *Sam MacManus* is torpedoed, and, following the explosion, Augie scrambles into a lifeboat the other occupant of which is one Basteshaw, the ship's carpenter, who, with a curious pedantry, holds forth in a high-sounding, pompous oratory. As the two drift along over the water together, Basteshaw speaks, for example, of a former girl friend who contracted pulmonary phthisis, a condition which, as he informs Augie, "in his lecturer's tone," entails increased temperatures that "often act on the erogenous zones spectacularly." Or, again, this megalomaniac — who has tried all his life "to be as much of a Renaissance cardinal as one can under modern conditions" — undertakes to instruct Augie on what he calls "the reality situation" and describes how his researches in the physiology of boredom eventuated in his learning how to create life, to create protoplasm — some of which had been on the *MacManus*, where he had been continuing his researches. Now that it floats somewhere in the ocean, he contemplates the possibility that he has initiated a new chain of evolution. So it is that this madman's rhetoric moves on, to ever greater peaks of extravagance and intensity, till Augie at last thinks weariedly to himself, "Why did I always have to fall among theoreticians!" And one cannot help noticing how frequently at many other points Mr. Bellow's fiction wants to express a sense of something ambiguously threatening and baleful in the Idea and in those of its servants

31

whose zeal is unqualified and absolute. In his monologue called "Address by Gooley MacDowell to the Hasbeens Club of Chicago," [4] Gooley speaks of the "dome of thought" around our heads, "as thick as atmosphere to breathe. . . . [P]lenty are dying of good ideas. We have them in the millions. . . . Look at us," he says, "deafened, hampered, obstructed, impeded, impaired and bowel-glutted with wise counsel and good precept, and the more plentiful our ideas the worse our headaches. So we ask, will some good creature pull out the plug and ease our disgusted hearts a little?" And a similar note is struck in *Seize the Day* and *Henderson the Rain King* and *Herzog.*

Yet, despite his penchant for viewing with alarm the brutalizing power of the intellect and the desiccating effects of modern rationalism, Mr. Bellow is himself perhaps the outstanding "theoretician" amongst the major novelists of our period, and his books are drenched in speculation. This is not to say that he conceives of the novel as an essentially expository medium or that he is a "philosophical novelist," in the usual sense of that term, for the immediate stuff of his art is not an affair (to use a phrase Lionel Trilling has somewhere employed) of those "pellets of intellection" which are the material of systematic thought: it is, rather, an affair of enormously larky and vital characters and of the interesting relationships into which they are brought with one another and with the world of the American metropolis. But these characters themselves are personages whose most fundamental interest is a "theoretical" interest, and therein, Mr. Bellow seems to feel, is the real wellspring of their humanity.

Joseph, in *Dangling Man*, commits to his journal the reflection that "we are all drawn toward the same craters of the spirit — to know what we are and what we are for, to know our purpose, to seek grace." This is indeed the gravitating passion by which Mr. Bellow's people are moved. Augie March has a great need to ferret out the "axial lines" of life — which is precisely the sovereign aspiration by which Asa Leventhal and Tommy Wilhelm and Eugene Henderson and

[4] In *Hudson Review*, vol. 4 (Summer, 1951).

Moses Herzog are guided. And, as Joseph says, "if the quest is the same, the differences in our personal histories, which hitherto meant so much to us, become of minor importance." So it makes little difference at what point the reader enters Mr. Bellow's fiction, since, wherever he makes his way into it, he encounters people like the protagonist of *Seize the Day* — who is, we are told, a "visionary sort of animal. Who has to believe that he can know why he exists"; one encounters "theoreticians" whose most passionate commitment is to a very urgent kind of *Lebensphilosophie*, to the kind of vitally *existential* "theorizing" which is a hallmark of many of the central personages in twentieth-century fiction, of Musil's Ulrich and Joyce's Stephen Dedalus, of Lawrence's Birkin and Mann's Hans Castorp, of Malraux's Hernandez and Vincent Berger, of Camus' Rieux and Penn Warren's Jack Burden.

It should be stressed that the inquiry into the meaning of human existence carried forward by Mr. Bellow's protagonists is not, experientially, a bootless thing of abstract dialectic: instead, it is a search they are plunged into by the pressure of concrete circumstance, by the wreckage of hope and the bitter taste in their own lives of inauthenticity. One among them tells himself, on a certain crucial day of awakening, that he must undertake a great new effort, that otherwise it is likely his life will simply wither away, with nothing remaining — "nothing left but junk." Indeed, the character of rubble, of mess, of disarray, defines a part of what is initially problematic in the situation of Mr. Bellow's people: they have stumbled into one or another dark and airless pocket of the world — where confidence is broken by piles of little disappointments, where nerves are rubbed raw by the cheats and condescension suffered at the hands of duplicitous friends and relatives, and where the spirit is smothered by all the pledges and promises it has made and found impossible to fulfill. "The world is too much with us, and there has never been so much world," Mr. Bellow remarked a few years ago in a review of Philip Roth's *Good-bye, Columbus*; and this is very much the sort of complaint one imagines his own characters wanting weariedly to express, as they face the human bustle and density of their drab little space amidst the great, noisy, sprawling urban wilderness — which, whether encountered in Chicago by an Augie March or in New York by a Tommy Wilhelm, requires to be thought of as a "somber city." "Hot, stony odors" rise up from subways, and traffic seems to "come down . . . out of the sky": everything is draped with soot, and nowhere does one hear any happy "epithalamium of gentle lovers." The scene or site of the novels is, in short, where it is in Joyce's *Ulysses*, in Canetti's *Auto da Fé*, in Dos Passos' *The Big Money*, in Graham Greene's *It's a Battle-field* — "a populous and smoky city," where one would not have thought "death had undone so many."

The stars are capricious, and the burdens that people must bear exact, therefore, a geat expense of spirit: as a consequence, their fingernails are bitten and their eyes red-rimmed, and they often do not feel well, suffering a sense of "congestion" or extremes of fatigue, an obscure pain in the side or a raging headache — signs that they have not done well in their isolateness. Joseph, the young man whose diary (composed in the months during which he awaits his call-up into the army) forms Mr. Bellow's first book — the novel of 1944, *Dangling Man* — no longer takes any real delight in his devoted wife Iva: he explodes at the members of his family and picks quarrels with his friends, "storing bitterness and spite which eat like acids at [his] endowment of generosity and good will." Gripped by a strange "narcotic dullness," he is growing fat and slovenly, as more and more — like Beckett's Murphy — he becomes "rooted to [his] chair." Or, again, Asa Leventhal, the unheroic hero of Mr. Bellow's second novel, *The Victim* (1947), has slipped into early middle age as one who has just barely missed failure in the world of the city's job market: he edits a small New York trade paper, but his competence at the job does not altogether allay his intermittent anxiousness about the security of his tenure. He is attentive to his brother's wife and children in the brother's absence, but grudgingly so; like the young protagonist of *Dangling Man*, he turns a dour peevishness and spleen upon his friends and is given to nursing imagined slights and insults, for he is a "bitter and suspicious" man; he often does not even trouble to answer the friendly greeting of a waitress in a restaurant, though he tells himself that he ought to be more responsive; his burly, disheveled figure presents an appearance which is "unaccommodating, impassive," and, in the oppressive heat of a New York summer, he sweats profusely and suffers headache and heart tremor and a sense of his very head being filled with the pungent odors of the city. But even more blistered by experience is Tommy Wilhelm, the protagonist of the brilliant *novella* of 1956, *Seize the Day* — a man without work and very nearly penniless; badgered for money by the wife from whom he is separated and scorned by his smug, unfeeling father; ruined in physique and going to seed in every way, yet desperately scrounging about New York for some merest foothold — a man whose throat is nearly bursting with a "great knot of ill and grief" as his "day of reckoning" approaches. And that great Tarzan of a man whom we meet in *Henderson the Rain King* (1959), for all his millions and his rude health and energy, knows how onerous it is to "lie buried in yourself" and is filled with an aching need to "burst the spirit's sleep." Indeed, not even the irrepressible little *picaro* of *The Adventures of Augie March* (1953) is untouched by the generalized *malaise* of Mr. Bellow's world, for, at every turn, he finds himself surrounded by "destiny moulders . . . and wizard evildoers, big-wheels and imposers-upon," and the city against the background of which most of his drama is played out is a place of crime and violence and suffering. The world this fiction takes us into puts us in mind of the old monition, "Though he believe it, no man is strong."

Yet the effect of these books is never depressive and enervating, and their *personae* are not felt, in the end, to be denizens of the Underground. Indeed, I first spoke of their great vitality and — using a piece of Mr. Bellow's favorite slang — of their "larkiness." And this, curiously, is the final impression they make upon us, of being, most of them, very larky people. The sense of animation and exuberance comes, of course, in part from the buoyant language of which Mr. Bellow is so brilliantly vivacious an impresario. In many of the marvelously subtle and perspicacious essays making up his book of 1962, *The Barbarian Within*, Fr. Walter Ong, in a very profound way, is reminding us of a truism frequently forgotten by a generation whose most characteristic mentors in criticism have taught us to believe "that it is neither the potter who made it nor the people, real or fictional, to whose lives it is tangent, but the well wrought urn itself which counts. . . ."[5] The great preoccupation of contemporary criticism has been with *the text*, with the work of art *as such*, for it has been supposed that only by squinting at the poem or the novel as an *object* could criticism locate norms by which its discourse might become really corrigible. But this kind of thinking has long been overdone, so it is good that a theorist such as Fr. Ong should now remind us that a work of literary art, in its most primitive reality, is something "said" — not simply an object clearly and distinctly framed in space, but a "word" spoken *by one man*, "a moment in a dialogue."[6] The "voice" of the artist is conveyed, of course — as Fr. Ong fully understands — through the "objective" structures of poetry and fiction and drama, which is to say that its invocations and evocations are accomplished through the artist's various "masks." But the writer's mask is not itself vocal: it is an instrument (whether of plot or scene or "point of view") whereby the voice is enabled to register interesting variations in tone and pitch and rhythm and stress, but it does not itself modify the authorial voice in the way a mute modifies the sound of a violin.[7] So, given the primitively vocal and aural character of literary experience, it is the *voice* heard in a work of art that remains one of the principal realities inviting the disciplined attention of that uncommon reader whom Virginia Woolf generously called "the common read-

[5] Walter J. Ong, S. J., *The Barbarian Within* (New York: Macmillan Co., 1962), p. 15.
[6] *Ibid.*, p. 36.
[7] The analogy is Fr. Ong's, though his use of it differs somewhat from mine: *ibid.*, p. 60.

er." And it is, I want now to say, the voice that one constantly hears, and overhears, in Mr. Bellow's fiction which in part gives us so great a sense of the lively suppleness of the human reality being portrayed.

Here, for example, are the opening lines of *The Adventures of Augie March*:

> I am an American, Chicago born . . . and go at things as I have taught myself, free-style, and will make the record in my own way: first to knock, first admitted; sometimes an innocent knock, sometimes a not so innocent. But a man's character is his fate, says Heraclitus, and in the end there isn't any way to disguise the nature of the knocks by acoustical work on the door or gloving the knuckles.

These sentences, in their cascading bounce and friskiness and wit, could, by no stretch of the imagination, be thought to have come from the pen of a Hemingway or a Faulkner or a Penn Warren, or indeed from that of anyone other than Saul Bellow. The voice (though "masked" by the *persona* of the novel's hero) is unmistakably his — a voice that says, "Gee, what a funny, mysterious, surprising bloke man is, even when he's on his uppers! What shrewdness it takes to keep up with his craft and enterprise! How inspiriting it is to think that, maybe, things finally will give way — before intelligence and good humor and *esprit*; but how necessary it is not to tell ourselves lies and not to lose our sense of how wonderful is the gift of life!" This is the voice one hears throughout these books, even when it is speaking of suffering and humiliation and despair; and it is, I say, this voice that makes even an Asa Leventhal or a Tommy Wilhelm somehow larky.

What is most decisive in the shaping of character in Mr. Bellow's fiction, however, is the resoluteness with which he refuses to allow his people merely to wriggle in their despondency and dispeace. The texture of their lives is banal and gritty, because, one imagines, this is what Mr. Bellow takes to be the general quality of life in our great metropolitan communities, and his people therefore bear upon themselves the characteristic stigmata of the age — its *anomie*, its nostalgia, its alienation. But he will not permit them to *rest* in their distress: they carry great burdens, but Mr. Bellow's way of plotting the human story requires that they be brought to the point of attempting *dis*burdenment; though they are nagged by the "feeling of alienation," a way is prepared by which they may come to understand, as the young protagonist of *Dangling Man* says, that "we should not make a doctrine of our feeling." So the old journalist Schlossberg, in *The Victim*, says: "Choose dignity." And there comes a time when Henderson feels called upon to say sternly to himself: "Henderson, put forth effort." Moses Herzog, for all his "schooling in grief" and weighed down as he is by trouble, is finally brought, like Asa Leventhal, to "a kind of recognition," that he owes the powers that created him "a human life." And it is a similar *anagnorisis* towards which the human drama tends generally to move throughout Mr. Bellow's work.

This drama becomes explicitly a drama of reconciliation, however, only in the late books, in *Seize the Day* and *Henderson the Rain King* and *Herzog*; in the early books Grace is more a hope than a reality. And it is in *Dangling Man* that we get the most tenuous and muted expression of this hope. Here, the central figure is, of course, Joseph, a young "apprentice in suffering and humiliation," who, at the outbreak of World War II, gives up his job in a Chicago travel bureau to await his draft call. In the months that follow, he retires to the little cell he and his wife occupy in a rooming-house, there to become an "earnest huntsman of himself," as he anticipates "the minor crises of the day" (". . . the maid's knock, the appearance of the postman, programs on the radio. . . .") and contemplates what may be involved in the vocation of a good man. But he soon falters in his "retreat," and, far from becoming a happy experience of deepened self-recognition, it proves instead to be a sterile cul-de-sac in which Joseph finds himself increasingly defenseless before a strangely disabling inertia that settles down upon him. His predicament begins, paradoxically, to be that of a man *trapped* — in his freedom. And he is quite free: Iva, his wife, earns their living; so he is free of any formal daily appointments; and, keeping his distance from friends and family (except for an occasional encounter), he is free of virtually all human involvements. His solitude is not a rich and fecund thing, however, but something arid and debilitating: as he admits in his diary, "I have begun to notice that the more active the rest of the world becomes, the more slowly I move. . . . I grow rooted to my chair." And though, as he says, "I am unwilling to admit that I do not know how to use my freedom," nevertheless, day after day, as he sits in his room, rooted to his chair and anticipating the minor crises of the day, his freedom becomes a cheerless void — in which this descendant of Dostoievski's Underground Man and Goncharov's Oblomov and Svevo's Zeno simply dangles. He is jailed in the prison of his own ego, and, thus doubled back upon himself, it is no wonder that "bitterness and spite" corrode his "endowment of generosity and good will." He thinks that the end of all our striving, the goal towards which man perennially has to struggle, is "pure freedom." But at last, soured as his life is in the acedia of its isolation, he cannot put aside the realization that, if indeed freedom is the proper goal of man, this must surely be a freedom *from* precisely that into which he has too deeply entered — namely, one's own private selfhood. The self needs somehow to escape its own cage, to avoid being "humped protectively" over its own life. He is forced, in short, to admit: "I had not done well alone." Thus, in its stress on the need for self-transcendence, the book takes a step towards what were to be the principal emphases of Mr. Bellow's later fiction. It is only the merest step, however, for Joseph's illumination issues in nothing more than a hastily written note to his draft board requesting that he be called up "at the earliest possible moment." On his last civilian day, as Iva is packing his things, he inwardly exults at being now "in other hands": "Hurray for regular hours! And for the supervision of the spirit! Long live regimentation!" But not even the manifest irony with which these final lines are carefully fringed can quite obscure the paltriness of the Army as a redemptive principle, in the kind of spiritual context which Mr. Bellow's narrative so brilliantly establishes. So his book of 1944 strikes us as making a testimony which is, finally, too provisional, and as thus lacking an ultimate cogency. But, in the degree to which it finds its center in a "theoretician" whose great hope is for a new "colony of the spirit," it can now be seen to have been presaging the main course of Mr. Bellow's later fiction.

His second novel, *The Victim* (1947), is no less provisional and indecisive, in its embrace of a cathartic principle, than *Dangling Man*. But Mr. Bellow here implicates his protagonist Asa Leventhal — like Joseph, a "theoretician" who hovers over "craters of the spirit" — in a complex structure of human actions and relationships which requires him to do something more than merely engage in a continuous self-interrogation. He is by no means exempted from the embarrassments of self-arraignment, however. For one hot summer evening, in the little neighborhood park near his New York apartment building, he is suddenly approached by a shabby bystander whom, with some exertion of memory, he recognizes as a man he had known very slightly a few years earlier, Kirby Allbee. Allbee was then working on the staff of a trade magazine, and he had arranged for Leventhal, who was unemployed at the time, to be interviewed by his editor. The interview went badly, with Asa responding irately to the provocative boorishness of Rudiger, and the anger of these exchanges did in fact lead the editor not only to throw Leventhal out of his office but even to fire Allbee for having proposed the meeting. Now Allbee, meeting Leventhal for the first time in several years, accuses him of bearing the real responsibility not only for his dismissal from *Dill's Weekly* but also for his subsequent decline, irreversibly, into failure and hand-to-mouth impoverishment. Indeed, Allbee charges Leventhal — to Asa's utter astonishment — with having deliberately undertaken, on the day of that interview, to ruin him, in retaliation for his outburst of anti-Semitism at a party a few nights earlier that he knows Leventhal overheard. It is a strange indictment, in response to which Leventhal can only splutter out confusedly: "I haven't thought about you in years, frankly. . . .

What, are we related?" And, laughing surlily, Allbee answers: "By blood? No, no . . . heavens!"

But how, then, are they related? This is the issue the novel wants to explore. Here is a New York Jew — an obscure functionary in the great machine of the city's business — living a careful, conventional, apparently irreproachable life. And then, suddenly — like the abrupt appearance of Joseph K.'s accuser at the beginning of Kafka's *Der Prozess* — a paranoiac anti-Semite accosts him and bitterly complains of the injury he has suffered at Leventhal's hands. Nor do matters end there. In his wife's absence — Mary is helping her recently widowed mother move from Baltimore to Charleston — his self-declared victim, claiming no longer to have shelter, invades his flat, soiling it with his personal filth, upsetting the normal routines of Leventhal's tidy life, secretly ransacking personal papers to take possession even of the intimacies of Asa's marriage, and finally even taking over his bed to couple with a woman whom he brings in from the streets. Strangely, Leventhal acquiesces in all this outrageous plunderage. For the force of Allbee's reiterated accusations unsettles him to the point of compelling him to look back into the past. And, as he inquires into his own motives and solicits the judgments of friends who were privy to the circumstances of a few years ago which Allbee has now called up, he indeed begins to feel that perhaps this man is not, as he first claims, solely responsible for his own misfortune, that perhaps he, Asa, has himself in some measure contributed to it. This uncouth paranoiac is not wholly right in his furious allegations, but then he may not be wholly wrong — and, once he begins inwardly to make this admission, Leventhal's defenses against his adversary are effectively broken, and he is entrained towards discovering the true meaning of his own humanity.

In what ways are we really members one of another? If we shoot a bird, do we wound ourselves? How is a man related to his neighbor? What is the full meaning of responsibility? These are the questions that bristle before this perplexed defendant. At first he wants simply to say: "Why pick on me? I didn't set this up any more than you did. Admittedly there was a wrong, a general wrong." But Allbee will not let him off the hook and persists in saying *You!* . . . *You!* . . . *You!*

One Sunday afternoon, as Leventhal sits in a restaurant with a group of friends, he listens to the wise old journalist Schlossberg reflecting on the difficult equilibrium that man's nature requires him to seek: "It's bad to be less than human and it's bad to be more than human." And there comes a time when Leventhal's conscience begins to enforce upon him the hard truth that to be "human" is indeed to be "accountable in spite of many weaknesses," is to be in fact one's brother's keeper. But is there, then, a point beyond which the keeping of one's brother becomes "more than human"? So it would seem. For one night Leventhal wakens to find gas pouring out of his kitchen oven: in an attempt at suicide Allbee would have murdered him as well, so he throws him out. Further to temporize with this unhappy creature would be both more *and* less than human.

Then, a few years later, Leventhal (now solidly successful) and his wife are in a theatre one evening where, after the second curtain, by chance they meet Allbee in the lobby. This final episode is curiously tentative and indistinct. Though Allbee, having apparently made some sort of recovery, is elegantly dressed and squiring about a once-famous actress, Leventhal, as he faces him, is given a sense of decay. And though Allbee, as he recalls that earlier period in his life, faces Leventhal shamefacedly and with self-mockery, he yet manages to say, as he presses Asa's hand, "I know I owe you something." And so he does; but each is in the other's debt. For it was through Allbee's demoniac agency that Leventhal was brought to a "kind of recognition" — that we cannot choose whom to love, that we are required to love all homeless men who require to be sheltered under our care, lest

> . . . we make a scarecrow of the day,
> Loose ends and jumble of our common world,
> And stuff and nonsense of our own free will. . . .

The initial phase of Mr. Bellow's fiction may, then, be considered to form a movement from the stiflingly solipsistic atmosphere of a first novel, marked by all the modish isolation-ism of the modern avant-garde, towards a substantially greater positiveness of affirmation — that "No man is an Iland, intire of it selfe. . . ."

Thus the way had already been prepared, really, for his magnificent book, published in 1953, *The Adventures of Augie March*. In his *New Republic* review of *Augie*, Robert Penn Warren remarked the extent to which Mr. Bellow's essay in "the apparent formlessness of the autobiographical-picaresque novel" represented a radical departure from "the Flaubert-James tradition" which he had turned to such brilliant account in his first two novels. This turning undoubtedly gave the public an astonished sense of a certain melodrama in the evolution of Mr. Bellow's career, for the tightness of structure and muteness of style charac-teristic of his early work seemed in no way to have presaged the pyrotechnical extravagance of language and narrative procedure marking *The Adventures of Augie March*: in 1953, it appeared to be the most surprising development in the literary life of the period. But, startling as the changes were in the basic style of his artistry, they would not have seemed quite so startling had *The Victim* been read more closely, for the moral meaning of that book might well have been taken, logically, to entail an inevitable turning towards a more open form.

Unlike the Joseph of *Dangling Man*, who is drawn into him-self and, as a consequence, is hard and inflexible, Augie is a tractable and resilient young man endowed not with "single-ness of purpose" but with an unquenchable hospitality toward experience. Thus he "circles" — uncommittedly, and believing that "gods [may] turn up anywhere" — from manag-ing a sport-goods shop in Evanston to training an eagle for iguana-hunting in Mexico, from running a Chicago coalyard to consorting with Trotsky's lieutenants in Mexico City, from vagabondage in Detroit to black-market operations in Paris, from Depression poverty to post-World II affluence. He is an ebullient *picaro* in search of a fate which he can regard as worthy of his natural endowments, and his insatiable appetite for adventure gives the novel its huge expansiveness, causing it to span continents and generations and to make room for nearly a hundred personages, altogether remarkable in their vital eccentricity and vividness of presence. Many years ago, in discussing Theodore Dreiser, Mr. Bellow expressed admiration for Dreiser's great "lifting power," for his ability to make his fiction "lift up" great masses of human actuality, of American experience, of social fact. And it is a similar "lifting power" that helps to make *The Adventures of Augie March* so impressive a feat of the novelistic imagination: it notices and names and evokes and gathers in so rich an abundance of material that its teeming world seems barely once removed from the existential reality of the modern world itself. Mr. Bellow says: "The great pleasure of the book was that it came easily. All I had to do was be there with buckets to catch it." And this is indeed the impression the novel makes upon us — this sense of a beautifully easy improvisation being, however (as Penn Warren reminded us in his review of the book), "a dramatic illusion . . . [which is] the last sophistication of the writer . . ."

But, though Augie never finds what he can confidently accept as "a worthwhile fate," he keeps the "opposition" that old Einhorn in Chicago discovered in him as a boy. Despite the pliancy which permits him to play the games of so many different people (the young book thief Padilla; the trade-unionist Grammick; the unbalanced millionaire and researchist on the "history of human happiness," Robey; the Trotskyite Frazer; the Armenian lawyer and black-marketeer, Mintouchian), there comes a point when he must always "offer resistance and . . . say 'No!'" to those who want to manage and manipulate his life — whether it be to his brother Simon, who wants him to make money and become a big wheel; to the Renlings, who want him to be their adopted son and heir; to Thea Fenchel, who asks a self-dedication to her special sort of underworld; or to various others under whose influence he is brought by the adventures of life. Thus the persistent rhythm of the book is (as the English critic Tony Tanner has acutely observed) "a drifting into things finally stopped by a sudden digging in of the heels or a sudden flight from attachment,"[8] for Augie does not want, as he says, to be "sucked into . . . [any] of those . . . currents where I can't be myself." As Einhorn says: "You've got *opposition* in you. You don't slide through everything. You just make it look so." Clem Tambow tells Augie that he "can't adjust to the reality situation," and to this he is not inclined to offer any rebuttal, for he knows himself to want "a charge counter to the central magnetic one and to dance his own dance on the periphery."

So Augie always has "trouble being still" and never has "any place of rest" — and this is why, I suspect, the novel over which he presides lacks any true conclusion. Yet this young "American, Chicago born," always wants very much to find a way of being still, since his great hope, he says, "is based upon getting to be still so that the axial lines can be found." And this, to be sure, is his most basic passion (as it is of all those "theoreticians" whom Mr. Bellow elects to a pivotal position in his books), finding the "axial lines" of life. But though, by the end, there is no evidence of Augie's having ever really found this lambent center of gravity, he persists, nevertheless, in his refusal to "live a disappointed life": as he says on the final page of the novel, with his characteristic insouciance, "I may well be a flop at this line of endeavor. Columbus too thought he was a flop, probably, when they sent him back in chains. Which didn't prove there was no America." Yet, finally, Augie has at least won the crucial insight that leads directly into the remarkable novels of Mr. Bellow's maturity — that, as he says, "When striving stops, there they are [i.e., the "axial lines"] as a gift."

Now it is just here that we are brought to what begins indeed to seem *the* axial line of Mr. Bellow's whole vision of the world, most particularly as it is expressed in the late books, in *Seize the Day* (1956) and *Henderson the Rain King* (1959) and *Herzog* (1964) — that, when striving stops, there it is, the infinitely poignant fullness and beauty of the very miracle of life itself. It begins to appear, in other words, that what

[8] Tony Tanner, *Saul Bellow* (Edinburgh: Oliver & Boyd, 1965), p. 48.

we confront in this whole body of fiction is a radically religious perspective on the human reality. For though Mr. Bellow's protagonist is, characteristically, like Joseph in *Dangling Man*, a "creature of plans" and projects, the recognition that he has ultimately to achieve, particularly in the late novels, is that his plans and projects must at last yield before those tidal rhythms of life which ordain (as it is put in one of the Anglican Prayerbook's most famous Collects) that "in returning and rest we shall be saved, in quietness and in confidence shall be our strength," and that we shall be brought by the Spirit to that Presence "where we may be still. . . ."

"Damn braces, bless relaxes," says a wise half-truth of William Blake's ("half," because, in certain areas of experience, it may be equally important to make the converse testimony). And in a similar way, increasingly, Saul Bellow is also wanting to say that there is a certain ultimate dimension in the life of the human spirit in which strenuousness is of no real avail; that true sanity of mind and heart is not won by grabbing at life, by jamming our barns full and packing our banks tight; [9] that moving about the world "with clenched fists even though we keep them in our pockets" [10] does not lead to abundance of life; that *fullness* of life cannot be accumulated "like bank notes or garments"; [11] that the kleptomania which prompts us to fill "our little backyards with all kinds of things" [12] which strenuousness can lay hands on only makes our last state worse than the first; and that, therefore, we must not "force the saw, flail the wind, beat the waves, uproot the seed": [13] for, when striving stops, there it all is, as a gift — of Grace.

In my citation of the Anglican Collect for Quiet Confidence and in my use of Martin Luther's famous formula — *sola*

[9] *Vide* Samuel H. Miller, *The Great Realities* (New York: Harper & Bros., 1955), p. 162. The quotations from this book which are cited in the four footnotes immediately following acknowledge my indebtedness to the language of one of the most beautifully written and brilliantly original essays in ascetical theology of our time.
[10] *Ibid.*, p. 160.
[11] *Ibid.*, p. 164.
[12] *Ibid.*, p. 162.
[13] *Ibid.*, pp. 164–65.

gratia — in the title of this essay, I may appear to be bringing the design of Mr. Bellow's thought into a distinctively Christian *ambiance*. But to attempt this would surely be an error in tact and in definition, for the ethos of his fiction is, of course, manifestly drenched in the life and lore of Jewish experience. One suspects, indeed, that Mr. Bellow's great sympathy for something like a doctrine of *sola gratia* is a consequence of his having been influenced, at some very deep level of his mind and sensibility, by the Hasidic strain of Jewish spirituality. But the essential thrust that I am here remarking need not be given any "denominational" tag at all. For it can be taken to be a "natural law" governing the life-world of the *homo religiosus*, that (as Simone Weil phrased it) "by pulling at the bunch, we make all the grapes fall to the ground," [14] and that the way into Truth and Felicity is therefore (to change the metaphor) the way of "letting oneself fall" — like "the first flight of a baby eagle, pushed out of the nest by its parents, and then discovering to its amazement that the invisible ocean of light in which it is dropping is capable of bearing it up." [15] At the Center of life there is no straining, no muscular effort, but only a certain kind of strict attentiveness and (as Gabriel Marcel terms it) *invocation*: there, at the Center, we consent to take our hands off our lives and simply to wait — for the stroke of Grace. Something like this is said in the *Bhagavad-Gita* and by Lao-tse, in the Hasidism of the Baal-Shem-Tov and by Meister Eckhart. "Damn braces, bless relaxes." And a kind of *falling*-into Peace also seems to be the essential reality dramatized in the later work of Saul Bellow.

It is perhaps in *Henderson the Rain King* that this salient principle of Mr. Bellow's fiction finds its clearest rendering, though it is their inattentiveness to its presence in *Seize the Day* which has, I suspect, led many of his critics to be so baffled, finally, by that brilliant *novella*. Mr. Bellow tells us

[14] Simone Weil, *Gravity and Grace*, trans. Arthur Wills (New York: G. P. Putnam's Sons, 1952), p. 171.
[15] Karl Heim, *The Transformation of the Scientific World View* (London: S.C.M. Press, 1951), p. 167.

that "shoulders are from God and burdens too," and the harried protagonist of Seize the Day, Tommy Wilhelm, seems to have received more than his share of God's largesse. This ex-actor and ex-salesman is unemployed and, having fallen behind in the world's rat race, at forty-seven years of age is without any hopeful prospect at all: he is down to his last seven hundred dollars, and the wife from whom he is separated is brutally pressing in her insistence upon absolute promptness in his rendering of the support payments; nor will the cold little Philistine who is his father — a formerly distinguished physician now living in comfortable retirement — assist him in any way at all, not even with the cheap help of words of encouragement. In addition to all the external disarray in Tommy's life, he is himself, despite desperate attempts to keep up appearances, fast going to seed, his body spoiled with fat and broken-windedness, with neurotic overeating and phenobarbital.

Indeed, the day recorded in Mr. Bellow's narrative is the "day of reckoning" that has rapidly been drawing near: "A huge trouble long presaged but till now formless was due." "I'm so choked up and congested . . . I can't see straight," Tommy moans, as he contemplates the wreckage of his foundered life and grows terrified by the thought that he may even have thrown away his last seven hundred dollars, in permitting the self-declared psychologist, Dr. Tamkin, to manage it in stock-market speculations. Nor does this surmise prove to be amiss, for, when he goes in search of the wily little confidence man ("full of high sentence" about "seizing the day"), he finds that he has absconded. And it is as he is chasing Tamkin along Broadway on a hot, bright afternoon that he finds himself suddenly shoved by the crowds into a funeral parlor, where a ceremony happens just then to be in progress. Looking down at the dead man, Tommy's "eyes shone hugely with instant tears," and "standing a little apart," he begins to weep.

> He cried at first softly and from sentiment, but soon from deeper feeling. He sobbed loudly and his face grew distorted and hot, and the tears stung his skin. . . .

Soon he was past words, past reason, coherence. He could not stop. The source of all tears had suddenly sprung open within him, black, deep, and hot, and they were pouring out and convulsed his body, bending his stubborn head, bowing his shoulders, twisting his face, crippling the very hands with which he held the handkerchief. His efforts to collect himself were useless. The great knot of ill and grief in his throat swelled upward and he gave in utterly and held his face and wept. He cried with all his heart. . . .

The flowers and lights fused ecstatically in Wilhelm's blind, wet eyes; the heavy sea-like music came up to his ears. It poured into him where he had hidden himself in the center of a crowd by the great and happy oblivion of tears. He heard it and sank deeper than sorrow, through torn sobs and cries toward the consummation of his heart's ultimate need.

One feels that these concluding lines of the story might well have been given such a postscript as T. S. Eliot's "Shantih shantih shantih," for, as they speak of "the consummation of his heart's ultimate need," they announce that this unhappy man has finally been touched by a "Peace which passeth understanding." But, though this peace surpasses the understanding in precisely the way of all miracles of Grace, it ought not, *in this way*, to have surpassed the understanding of so many of Mr. Bellow's critics who have fidgeted over what they have taken to be its gratuitousness and have sometimes, in exasperation, simply dismissed it out of hand, finally, as an illicit tour de force. The point is — the *dramatic* point is — that, in the hour of his great extremity, Tommy Wilhelm, by the sheer force of his heart's pain, is disarmed into taking his hands off his life, into giving up his struggle, into surrendering, simply surrendering, to the mystery of his own existence. When, in short, striving stops, there it is — the consummation of his heart's ultimate need, a strange new kind of peace, inevitably at first inchoate and indistinct, which promises that he may yet survive his distress: he is by way, willy nilly, of *falling* into blessedness.

It is, essentially, the same sort of adventure in atonement which is being dramatized in *Henderson the Rain King*, and, again, when the book appeared in 1959, it was somehow very well received, despite the confusion with which many of Mr. Bellow's critics rubbed their eyes and wondered what it is really about. But, if his commitment to the principle of *sola gratia* be remembered, the novel should then not be found to present any great puzzle. Its hero, Eugene Henderson — Mr. Bellow's only Gentile protagonist — is a great titan of a man whose fortune runs into the millions and whose life is cluttered not only with money but with wives and children and mistresses and estates and servants: yet he suffers a great sense of insufficiency; there is a voice within him constantly crying, "I want, I want, I want"; and he feels a nagging compulsion to "burst the spirit's sleep." So he goes off to Africa, "the ancient bed of mankind," in quest of a Great Awakening. And, there, his tutelage falls into the hands of two tribes, the Arnewi and the Wariri.

The Arnewi are a benign, easy-going, placid people whose quiet life is badly ruffled by the strenuous dynamism of this chaotic Yankee. They are cattle-raisers, but they do not eat beef, for they regard their cattle as their relatives, not as domestic animals. At the time Henderson enters their village the people are stricken with grief, for they are unable to water their cattle, which are rapidly dying of thirst. The cattle cannot be watered because a great batch of frogs has gotten into the village cistern, and the people appear to be prevented by religious scruples from removing the frogs, though they believe the frogs to be contaminating the water: they think they are suffering a plague sent by the gods. Henderson determines to come to their assistance — but, in attempting to explode the frogs out of the water, he blows up the cistern as well. And, having visited this disaster upon the Arnewi, he must then, of course, leave. But, before his short stay amongst them is thus concluded, he has an interview with Willatale, the old lady who with an impressive dignity presides over these people as their Queen. This interview brings him great solace, because of what he feels to be the sensitive penetration with which the Queen perceives his heart's deepest aspiration, when she says to him, "Grun-tu-molani" — which means "Man want to live."

Henderson's most crucial encounter, though, is with the Wariri — who are, as his guide Romilayu tells him, "chillen dahkness." Indeed, their rites and manners are cruder, and much more savage and violent, than those of the Arnewi. But their King, Dahfu, is a man of great gentleness and sophistication who makes Henderson feel immediately "that we could approach ultimates together." And so they do. After Henderson survives certain initial tests, Dahfu, with great patience, undertakes his education in the things of the spirit. "Granted, grun-tu-molani is much," says Dahfu, "but it is not alone sufficient. Mr. Henderson, more is required." And it is the additional virtues which he wants his American friend to have. So he prescribes a most exigent discipline. It involves a daily descent into the den of a lion which Dahfu has himself trapped and tamed and which he keeps in an underground vault beneath his palace. Henderson is "all limitation . . . contracted and cramped" — "self-recoiled" — and Dahfu perceives that this man who has all his life inwardly cried, "I want, I want, I want," must be taught how to relax. And his way of doing this involves his requiring Henderson each day to draw nearer and nearer to the lion, and finally to romp about the den on all fours, roaring and snarling as loudly as his lungs will permit. Thus it is that Dahfu takes Henderson to "the bottom of things," being certain that if his American visitor can learn, like the lion, "not [to] take issue with the inherent" and to relax, his fear will be overcome and his "consciousness [will be made] to shine": his excessive "ego-emphasis" will be mitigated, will be "loosened up" — and then he can move into the profound peace that comes when a man is no longer glued to his own finitude but when, having learned to submit to Being-itself, he can be claimed by a waft of Grace and delivered into perfect felicity. "Damn braces, bless relaxes": this is what Dahfu wants to say to his pupil. And, indeed, Henderson's last state is better than the first, for the importunate voice within — "I want, I want, I want" —

has been stilled. At the end, when the plane on which he is bound for New York stops at Newfoundland for fuel and he gets out to leap about "over the pure white lining of the gray Arctic silence," he is a man whose spirit's sleep has been pierced; no longer does he need to *rush* through the world in the old way, for he has broken out of the cycle of *becoming* and into the realm of *being* — because, back there, with Dahfu, he became (in Rilke's phrase) a "deeply kneeling man."

Here, of course, one feels that Mr. Bellow's eagerness to enunciate a principle of redemption released an allegorical passion so rampant as nearly to have overwhelmed altogether his commitment to the novel as a form; and, in retrospect, it seems that the exuberant sportiveness of the language in which the book is written and the rich inventiveness with which scene and incident are created may have produced the illusion of novelistic structures which in fact have been virtually suspended. Yet, if Henderson — with his size-22 collar and his enormous bulk and his aching teeth and his pig farm and his two wives and all his millions — is more a presence than a man, he is certainly the most memorable comic presence in recent fiction. And though his outrageous shenanigans and buffoonery sometimes come close to parodying Mr. Bellow's deeper meanings, this writer's *deepest* meaning may well be that the kind of nonchalance about itself which is expressed in self-parody can easily be afforded by a humanity whose "ego-emphasis" has been "loosened up" by the realization that the gift of life is to be had only "when striving stops."

Mr. Bellow's brilliant book of 1964, *Herzog*, carries forward the basic design of his thought, morally and religiously — though here it is expressed far more with the extremely subtle indirection characteristic of *Seize the Day* than with the allegorical simplicity of *Henderson*. Moses Herzog is a forty-three-year-old Canadian Jew whose life has largely been spent (sometimes) in the midst of and (sometimes) on the fringes of academic circles in Chicago and New York. He is an intellectual historian specializing in the Romantic movement, and his book *Romanticism and Christianity*, though it never made a great splash, had, at the time of its appearance, established him as a young scholar of considerable originality and promise. But Herzog, bearing as he does a "great bone-breaking burden of selfhood," lacks some necessary gift for success. As the novel opens, his life appears very nearly to have collapsed in utter failure: he is without any academic portfolio; he has squandered a patrimony of twenty thousand dollars on the unredeemable dilapidation of an isolated country house in the Berkshires; he has been cuckolded by his best friend and deserted by Madeleine, the beautiful and malevolent bitch whom he forsook his first wife Daisy to marry; and his scholarly researches on Romanticism have reached an impasse, so that he has virtually given up his work on the book in progress. Indeed, the pressures of life have taken so heavy a toll that "some people thought he was cracked and for a time he himself had doubted that he was all there."

But then, at what seems to be the end of his tether, he begins to write letters — which are never posted — to his former mistresses and to General Eisenhower, to professional rivals and to his dead mother, to Adlai Stevenson and Martin Heidegger, to his first wife and to Friedrich Nietzsche, to contemporary British physicists and to Russian intellectuals of the nineteenth century, and "to everyone under the sun," even to God himself. Through this discipline of letter-writing — and through the recollection of the past and the sorting out of his experience that this discipline entails — Herzog undertakes to gather up and re-order the scattered fragments of his life. And the novel largely consists of these letters — marvelously engrafted to the basic dramatic design — and of a plethora of flashbacks which gradually unfold the entire history of this man by means of a *montage* whose execution is a beautifully dazzling feat of narration.

What is so engaging about this erratic and charming scapegrace — this representative mid-century "anti-hero," who takes a vain satisfaction in his slightly faded handsomeness and who is so unadept at fending for himself in the rough and tumble of the world — is that, as he stands amidst the

débris of his imprudent life, though he must constantly resist
the invading pressures of madness, he steadfastly refuses the
"foolish dreariness" of "the Wasteland outlook." He has had
his "schooling in grief," but he will not "tout" the Void; and
he knows enough about the whole Romantic experiment to
understand that the modern fascination with the "florid ex-
tremism" of Crisis and Alienation leads only into another
blind alley. For all his failures as scholar and lover and husband and father, he has no desire to contract out of history.
The "transcendence" that beckons him is what he finds the
philosopher Jean Wahl calling "transcendence downwards":
our job, in other words, is not to get outside of life but to find
within the human situation itself a redemptive center and a
healing grace.

It is after his final confrontation with Madeleine that Moses
begins to find a new steadiness and serenity. He is suddenly
stirred one day by love for his little daughter, and he takes a
plane from New York to Chicago to pay her a visit. A friend
arranges with Madeleine for him to spend an afternoon with
the child. All goes well until, as he is returning June to her
mother in a rented car, he becomes involved in a minor collision. Since – for reasons which are fully explained – he
happens to have an unregistered revolver on his person, the
policemen who come to the scene are required to "book"
him: so June has to accompany him to the precinct station.
After his wife has come for the child and as he faces her
motiveless malignity and rage, he slowly begins really to see
that the brutal violence of this destructive woman has about
it "a fringe of insanity." Yet the very fire of her pointless
malevolence has a certain purgative effect, for it elicits from
him an inward act of rejection. He knows that he owes the
powers that created him "a human life," and he makes us feel
the dawning realization in himself that living "a human life"
involves, however quietly and unobtrusively, the making of a
sort of testimony – not to apocalypse and crisis and alienation, but in behalf of the "ordinary middling human considerations." So he goes back to his house in the Berkshires, there
at last to bring his letter-writing to an end and, like Candide,

to begin to cultivate his garden, with the beautiful Castilian Ramona Donsell, a successful New York businesswoman who adores him and for whose robust sensuality and delicious Shrimp Arnaud he has a fine appetite.

But, though Mr. Bellow's story is a story of salvation and of Paradise Regained and though Herzog's letters are dense with a very sophisticated kind of commentary on the lore and ideology of modern intellectual life (recalling in this respect the Mann of *Der Zauberberg* and *Doktor Faustus*), the novel is in no way a solemn morality. It is drenched in a fun and lightheartedness and wit which have that very Jewish sort of bounce and rhythm by which *The Adventures of Augie March* is so noticeably marked. And the gaiety and playfulness that give raciness to Mr. Bellow's language and élan to his deployment of character and situation are a part of what is substantive in his message: he wants to convey a most stringent judgment of that *Angst*-ridden mentality which has for so long been our fashionable mode of seriousness, and he wants to suggest that there is healing in laughter. Indeed, the comedy of *Herzog* is a comedy of redemption, a redemption whose catalyst is similar to that initiating the process of restoration in Mr. Bellow's earlier books — namely, the quitting of anxiety, of stress, of struggle. For Moses begins to hear "indefinite music within" and to be on his way towards blessedness once he decides "to surrender the hyperactivity of this hyperactive face. . . . just to put it out instead to the radiance of the sun." Then it is that a new peace settles over the novel, as he, in the final chapter — now back at his property in the Berkshires — begins to paint a piano for little June and walks quietly in the woods and makes arrangements with a local cleaning woman to put his house in order. "Whatever had come over him during these last months, the spell really seemed to be passing, really going." Indeed, the time even comes when he gives up his letter-writing. "Yes, that was what was coming, in fact. The knowledge that he was done with those letters." Now, "feeling that he was easily contained by everything about him," he has "no messages for anyone else. . . . Not a single word." By returning and rest and quietness, he is brought — by Grace — into a new domain of the spirit, where it is good to be, since here (as St. Bernard says) a man

  . . . . vivit purius,
Cadit rarius, surgit velocius, incedit cautius,
Quiescit securius, moritur felicius,
Purgatur citius, proemiatur copiosus.

Perhaps as a result in part of influences exerted on the English scene by F. R. Leavis and on the American scene by Lionel Trilling, there is a strange and clumsy usage that contemporary criticism has fallen into, of naming the writer a "moralist" who handles the art of fiction in such a way as to advance a serious comment on the meaning of human existence. So much has this designation become a part of our critical lexicon that I am almost now at the point of so denominating Saul Bellow. But *Webster's New International Dictionary of the English Language* tells us that a moralist is "one who moralizes; a teacher or student of morals; a writer seeking to inculcate moral duties." This is the exact meaning of the term, and so it should be used, if it is to be used scrupulously. But though the novelist is no doubt a "student of morals" — in the sense, however, not of "ideals" but of the actualities of human behavior — neither Mr. Bellow nor indeed any serious artist in fiction undertakes to "moralize" or "to inculcate moral duties." Such may in part be the job of a priest or a spiritual director, but it is not the job of the novelist. And in fact — in the passage I quoted earlier on from his monologue called "Address by Gooley MacDowell to the Hasbeens Club of Chicago" — Mr. Bellow has already recorded his belief that today we suffer from a surfeit of "wise counsel and good precept"; and thereby he has very clearly forsworn for himself the role of "moralist."

So it is not by this term that we shall properly express our sense of the weight and dignity of his achievement. What needs rather to be said, I think, is that that weight and dignity reside not in his enactment of the role of moralist but in the profundity with which his fiction negotiates (in Kierkegaard's phrase) a "teleological suspension of the ethical." What is substantive in his art is not, in other words, primarily to be located in the dimension of morality at all: it is, rather, to be found in the more ultimate dimension in which we search for what ought to be the fundamental orientation or posture of the human spirit towards reality. And here, in this dimension of things, Mr. Bellow's deepest engagement, as I have been attempting to suggest, appears to be with the mystery that Christian theology calls *Justification* (*through*-faith, *by*-Grace-alone), or that Hebraic spirituality comprehends in its concept of *teshubah* (the "turning" of the self, in quietness and humility, away from self-sufficient "striving" towards the mysterious reality of Grace). The daily *Tahanun* of the Jew's morning prayer says: "Our Father, our King, be gracious unto us and answer us, for we have no works. . . . Save us according to thy grace." And, despite its independence of any explicitly theistic position, Mr. Bellow's fiction moves in a similar direction. His novels do not exhibit, to be sure, the manifest indebtedness to a special dogmatic tradition that marks the fiction of a Bernanos or a Graham Greene; but they are not thereby prevented from forming one of the most profoundly religious renderings of experience in the literature of our time.

2

Bernard Malamud and the High Cost of Living

GILES B. GUNN

"And I know that the spirit of God is the brother of my own,
And that all the men ever born are also my brothers,
and the women my sisters and lovers,
And that a kelson of the creation is love. . . ."
Walt Whitman, "Song of Myself"

In a profoundly anxious and skeptical age such as our own,
Whitman's wonderfully celebrative lines sound strangely out
of place. We seem to have witnessed too many acts of human
barbarity and perversity to share his warm feeling for *Brudermensch*, to have experienced too many instances of cosmic
absurdity or indifference to accept his generous faith in the
essential goodness of life. For ours has been described as a
time when the only human community men have been able
to discover is a divided, fragmented or broken one, and a time
when the only God men have been able to acknowledge is an
impotent, an absent or a dead one. Thus our history and our
condition have given rise to the assumption that the only
kind of literature which can reach us, much less appeal to us,
is a literature which accentuates the extreme at the expense
of the commonplace, the perverse at the expense of the ordinary, the violent at the expense of the pacific, the intense at
the expense of the casual — in short, a literature which poses
the possibilities of existence, if possibilities there be, in terms
of irrevocable choices and ultimate finalities instead of tentative alternatives and proximate goals.

Yet a number of American writers have begun to receive
wide public and critical acclaim — writers otherwise as di-

verse as J. D. Salinger, Wright Morris, Ralph Ellison, Ken Kesey, Saul Bellow and Bernard Malamud — who seem united, if in nothing else, in the common effort to challenge this assumption about ourselves and the kind of literature we think we need. While none of them has betrayed any desire to overlook or discount the fearful antinomies which characterize modern experience, all of them have shared the conviction that life must somehow be made possible not merely in spite of those antinomies but even, perhaps, because of them. They have not tried to evade or escape from the nightmarish ambiguity of modern experience; they have simply sought, after fully confronting its irrational, demonic underside, to use that experience for the purpose of discovering not merely what man can endure by defying it, but also what man can learn, and by learning more fully become, by trying to live with it.

Their typical strategy has thus been to seek ways of somehow passing through and beyond what is grotesque and absurd and dehumanizing in contemporary experience, in order to reach the point where the frightful dimensions of our life can be comprehended imaginatively and then even used for the purpose of ennobling in however small a way the man who must contend with them. In this effort to evaluate and then to employ all the possibilities for both good and evil in modern life, these writers have frequently found themselves closer than we might otherwise expect to the Whitman who tried to absorb all of life's oppositions and contradictions in the body of his poetry. And whether or not they have consciously worked toward Whitman's joyful, life-affirming mysticism, they have shared his deep and generous feeling for life in all its minute and inconsequential particulars.

This is nowhere more evident than in the work of Bernard Malamud whose fiction is suffused with the feeling expressed in Whitman's lines. Indeed that feeling, reuniting man with his neighbor and the spirit of God with his creation, carries us to the very heart of Malamud's deepest sense about life, a sense or intuition which is expressed not so much through character, action or thought as through the underlying tone of his work, what the Yiddish tradition refers to as the *nigun* [1] — the voice behind and beneath his narratives which carries that deep undercurrent of sympathy, as in Whitman, for all that is human and which suffers simply because it is there. Yet in Malamud's best work — in *The Assistant*, "The Loan," "The Magic Barrel," "Idiots First," "The German Refugee," and parts of *A New Life* and *The Fixer* — this fundamental intuition about life is always implicit rather than explicit, a function of the way he has treated his materials rather than of the nature of the materials he has chosen. Indeed, the situations and meanings most representative of Malamud's materials have usually been at variance with this intuition, ironically qualifying and complicating it, and thus endowing it with the character of something earned instead of given, something achieved instead of simply assumed.

This is no more than a statement of the fact that nothing of value is acquired cheaply in the world which Malamud has created in his fiction. Whatever man gains, he gains through suffering and is always in danger of losing because of the way his present aspirations are tied to his past failures, his future ambitions to his present foibles. A victim of circumstance, man is also a victim of himself. Yet what ultimately seems to matter is that, being both, man is indelibly human and thus worthy of our respect, even of our compassion, for all that makes him so.

But the comparison between Malamud and Whitman may seem strained to those who have identified Malamud more particularly as a Jewish rather than as an American writer, as a writer whose most important characteristics stem from his affinities with the Yiddish tradition of Mendele, Aleichem and Peretz rather than from his relationship to the American tradition of Hawthorne, James and Faulkner. His most memorable characters — like Morris Bober in *The Assistant*, Leo Finkle and Pinye Salzman in "The Magic Barrel," Lieb the baker in "The Loan," Shimon Susskind in "The Last Mohican," Oskar Gassner in "The German Refugee," and Yakov Bok in *The Fixer* — all seem to possess too distinct an old-

[1] See *A Treasury of Yiddish Stories*, ed. Irving Howe and Eliezer Greenberg (New York: Compass Books, Viking Press, 1965), p. 48.

world quality, even when they are first- and second-generation American immigrants, to be imaginatively associated with the New World. The ethos, the condition, even the suffering of the East European *shtetl* clings to them like a suit of clothes, and Malamud seems to treat them in the classic Yiddish manner.

His fiction is everywhere characterized by that mixture of styles, and even modes, so characteristic of Yiddish literature — the fantastic with the actual, the absurd with the ordinary, the surreal with the natural, and even the ridiculous with the sublime. But Malamud's technique has not originated from any mere desire to imitate; it has arisen instead, so at least one critic has argued,[2] from his own essentially Jewish, almost mystical apprehension of the fearfully intimate relation between heaven and earth and perhaps even Hell, a relation so close that the sacred and the profane seem to intermingle in his fiction, imbuing even his most pathetic characters and their overwhelming circumstances with a certain hallowed quality.

Life envisaged in such terms becomes a frightfully precarious adventure, as it has always been for the dispossessed Jew, where man is ever poised between a hopeless past and a possibly redemptive future. Living in the insubstantial present which is always in danger of dissolving or disappearing before him, man is faced with the problem of sheer survival. To prevent his affliction and his uncertainty from engulfing him, the characteristically Yiddish figure in Malamud's fiction, the *schlemihl*, usually attempts to devise an elaborate defensive strategy of ritualistic gestures, symbolic shrugs and ironic witticisms. But these cannot suffice to curb his despair as he tries to cope with the pain of history and wait for the promised end which never comes. His only real possibility for enduring the present depends upon his ability to achieve through suffering that inner discipline over his own desires and expectations which alone can provide him with the ca-

[2] Alfred Kazin, "The Magic and the Dread," in *On Contemporary Literature*, ed. Richard Kostelanetz (New York: Avon Books, 1964), p. 439.

pacity to endure, not simply for himself but for all those other nameless victims of life who suffer with him. To achieve such discipline is to achieve the power to love, the one value, both in Malamud and in the Yiddish tradition as a whole, whose radiance can redeem life even when life itself seems bent upon destroying it.

Yet it is precisely because of his faith in the power of love that Malamud belongs so firmly to the American tradition of Walt Whitman as well. It was F. Scott Fitzgerald who first characterized America itself, in a phrase equally as descriptive of the deepest impulses in Malamud's fiction, as "a willingness of the heart,"³ but the emphasis upon sympathy and compassion so deeply embedded in the American grain can be traced back from T. S. Eliot's meditations upon the intersection of the timeless with the temporal through Melville's reflections upon Hawthorne's "boundless sympathy with all forms of being"⁴ to Jonathan Edwards' doctrine of creation. And, as in the Yiddish tradition, so, too, in the American: that "willingness of the heart" has not only been responsible for its basic impulse; it has also been responsible for many of its most typical virtues and shortcomings, virtues and shortcomings to which Malamud, in either case, has been heir — its profound sympathy for the dispossessed and the victimized, and its consequent tendency to sentimentalize their predicament; its deep identification with the problems of the heart, and its consequent suspicion of the intellect; its tendency to idealize the genuine and the simple, and its frequent disinclination to criticize mere uneducated innocence; its preoccupation with the moral and spiritual as opposed to the merely social dimensions of existence and its consequent inclination to oversimplify the social ramifications of moral and spiritual problems; its compulsion to defend the integrity and value of man, especially in a time such as ours when it has become modish to call them into question, and its consequent temp-

³ F. Scott Fitzgerald, *The Crack Up*, ed. Edmund Wilson (New York: New Directions, 1956), p. 197.
⁴ Herman Melville, "Hawthorne and His Mosses," in *The Portable Melville*, ed. Jay Leyda (New York: Viking Press, 1952), p. 404.

63

tation, as Alfred Kazin once put it, "to stand and deliver, . . . to end up in the great American sky of abstractions."[5] But if the major strengths and limitations of Malamud's fiction can be said to derive as much from the American as from the Yiddish literary tradition, so can his most characteristic narrative form. Indeed, the story which Malamud has told again and again in each of his novels simply mirrors in all its essentials what R. W. B. Lewis once called the authentic American narrative.[6] Based upon Whitman's fundamental apprehension of "the simple genuine self against the whole world," Lewis' prototypical story, like each of Malamud's novels, seeks to test the nature of that self when it is thrust into a world not of its own making. As in so many of the great American classics, from *The Scarlet Letter* and *Billy Budd* to *The Portrait of the Lady* and *The Great Gatsby*, all of Malamud's longer works concern the nature and possible destiny of an essentially innocent protagonist of mysterious or questionable origin who seeks to begin a new life when the old one has come to nothing. In *The Natural* (1952) this figure of innocence is Roy Hobbs, who returns to the major leagues fifteen years after he was first cut down by Harriet Bird's silver bullet to fulfill his ambition to be "the best there ever was in the game." In *The Assistant* (1957) he becomes Frank Alpine, the quixotic Italian immigrant, who appears one day in the Bober grocery store to begin his long apprenticeship in suffering. In *A New Life* (1961) Malamud's ever-present innocent emerges as S. Levin, the ex-drunkard from New York, who goes as far West as he can imagine, to Marathon, Cascadia, to forget his old life and begin a new one. In Malamud's latest novel *The Fixer* (1966), this figure is finally transformed into Yakov Bok, the little Jewish fixit man, who sets out for the big city in search of better possibilities after his barren wife leaves him for another man.

What unites each of these figures of innocence with many of Malamud's other memorable characters such as Breitbart

[5] Kazin, "Magic and the Dread," p. 438.
[6] R. W. B. Lewis, *The American Adam* (Chicago: University of Chicago Press, 1955), p. 111.

the bulb pedlar, Kessler the egg candler and Rosen the ex-coffee salesman, even as it qualifies their possibilities, is that they are all failures of one kind or another, people who have been victimized by circumstances or other people or even themselves to the point where in actuality they seem to have nothing to sustain them but the promise of further failure in the future. It is as though Malamud were trying to demonstrate his conviction that America is not the land of promises fulfilled but of promises betrayed. Yet Malamud is not interested in failure for its own sake. His concern is with the consequences of failure, not its anatomy, with the possibilities which can emerge as a result of an acknowledgment of the inevitability of failure. Thus the experience of failure in Malamud's fiction is simply the testing-ground of character; its purpose is to explore the possibilities for moral development and even spiritual regeneration which follow from a recognition of the fact of failure. Yet in this Malamud has simply developed the possibilities already inherent in the authentic American narrative he has employed whose function, whether in Cooper or Hawthorne, James or Hemingway, has always been the same: to test the character and integrity of the individual innocent, the typical or archetypical man, by determining what he can learn from experience.

The most conspicuously American of Malamud's novels, if also the least successful, is obviously *The Natural*. From the perspective of *The Assistant*, the novel which most firmly established Malamud's reputation as a writer, and now *The Fixer*, which has frequently been called an even better book, *The Natural* appears to be something of an anomaly. Its setting is not the claustral atmosphere of the Jewish ghetto but the open air of the baseball diamond. Its style does not reflect the anguished movement so characteristic of Malamud's other stories where, as Ihab Hassan once remarked, "Pain twisted into humor twists humor back into pain."[7] It is, rather, marked by the expansive, zany, high-spirited rhythms of the mythology of sports. Its protagonist is not

[7] Ihab Hassan, *Radical Innocence* (Princeton: Princeton University Press, 1961), p. 161.

65

Malamud's usual victim of the Diaspora who must eke out his marginal or sub-marginal existence by running some down-at-the-heel grocery store, confectionery shop or shoe-making establishment, but is rather that quintessential American hero who is committed almost without qualification to his own idealized conception of himself.

Roy Hobbs fails as a hero because he is unable to learn from his experience; the novel fails because it never answers in anything but an indirect way the question which, so Malamud has confessed, originally provoked it — the question raised in one of Arthur Daley's columns in the *New York Times* about why a good man sells out.[8] Roy Hobbs, the naive but potentially heroic natural of the story, takes a bribe to throw the last game of the pennant race and loses his dignity in the process, but the motives behind his action remain somewhat obscure. There is a strong suggestion throughout the novel that Roy is an overreacher in the classic American style — a young man filled with the ambition to rewrite the record books in his own name — who is corrupted, in fact quite literally, by his own natural appetites; but this suggestion is all but buried under the mythic framework which Malamud has provided his story. The problem with the novel is that Malamud's technique works at cross-purposes with his intention. Instead of permitting him to build sympathy for Roy by exploring in depth the all-too-human motives behind his self-betrayal, the mythic and allegorical framework of the novel tends to separate us from Roy by turning him into a type whose destiny is fated from the very beginning.

Roy is variously described as an Achilles before Troy who is given to sulking and undergoes a slump when his talents are most needed by his team, as a Sir Percival in quest of the Holy Grail which for him is simply "to be the greatest there ever was in the game," as a latter-day Babe Ruth who promises to hit a home run for a young boy in the hospital, and

[8] Marcus Klein makes the same point about the novel's failure in *After Alienation* (Cleveland: Meridian Books, World Publishing Company, 1965), pp. 255–56.

even as a Shoeless Joe Jackson who (as he leaves the ballpark after throwing the last game of the pennant race) is exhorted by a newsboy with the words, "Say it isn't true, Roy." Roy's team, the New York Knights, is managed by Pop Fisher, a thinly disguised Fisher King, who presides over the fate of his players and the land where they work in what he calls "a blasted, dry season."

"No rains at all. The grass is worn scabby in the outfield and the infield is cracking. My heart feels as dry as dirt for the little I have to show for all my years in the game."

In the allegorical framework which Malamud has provided for his novel, Roy's function is to restore health and vitality to the land of the Knights by removing the jinx which has been placed upon it by that incident long ago known as "Fisher's Flop" when, as a young player himself, Pop Fisher "fell" on the base path trying to make home plate on an inside-the-park home run. To remove the jinx, so Pop Fisher contends, Roy must make it possible for the Knights to win one pennant. And Roy gives every promise of doing so the first time he steps to the plate when he knocks the cover off the ball with Wonderboy, his miraculous bat which, like Achilles' shield, has been tempered by lightning, and thus brings rain by the bucketfuls.

Yet, like his mythic predecessors of old, or even his surrogate father Pop Fisher, Roy is doomed to fail or, better, fall. Though a natural, he is "somewhat less than perfect," according to Red Blow, "because he sometimes hit at bad ones. . . ." Roy's temptation to swing at bad ones stems from his vaulting ambition, his insatiable appetite for glory, which is dramatized by his fatal attraction to women. Roy's first temptress, his first Helen, is Miss Harriet Bird, who, after learning of his presumption and watching him strike out the American League's leading hitter, Walter "the Whammer" Wambold, on three consecutive pitches, lures him to her apartment with the promise of love and then nearly kills him instead by shooting him in the stomach with a silver bullet. When Roy miraculously reappears fifteen years later to make good his ambition, his second temptress Memo Paris also seeks to destroy him by giving him a pain in the gut. But this time the cause is overeating, Roy's compensation for his frustrated sexual desire, which hospitalizes him for a time at the end of the season and all but ruins his team's chances for the pennant. With Roy in the hospital the team loses the remaining three games, and the pennant race ends in a tie.

With his illusions destroyed Roy yields to the pressure from Memo and her fellow conspirator, the fatuous, hypocritical, mysterious owner of the Knights, Judge Goodwill Banner, and decides to take a bribe to throw the playoff game. His motive is simply to obtain enough money to win Memo for himself. When Roy changes his mind late in the final contest and decides that it is more important to win the game instead, it is already too late. As if to underline his fatedness, his hopeless destiny, Wonderboy breaks in two and, without its assistance, Roy is struck out in three consecutive pitches his last time at bat by a rookie relief pitcher named Herman Youngberry, just as Roy himself had struck out "Whammer" Wambold fifteen years before. When the baseball commissioner announces that Roy "will be excluded from the game and all his records forever destroyed" if the rumor of his sellout proves true, the book comes full circle. As Jonathan Baumbach suggests, Roy is made to suffer the ultimate defeat for a mythical hero "who had hoped . . . to live eternally in the record of his triumphs." [9]

But if the fact of Roy's failure is clear, the reasons for it are not. Apart from the sense of inevitability which Malamud's mythic framework gives to everything that happens in the story, all it demonstrates besides is that Roy, in re-enacting his past deed for deed, thus proves himself incapable of learning from experience. Bump, Memo, and Pop Fisher are simply later avatars of "Whammer," Harriet, and Sam Simpson, the scout who originally discovered Roy. The mysterious origins, the sense of unlimited possibilities, the fantastic presumption, the spectacular achievement, the sexual temptation, the im-

* Jonathan Baumbach, *The Landscape of Nightmare* (New York: New York University Press, 1965), 110.

68

plied emasculation, and the final defeat — all are merely re-peated fifteen years later, as though nothing had been learned in the interim.

The only explanation which Malamud seems to offer for Roy's obduracy is to be found in the line of action which runs tangential to the mythic and allegorical movement of the novel, the action which concerns Roy's relationship with Iris. Though Iris is another "snappy goddess" who at one point recommits her hero to battle by restoring his faith in himself, and at another confesses that "without heroes we're all plain people and don't know how far to go," it is clear that her main function in the novel is ultimately more realistic and less mythical. For despite her hatred of seeing a hero fail — "There are so few of them," she remarks — Iris knows that the only possibility of averting failure is through knowledge which is gained by experience and which requires suffering. Iris has earned her wisdom the hard way — through a mistake with a stranger in the park one night which gave her a child before she was seventeen — but Roy is deaf to what she says.

> "We have two lives, Roy, the life we learn with and the life we live with after that. Suffering is what brings us toward happiness."
>
> "I had it up to here." He ran a finger across his wind-pipe."
>
> "Had what?"
>
> "What I suffered — and I don't want any more."
>
> "It teaches us to want the right things."
>
> "All it taught me is to stay away from it. I am sick of all I have suffered."

Roy refuses to accept the lesson his suffering can teach him, preferring instead simply to avoid the possibility of further suffering in the future. Consequently he never learns "to want the right things" until it is too late. Infatuated with an ado-lescent dream of glory and heroic immortality, one aspect of the American dream itself, Roy spurns the lessons of ex-perience and thus remains an adolescent to the very end, when he is forced to discover that life will not fulfill the demands his childish imagination makes upon it without exacting a price of its own in the process.

Yet Roy's obduracy does not diminish the fact that Iris' wisdom is essentially the wisdom which all of Malamud's protagonists must learn if they are to achieve authentic moral existence. And the nature and meaning of moral existence is the subject of all of Malamud's best fiction. But the full content of Iris' wisdom, like the full elaboration of the kind of hero who can learn it, lies elsewhere in Malamud's work.

Its first full-scale adumbration is to be found in Malamud's powerful second novel *The Assistant.* The spokesman for this wisdom, and one of its most effective embodiments in Malamud's fiction, is Morris Bober, the sixty-year-old grocer who awakens an hour early every morning to sell a three-cent hard roll to a "sour-faced, grey-haired Poilisheh" who is always impatient with him. But her testiness is nothing new to Morris, for everyone is impatient with him — his wife Ida because he dragged her out of their former Jewish neighborhood into their present Gentile community where their luck has changed from bad to impossible; his daughter Helen because his failure to make anything of himself has forced her to forego a college education and get a job to help support them; his assistant Frank Alpine because Morris appears so inured to the poverty and affliction he shares with his few friends, Breitbart the bulb pedlar and Al Marcus the paper products salesman, that he seems to live for nothing more than his suffering: "That's what they live for, Frank thought, to suffer. And the one that has got the biggest pain in the gut and can hold on to it the longest without running to the toilet is the best Jew." Morris is so utterly dejected that, when he is first robbed by Frank and Ward Minogue and then beaten, he can only fall to the ground without a cry, thinking to himself, "The end fitted the day. It was his luck, others had better."

Morris' situation is similar to Sam Tomashevsky's in "The Cost of Living." Another poor grocer, Sam lives with his wife Sura in a failing neighborhood on the very brink of destitution. He is ruined when his friend the barber finds it necessary to sign a lease with a grocery chain to open a new store next door. The barber is not an evil or unfeeling man; he simply cannot afford to lose more than seven months' rent from his empty store. His need is the grocer's destruction, and when Sam looks back upon his life and contemplates the waste of it, he might as well be speaking for Morris as well as for himself:

> ". . . after all the years, the years, the multitude of cans he had wiped off and packed away, the milk cases dragged in like rocks from the street before dawn in freeze or heat; insults, petty thievery, doling of credit to the impoverished by the poor; the peeling ceiling, fly-specked shelves, puffed cans, dirt, swollen veins; the back-breaking sixteen hour day . . . the work, the years, my God, and where is my life now?"

Morris and his family inhabit a world which is everywhere drab, desolate and bleak. Its only light derives from the clarity of Malamud's own vision which permits him to depict the victims of this world, in all their degrading and paralyzing circumstances, with compassion and tenderness. For Malamud will not relinquish his hold on his characters, his sense of the evanescent actuality of their lives, even if they are always in danger of losing their own hold on the reality which forever seems to be slipping away from them. The precariousness of their situation stems from their common predicament in a world where possibilities always seem to dissolve before they can be actualized, where promises are made only so that they can be broken, where new beginnings are continually frustrated by the emergence of old habits, where Spring is merely one of the deceptions of Winter. The God of this world in which appearances possess more tangibility than facts is simply a remorseless kind of bad luck which wears its victims down to the point where they tend to become as insubstantial as the circumstances which conspire against them. Thus, when Morris reaches the end of his tether and goes out in search of an extra job to feed his family,

71

he is blown about by the wind as though he were no more palpable than a dry leaf:

> The March wind hastened him along, prodding his shoulders. He felt weightless, unmanned, the victim in motion of whatever blew at his back; wind, worries, debts, Karp, holdupniks, ruin. He did not go, he was pushed. He had the will of a victim, no will to speak of.

The problem for those who must inhabit such a world is simply the problem, as Marcus Klein has remarked, "of holding on . . . in a world that exists just this side of nothing,"[10] a world where everything is on the verge of dissolving and disappearing, like the arsonist's celluloid, without a trace.

The wisdom Morris has gained in coping with such a world is not very profound, but it is perfectly suited to the task it must perform. It is a wisdom which is not only engendered by suffering but is also founded upon the fact of suffering. It is built upon the proposition, as Morris explains to Frank, that to live is to suffer, and that to suffer for yourself is to suffer for all the others who suffer with you. Suffering in this case — and there aren't any others — is the one mode of both engaging the world and surviving it. It is the name of what you must endure to live at all and of what you can achieve if you are fully human. For suffering is not more nor less than "good-willed and deliberate acknowledgement and acceptance of the common life of men. It is expression of the way in which men are bound together, in their loss."[11] Thus when Frank asks Morris for whom he suffers, Morris simply replies, "I suffer for you." And when Frank asks him to elaborate, Morris calmly suggests, "I mean you suffer for me."

Morris has acquired this knowledge not merely from his experience of life but also from his faith as a Jew. It is to be found in the Law which exhorts man, as he puts it, "to do what is right, to be honest, to be good. This means to other people. Our life is hard enough. Why should we hurt somebody else?" Even though they are few in number, Morris'

[10] Klein, *After Alienation*, pp. 276–77.
[11] *Ibid.*, p. 263.

preachments would remain inconsequential, were they not the real basis of his actions. But the fact that he is willing to awaken before dawn for the irritable "Poilisheh," that he extends credit to poor customers even though he is close to bankruptcy, that he sympathizes with Frank Alpine and takes him in (even though Frank begins by stealing his precious bread and milk), and that he feels great remorse for all that he and his bad luck have inflicted upon his family — these facts and many others like them demonstrate that Morris has earned his wisdom, that, indeed, he incarnates it. And thus it is that Morris can become an example for Frank Alpine, as he makes his own tortuous way from the impossibility of commitment to what one can only call a kind of commitment to the impossible.

In the beginning Frank Alpine appears to be a most unlikely candidate for initiation into either the Bober existence or the Bober wisdom about how to endure that existence. An orphan and a drifter who is tempted by semi-adolescent notions of grandeur and self-importance, Frank shares many affinities with Roy Hobbs — a similarly mysterious background of failure and disappointment and consequent desire to improve himself, a comparable innocence about the nature of experience and a resultant problem in coming to terms with a world not of his own making. But Frank also evinces a much larger capacity for suffering than Roy and a greater willingness to learn what it has to teach him. He is more intensely aware of his own mistakes and is thus able to exhibit a greater sympathy for the plight of others. Consequently, Frank is not only able to learn "to want the right things"; he is also able, so Malamud would have us believe, to pay the price of attaining them — the price of self-sacrifice and self-discipline — which in a world of bitter defeats and ironic reversals must suffice as its own reward.

But Frank's way toward the particular kind of moral and spiritual redemption which is possible in Malamud's world is full of obstacles. The pull of old habits and old lusts is so strong that he continues to steal from Bober after he secures employment in the store and acquires an almost unbearable desire for Helen as he watches her struggle pathetically to endure her drab life. The more he is influenced by Morris and the store, the more he simultaneously feels regret for his past mistakes and loathing for his present circumstances. Thus he is by turns beset with hunger and remorse, aspiration and guilt. Under Morris' benign tutelage Frank slowly begins to realize the necessity of discipline and the concomitant importance of confession; but he is unable to act until, like everyone else of consequence in the novel, he has lost all that is important to him. In his case this means his place in the store and thus his twofold possibility of winning forgiveness from Morris and love from Helen. This occurs when the "Alpine Fate," simply a mirror image of the "Bober Fate," reasserts itself, shattering all his former illusions. Morris catches him stealing from the cash register and fires him, even though he was simply taking back some of the money he had moments before deposited as payment on what he had previously stolen. Later the same night, Helen also turns against him when he forces himself upon her, even though he had just saved her from a similar fate at the hands of Ward Minogue and only took her himself out of a sense of frustrated desire which he had reason to believe she shared. Frank's loss thus becomes complete, and he now finds himself in a position roughly analogous to Morris':

> His goddamned life had pushed him wherever it went; he had led it nowhere. He was blown around in any breath that blew, owned nothing, not even experience to show for the years he lived. . . . The self he had secretly considered valuable was, for all he could make of it, a dead rat. He stank.

It is only when Frank is able to realize that no amount of confession can ever fully mitigate the stench of his guilt — "there would always be some disgusting thing left unsaid, some further sin to confess" — that he is prepared to accept and implement the "terrifying insight" which suddenly dawns upon him: "That all the while he was acting like he wasn't, he was really a man of stern morality." While this insight does not immediately transform Frank into a moral man, it does shock him into a recognition of the necessity to undertake a moral life. Thus he returns to the store to take up his own burden of suffering by making a clean breast of things to the Bobers, by repaying his debt to the business, by attempting to regain Helen's respect, and by seeking to earn Morris' forgiveness. The redemptive pattern of the book seems to complete itself after Morris' death when Frank clearly assumes the old man's place in the store, takes over his role as father to Helen, and adopts his style of humanity, his Jewishness, as his own.

But if this represents a tentative form of salvation for Frank, it is obvious that Malamud is at pains to qualify it to the bone. For there is a certain contrivance and artificiality about the way Frank seems to wallow in his own degradation and reprehensibility. When he reverts to his compulsive stealing after he returns to the store and then resumes his spying upon Helen after Morris dies, it is almost as though he was propelled, like a character out of Dostoevsky, by some hidden psychological necessity that compels him to continue to do wrong only so that he can feel right when he punishes himself for it, thereby proving that he is a moral man after all. There is a trace of sentimentality here, and it is increased by the fact that, in following Morris' example, Frank may simply be emulating a man who, despite his wisdom, ultimately preferred to yield to his circumstances rather than attempt to resist them. For there is more than a modicum of truth as well as bitterness in Helen's words after the funeral, when she remarks about her father:

> "People liked him, but who can admire a man passing his life in such a store? He buried himself in it; he didn't have the imagination to know what he was missing. He made himself a victim. He could, with a little more courage, have been more than he was."

And thus it is that Frank's conversion at the end of the novel is strongly tinged with irony. For while his circumcision can be taken as an act of self-purgation or initiation, it is also possible to consider it as "an act of self-repudiation, if not, as some may be tempted to say, of symbolic castration." [12]

Yet, in spite of the ambiguities which prevail throughout the novel, it seems certain that Frank's conversion at the end is no more specifically Jewish than it is, say, Christian. In accepting self-immolation, Frank simply takes the way of all those who have always believed that one finds his life only by losing it. In this Frank does no more than follow the example of his patron saint Francis of Assisi, who, like himself, began his life as a wastrel and a knave and achieved salvation only by disciplining himself to the rule of poverty and by learning to love through suffering. The identification of Frank with St. Francis is clearly indicated from the very beginning of the novel, but it becomes unmistakable when Frank commits himself — first out of a sense of guilt, then out of a sense of responsibility — to the hopeless, cheerless life of the Bobers. Since he cannot have Helen as his wife, he takes the family's poverty as his bride and then undergoes a ritual death and rebirth when he accidentally falls into the grocer's grave and miraculously reappears after the funeral in the grocer's place behind the counter of the store. Thus, as the new grocer-in-charge, Frank becomes a kind of sacrificial lamb who must now begin his own unending ordeal of suffering for Morris the way Morris first suffered for him.

The same redemptive pattern is repeated under drastically different circumstances but with only minor variations in Malamud's third novel *A New Life*. The scene has changed from a kind of immemorial urban ghetto to the magnificent surroundings of the far Northwest, but the central moral and spiritual preoccupations remain the same. Seymour Levin is another of Malamud's hapless, lonely, loveless innocents in search of a new beginning, a fresh start in life, who must eventually accommodate himself to the knowledge that the possibility of a future always depends upon one's willingness to accept the burdens of the past. In order to acquire this knowledge, Levin, like Frank Alpine, must survive his initiation into the world of the novel at the hands of its most un-

[12] Hassan, *Radical Innocence*, p. 168.

fortunte victim. Levin's Morris Bober is Leo Duffy, the radical young English instructor who had been summarily dismissed from Cascadia College just before Levin arrived, for
what faculty handbooks usually refer to as "moral turpitude."
And when Levin takes Duffy's office, then his former mistress,
and finally his crusading role in the department, it becomes
obvious that he is fated to relive Duffy's humiliating downfall
in order to redeem his failure.

A former alcoholic from New York whose mother went
crazy and killed herself after his father died in prison a petty
thief, Levin seems no better prepared for his *rite de passage*
than Frank Alpine was. He is constantly plagued by memories
of failure, tortured by feelings of remorse and victimized by
his own desires. After a series of comic sexual misadven-
tures — first with a barmaid in a haystack, then with a female
colleague on the floor of his office, and finally with an under-
graduate student in a motel by the Pacific — Levin achieves a
brief moment of self-fulfillment when he makes love to Pauline Gilley in the late afternoon rain under the pine trees on
the outskirts of town, in a scene which is resonant with overtones of the promise of pastoral felicity inherent in the benign
aspect of the wilderness myth: "He was throughout conscious
of the marvel of it — in the open forest, nothing less, what
triumph!"

But Levin's affair with Pauline Gilley is only the beginning
of his arduous struggle toward self-recovery and moral regeneration. For Pauline is the flat-chested, unsatisfied, discon-
tented wife of the man who initially hired Levin in the English department, and, while Gerald Gilley is constantly cari-
catured throughout the novel as something of an overgrown
but unprincipled academic adolescent who prefers teaching
"comp to lit" and is preparing a picture history of American
literature, it is apparent that Levin's affair with Pauline represents a betrayal of the man on the faculty who had first be-
friended him. Still more serious, their affair immediately
jeopardizes Levin's place in the college, especially after he
becomes deeply involved in curriculum policy and starts to
work for needed reforms, as Leo Duffy had before him.

Within a matter of months after his arrival in Cascadia, Levin is therefore confronted with a kind of exigency frequently encountered in Malamud's fiction: to retain his position in the English Department, a position which represents his one last chance to succeed in "the career of his choice," he must give up the only woman he has ever loved. The reward for this self-sacrifice is the realization all of Malamud's successful protagonists in some sense achieve: that there is a grace in renunciation and a beauty in that goodness which comes from the form given one's life by a moral act. But Levin does not fully earn this awareness until later. It is only after he has fallen out of love with Pauline and then, in spite of his feelings, consented to marry her when their affair is exposed — it is only then that he attains his full moral stature. Malamud carefully arranges Levin's situation in such a way that his decision may be seen to cost him very nearly everything. For in order to obtain custody of the children for Pauline, Levin must accede to Gerald's unreasonable demand to give up college teaching altogether. And when Gerald asks him in all amazement why he is willing to consent to this preposterous proposal — "An older woman than yourself and not dependable, plus two adopted kids, no choice of yours, no job or promise of one, and other assorted headaches. Why take that load on yourself?" — Levin expresses the quixotic nature of his own heroism by his reply: "Because I can, you son of a bitch."

Jonathan Baumbach suggests that by "leaving Cascadia with Pauline and her two adopted children, Levin is fulfilling his implicit commitment to Duffy," and thus by "completing the broken pattern of Duffy's life, Levin redeems his spiritual father's failure." [13] But the nature of Levin's commitment to Duffy extends beyond their mutual relationship with Pauline to the liberal and humanistic principles they share in common, and Levin is finally no more capable of implementing them than Duffy was. Moreover, when Levin accepts Gerald's unfair ultimatum (that he withdraw from teaching), he agrees in effect to relinquish the possibility of implementing

[13] Baumbach, *Landscape of Nightmare*, p. 105.

78

his principles, in education at least, ever again. Thus there is a sense in which Levin's departure from Easchester does not redeem Duffy's failure but only repeats it. For he, too, discovers, as Duffy's suicide note puts it, that "the time is out of joint" and that, as a result, it is necessary to leave "the joint" in order to save himself. The preservation, not to say the redemption, of his own personal integrity requires within the terms of the novel itself that he abandon his public and political commitments, and thus his tentative salvation can only be earned at the expense of a profound kind of emasculation as well.

Until the appearance of *The Fixer*, one could have argued that the process of moral regeneration and redemption in Malamud's fiction is always an exclusively personal affair which has little or no impact upon the social actuality in which his characters are so firmly immersed. Whatever measure of moral development his characters seem capable of experiencing enables them to bear their circumstances, but it never compels them to try to change those circumstances. Social reality appears to be a fixed quantity, and man's problem is simply that of learning how to live with it and in it, even in spite of it.

Yet in his most recent novel, Malamud seems bent upon changing all this. *The Fixer* has a much larger social background than Malamud has ever employed before and appears to express a self-conscious attempt to demonstrate that the process of moral and spiritual regeneration inevitably entails the transmutation of the private personality into a political self. "One thing I've learned," Yakov Bok muses in conclusion, "there's no such thing as an unpolitical man, especially a Jew. You can't be one without the other, that's clear enough. You can't sit still and see yourself destroyed."

Yakov Bok is Malamud's most extreme victim of circumstance and of self. A Jewish handy man who breaks what he fixes and can't fix what is broken, Yakov decides to leave his small Jewish community near Kiev after his wife deserts him, and he moves to the city to look for better possibilities. But like all of Malamud's protagonists, his good intentions and high expectations are relentlessly betrayed. No sooner does he ingratiate himself with Nikolai Lebedev, a member of the violently anti-Semitic Black Hundreds organization, than he is unjustly charged by the police with the ritual murder of a neighborhood boy who, following torture, was bled to death. The authorities are bent upon turning what is in truth a case of familial barbarity and perversity into a case of Jewish blood sacrifice so that they can start another pogrom in the ghetto, and Yakov seems the perfect victim. He is unknown in the city, lives in a district forbidden to Jews, has entertained an old Hasid (another recipient of his compassion) in his garret above the brickyard where he is an overseer, and professes to be a free thinker. Thus he is immediately incarcerated to await indictment.

But Yakov's indictment is more than two years in coming because the authorities know they have no case. Their only hope for a conviction depends upon a confession, and in order to extort it from Yakov they submit him to a series of increasingly degrading and cruel tortures. He is beaten by fellow prisoners, placed in solitary confinement, refused reading materials, deprived of any means of sanitation, searched as many as six times a day, at one point poisoned, and finally chained to the wall. When this fails, he is tempted with the possibility of suicide and then bribed with sex and the promise of leniency. But, as the authorities grow more willing to excuse him if he confesses, Yakov grows more adamant in his decision to maintain his own innocence. And thus it is that Yakov Bok finally becomes a man who will not break, even under the most extreme pressure, and a man who thereby achieves his true vocation as a fixer who is committed to righting what is wrong.

In the climax of the book, during an imaginary interview with the Tsar as Yakov is borne through the streets on the way to his trial, the old ruler asks Yakov to understand his difficult position as a man who "never wanted the crown." "After all," he remarks, "it isn't as though you yourself are unaware of what suffering is. Surely it has taught you the meaning of mercy?" Though the same question might have been asked by the implied author of any one of Malamud's earlier novels, Yakov's immediate reply indicates that he, like Malamud, has now lost patience with such reasoning: "Excuse me, Your Majesty, but what suffering has taught me is the uselessness of suffering, if you don't mind me saying so. Anyway, there's enough of that to live with naturally without piling a mountain of injustice on top." As if to underline the revolutionary implications of his new insight, Yakov concludes his interview by shooting the Tsar through the heart and then thinks to himself:

> Where there's no fight for it there's no freedom. What is it Spinoza says? If the state acts in ways that are abhorrent to human nature it's the lesser evil to destroy it. Death to the anti-Semites! Long live revolution! Long live liberty!

Yakov's militant radicalism at the end of *The Fixer* provides a striking contrast with Frank Alpine's passive acquiescence at the end of *The Assistant* or Seymour Levin's stoic resignation at the conclusion of *A New Life*. All three protagonists have been required to submit to the discipline of suffering in order to learn, as Iris Lemon puts it, "to want the right things," but the same ordeal which was meant to teach Malamud's earlier heroes to accept their fate is now intended to instruct them to resist it. Yet there is a sense in which Yakov's meditations upon the meaning of freedom and responsibility, together with the inward transformation they are meant to imply, remain the least convincing elements of the novel. For there is a note of contrivance and formality which creeps into his discussions with himself, especially when he turns to the ideas of his beloved philosopher and fellow sufferer, Spinoza; in these "profound" moments he is transformed from a simple Jewish fixit man who is struggling merely to survive into something more nearly like a college sophomore wanting to justify God's ways to men. Conceived as a representative of suffering humanity, Yakov becomes too quickly an apostle for freedom and liberation and thus loses his potentially beautiful and disarming specificity as a concrete, particular individual. Yakov retains that specificity when he answers his father-in-law's reminder not to forget his God with the angry question, "Who forgets who? What do I get from him but a bang on the head and a stream of piss in my face." Yet he loses it later on in the novel, where the idiomatic gives way to the speculative and the same subject evokes a more responsible but far less vivid reply:

> Nature invented itself and also man. Whatever was there was there to begin with. Spinoza said so. It sounds fantastic but it must be true. When it comes down to basic facts, either God is our invention and can't do anything about it, or he's a force in Nature but not in history. A force is not a father. He's a cold wind and try and keep warm. To tell the truth, I've written him off as a dead loss.

But the major problem with *The Fixer* is the problem it shares with all of Malamud's longer fiction. In an effort to evoke a sense of the tedium of holding on in a world where everything is in conspiracy against the individual, where circumstances are so oppressive that they all but bury the people they victimize, Malamud risks becoming tedious himself. With the possible exception of *The Natural*, his novels tend to drag in the middle, to bog down under the leaden weight of misery and affliction they so frequently express; and thus they lack that rush of movement toward a moment of final and irrevocable illumination and that sense of urgency about the knowledge to be gained under such circumstances which characterize the best of his remarkable short stories.

In many ways the stories of *The Magic Barrel* (1958) and *Idiots First* (1963) merely repeat the major themes and motifs of his longer works of fiction. There is the same concentration on the moral as over against the social dimensions of experience, the same preoccupation with the possibility of personal self-discovery and self-renewal, and the same awareness of the way the past impinges upon the present and the future, ironically binding a man to his earlier mistakes at the very moment when he appears to have succeeded in overcoming them. Like his novels at their best, his stories gain their power from his unquestionable ability to use the full imaginative resources inherent in Yiddish speech rhythms and colloquialisms to convey a sense of what it feels like to exist in a particular fashion. But many of his short stories are more successful than his novels in expressing that sense in all its felt immediacy, simply because they permit him to economize as a writer, to reduce action, scenic description and character development to the bare bone. Thus, without any wasted motion or extraneous comment, Malamud is able to achieve in a shorter form that compressed dramatic intensity which his novels frequently lack.

Here, "The Magic Barrel" provides a perfect example. As in each of the novels, there is the same, familiar figure of the apprentice who, in search of experience and what it can teach him, must undergo initiation in his world at the hands of another who is wiser than himself. But Pinye Salzman's wisdom is even more a part of his very being, of his way in the world, than either Morris Bober's or Leo Duffy's. He is a shaman and a savant, a prophet and a procurer at the same time. As matchmaker, Salzman's function is to find a wife suitable for Leo Finkle, the young rabbinical student who discovers that he has never loved God because, apart from his parents, he has never in fact loved anyone. As tutor and guide, Salzman's function is to lead Finkle toward an understanding and then acceptance of the fact that love and death, good and evil, hope and despair, all occupy the same place.[14]

Finkle achieves that understanding when he falls in love with one of the photographs from Salzman's "magic barrel" of marital candidates, ironically a photograph of Salzman's own daughter Stella, "a wild one — wild, without shame." Stella is obviously no bride for a rabbi, but Finkle is arrested and then captivated by her picture because he can perceive that she "had *lived*, or wanted to — more than just wanted, perhaps regretted how she had lived — had somehow deeply suffered. . . ." And thus he suddenly realizes, as Salzman has known all along, that by committing himself to Stella and thereby submitting to the tribulation involved in that

[14] See Klein, *After Alienation*, p. 277.

commitment, he, too, may learn what it is like to live by suffering for what he loves — indeed, by loving what makes him suffer. As a kind of latter-day Hosea, who must marry a prostitute to learn the meaning of *agape*, Finkle can therefore picture in Stella his own redemption. But when he rushes forward at the end, just as the story does, "with flowers outstretched," Salzman can only watch from around the corner, chanting prayers for the dead. For the wily marriage broker knows already what Finkle can only learn through suffering, that in choosing the girl whose eyes, like her father's, are "filled with desperate innocence," Finkle, though he may be electing his true vocation, is also embracing what may prove, finally, to be his self-destruction. In choosing the one he must inevitably choose the other, for such is the ambiguity inherent in the very nature of life itself in this kind of world.

Finkle's choice is precisely the kind of difficult and expensive choice which all of Malamud's protagonists must make. What enables Malamud to be so cogent in his dramatization of these choices is his firm sense of what they cost. To live in Malamud's fictive universe is to suffer loss, and that loss is frequently irreparable. All one can do is seek to comprehend it and, by the span of that knowledge, possibly to transcend it. Thus in "The Loan," another of Malamud's miracles of compression and intensity, Kobotsky and Lieb are each rendered speechless by the realization of what the other has suffered. Unable to assuage or mitigate it, they simply acknowledge their suffering by meeting for a brief moment in a mute embrace: "They pressed mouths together and parted forever." Yet what comes through in this story, as in so many of Malamud's others, is more than a mere comprehension of suffering, of loss; what is created is a memorialization of it as well which testifies in a language virtually beyond words that nothing is finally lost, nothing is absolutely irredeemable in a world such as this where the anguish of loss, however bitter it may be, can finally be allayed by the power of *agape*.

To speak of the love in and through which Malamud's most vivid characters are presented, the love which undergirds his fiction as the ultimate carrier of its deepest meaning, is to recall those sonorous lines from Whitman's "Song of Myself" that form the epigraph with which this essay begins. Nor is this recollection merely fortuitous. Malamud himself employs these lines in his tragic story of Oskar Gassner entitled "The German Refugee." After being forced, as a Jew, to flee Germany in order to escape the Nazi persecutions, Gassner turns out still to be a victim — of his own lack of faith. For he had suspected the wife whom he left behind in Berlin of sharing her mother's violent anti-Semitism, but he discovers, after emigrating to the States, that she became a Jewish convert following his departure and was subsequently martyred by the Nazis. And the guilt that he feels at having deserted her proves so unbearable that he takes his life, for he cannot endure the knowledge of how profoundly his actions have betrayed his words, the words from Whitman's poem which he has creedally professed as his basic faith. But though Gassner betrays this profession — what he calls Whitman's "faith in *Brudermensch*, his humanity" — by failing to keep faith with his wife and thus kills himself in despair, the essential compassionateness of the statement made by the story as a whole is in no way diminished. For the Whitman-esque faith in one's fellow men which Gassner professes but cannot implement is the same faith which constitutes the sovereign principle of Malamud's art. And it is this devotion to what Hans Urs von Balthasar calls "the Sacrament of the brother," [15] it is this radical faith in the sacredness of the human presence, that gives to Gassner's story a searing poignance which makes us feel that he, too, like so many of Malamud's other characters, is, in Conrad's words, "one of us."

[15] See Hans Urs von Balthasar, *Science, Religion, and Christianity*, trans. Hilda Graef (Westminster, Md.: Newman Press, 1958).

3

Comic Escape and Anti-Vision: The Novels of Joseph Heller and Thomas Pynchon
JOHN W. HUNT

It seems now that the contemporary novel exhibits the comic spirit in very much greater force than do those works we think of as forming the classic canon of modern fiction. True, a mood of desperation distinguishes current comedy, and the comic response itself arises, indeed, from many of the same perceptions about the absurd character of our fragmented lives which writers of a generation ago shared. Levin in *A New Life* making love with a pain in his arse, or neatly folding his trousers over the branch of a tree before pouncing upon the waiting Pauline; Leverett's drive to Sambuco in *Set This House on Fire*; Peter Caldwell's discovery of Pandora's box in *The Centaur*; the dismantling of Earl Horter's car in *Love Among the Cannibals*; the Negro boy's comment on Gauguin in the title story of *Goodbye, Columbus*; the protagonist's bombing of the frogs in the cistern of the Arnewi village in Bellow's *Henderson* — all of these (and each reader can make his own list) are scenes of comedy played against a background of concern about how the business of a meaningful life can be transacted in the modern world.

In recent years theology has attended closely to the modes in which religious issues are present in literature, especially in the novel. In general, critics of the novel have not shown a parallel interest in theology, and yet inadvertently, by close textual readings, they have helped enormously in making insights peculiar to the literary mode available for theological discussion. This situation arises from a strange reluctance on the part of secular intellectuals to call a religious issue by its proper name. As Nathan Scott has told us, when it comes to deciding what is and what is not of a religious nature in literature, "none are more fastidious," none are more "orthodox" than those "for whom the issues of religion are of no real account at all." "In matters of religious discrimination," he says, "theirs is a sense of the proprieties whose impeccableness would often seem to put the orthodox to shame."[1] And Dr. Scott's judicious observation reminds us that, for the discrimination of theologically important content in our current literature, we should go directly to the works themselves, and there be alert to the new guises — baffling to rigidly "orthodox" secular intellectuals — in which the religious issues are present. Some of our writers, admittedly, such as Updike, are strongly attracted by a traditional faith, but for many — like Heller and Pynchon and Ivan Gold, and Malamud and Bellow and Roth — before there is a conversion we are going to have to wait until some Ozzie Freedman among them climbs to the synagogue roof and threatens to jump.

It is to the contemporary novel that we must be most alert for the simple reason that our new writers are beginning at last to disengage themselves from the compelling example of the classic moderns — such as Faulkner and Hemingway and Fitzgerald — and to employ new techniques and find new uses of language which result in new perceptions. One of the difficulties for both writer and reader is that, as Louis D. Rubin, Jr. points out, while the version of reality afforded by the classic moderns "will not quite do any more," in fact "to a large extent this mode *still* suffices, and yet the times *are* changing and have changed since the years when those writers were learning how to see their world."[2] Thus there is a temptation for the writer to continue in the old mode and for the reader to canonize both the techniques and the vision of the modern classics.

At stake here is the question whether or not the con-

[1] *Ernest Hemingway* (Grand Rapids, Mich.: Eerdmans Publishing Co., 1966), p. 40.
[2] "The Curious Death of the Novel: or, What to Do about Tired Literary Critics," *Kenyon Review*, 28 (June, 1966): 311.

temporary novelist can find modes appropriate to his own reality, modes not overly prejudiced by the perceptions and language of his predecessors. I am not suggesting that such modes will be or can be discontinuous with what has gone before. But I am convinced that, until we are willing to learn more from our new writers about "what a novel ought to be" and to read them with the same kind of attentiveness that Faulkner and Hemingway finally exacted from their critics, we will continue as readers to live under the shadow of an antique vision and to miss the new disclosures that are coming from contemporary writers.

Yet the matter is not closed with the assertion that, because experience of reality is now different, new modes are necessary to capture it in literature. The reverse is also true: only when new modes — conceptual or poetic — are available to deal with experience *can* it be different. Durrell's character Clea puts this in its typically radical form when she says "events are simply a sort of annotation of our feelings."[3] That is to say, our feeling, our attitude, what we make of events constitutes their human significance, for, apart from the way they are related to one another, facts "mean" nothing. The nature of our experience, particularly its meaning, is largely dependent upon the connections we see, the modes of interpretation we can bring to the experience. And in literature these interpretive modes come to us not as ideas per se but as scene, episode, character, image, symbol, plot and the like.

A clear difference between current writers and their predecessors of a generation ago is to be found in their treatment of the absurd. David Galloway has suggested that the difference between the optimistic and the pessimistic in absurd literature is determined by who emerges victorious "in the conflict between man and his 'absurd' environment."[4] If nihilistic rather than humanistic impulses predominate, if the fragmented character of human experience is really absolute,

[3] Lawrence Durrell, *Justine* (New York: E. P. Dutton & Co., 1957) p. 242.
[4] *The Absurd Hero in American Fiction* (Austin: University of Texas Press, 1966), p. vii.

89

then a pathetic quality enters which precludes regeneration. The notion of "the absurd" as it was first given currency by Sartre, and especially by Camus, is metaphysical in character and says that the absurd nature of the universe emerges with the recognition of a disparity between hope and fact. The fact of death is itself enough to preclude a necessary connection between the universe and human value and meaning. Only when all the deadwood of expectation is cleared away, only when the Kantian notion of human meaning as supported by objective reality is abandoned, can one find a basis for heroism that is not subject to cancellation by the contradiction between human intention and reality. Thus Camus responds with a stoic strategy of imposing a meaning upon life which it does not itself bear. And a good deal of the power of his fiction lies in his characters' discovery of metaphysical absurdity and in their various responses to it.

Our younger comic novelists — Barth, Hawkes, Vonnegut, Friedman, Donleavy: the "black humorists" — deal differently with facts which contradict desire. Although they tend to accept the absurdist premises of existentialism, some — and notably Joseph Heller and Thomas Pynchon — have found that the assessment of contemporary experience through the comic mode can make meaningful life once again possible in spite of evil and death, even though the laughter their comedy evokes is often so dark it is nearly a cry of pain. When we turn to the novels of Heller and Pynchon specifically to discover the versions of reality embodied there, we find that they have been engaged in dramatizing the very problem I have outlined. That is, each has isolated discontinuity, the lack of connection and therefore of meaning and morality, as distinguishing the experience of men in our time. This gives them affinities with the existentialist mood of the contemporary novel, but they are novelists of the absurd only in a special sense.

Heller and Pynchon have no quarrel with Camus; with a significant number of other contemporary American authors they give body to the notion of the absurd as he outlines it. However, Heller shows little interest in the metaphysical nature of absurdity; as a child of his time, perhaps, he takes it for granted. What does interest him is the disparity between human intention and reality within the social structure, the actual inversion of professed values, the defeat of meaning by the strategies used to protect it. The irony present in such a situation is, of course, a classic material for comedy, and Heller shows that our experience of discontinuity, though radical, arises from the unnecessary abandonment of reason in the human enterprise. Pynchon, too, is a child of his time who finds the absurd nature of life something with which he begins rather than ends. He is more openly interested in metaphysics than Heller, and certainly he is more pessimistic. We experience this fragmented world as absurd, he seems to say, and we should leave it at that; attempts at rational connection should be avoided not because they are unsuccessful but because they are too successful. Pynchon focuses upon the maddeningly elusive *apparent* connections which seem to threaten the disconnections with which his characters have learned to live.

Nor should it be surprising that, as absurdity assumes more and more the position of premise rather than conclusion, the response of writers like Heller and Pynchon is to turn to comedy as a means of placing it in ultimate perspective. In the Christian tradition, as in many of the other great traditions of faith, the destructive aspects of life have often been conceived to be only phases of the full drama of redemption which, as Dante knew, requires comic structures for its completest expression. Typically in the novels of Heller and Pynchon the obstacles in the way of the comic protagonist are as serious as in any tragedy, and often genuinely tragic elements are present. But the achievement of these writers has been the creation of forms that fulfill again the ancient function of comedy, if not in a new way — for certainly one can find their antecedents in Rabelais and Swift and Voltaire — then at least with a new vigor and in the face of a new understanding of the threats to meaning.

The initial response to *Catch-22*, when it was first published in 1961, tells us a great deal about the degree to which the notion of the absurd was accepted as an adequate analysis of experience. It may be unfair to hold reviewers for our national weeklies closely to their hastily written words, but it is significant that few of them felt it necessary to hedge. Most of the reactions were extreme, with little middle ground. Because the novel was too complex in technique for the quick look and short appraisal, some, such as Richard G. Stern, found it "an emotional hodgepodge," lacking in design and gasping "for want of craft and sensibility."[5] Stern refused to call the book a novel at all, while Whitney Balliett in *The New Yorker* would not even call it a book.[6] It was also too subtle in theme for the reader who is content only with clear and ultimate solutions. Robert Brustein and a few others saw this, but most, such as the anonymous reviewer of *Daedalus*,[7] could not see beyond the caricatures, the stale jokes, and the *non sequiturs* to the purpose for which they were being used. Many reacted with what can only be called outrage, almost as if the mixture of tragic and comic elements violated some sacred purity of form the presence of which is one of our most cherished guarantees that art will not bring us too close to life. In a sense Heller got from these readers the response he was looking for: the realization, as their laughter subsided, that what they were laughing at was their own absurd world.

The story itself has a classically comic structure. The focus is upon John Yossarian, a bombardier stationed on the fictitious Mediterranean island of Pianosa during the Second World War. Yossarian opposes his society and seeks ways of escape. The novel's action arises from his various attempts to overcome the obstacles standing between him and the kind of new world he would like to live in. Obstacles are everywhere; everyone and everything is out to murder him. "The enemy," he says, "is anybody who's going to get you killed, no matter *which* side he's on."[8] Besides the Germans who

[5] *The New York Times Book Review*, October 22, 1961, p. 50.
[6] December 9, 1961, p. 248.
[7] Winter, 1963, pp. 155–65.
[8] Joseph Heller, *Catch-22* (New York: Simon & Schuster, 1961), p. 22.

shoot at him, and his colonel who keeps increasing the number of missions the men must fly, there are other enemies; the whole universe, in fact, is designed for murder, down to the very cells of one's own body, each one of which is "a potential traitor and foe" (p. 171), because it can contract a fatal disease. The novel's denouement comes with Yossarian's decision to answer his dilemma rather than solve it, to withdraw from his society, that is, rather than to try to live within it. His decision is possible because of a turn in the plot in which he discovers that his tentmate Orr — representative to him of the simple-minded good people of this world — has successfuly escaped to Sweden. The character of reality in Sweden is left vague; we know it only as a place without war and more desirable than Pianosa. We are told that the war is almost over, so that Yossarian's decision to desert becomes, in context, a refusal to participate in a society which he can no longer help and which, if he stays, will only kill him. When he learns of Orr's escape, his decision to make a separate peace is confirmed, and, taking Nately's whore's kid sister with him, he bids his own farewell to arms with hope in his heart.

Within this comic framework, the story could be told in many ways. Heller has chosen to write what Henry James called a "novel of saturation," and to include at face value elements of fantasy in both description and incident which appear initially not only to undercut the narrator's reliability but also to make the whole performance lacking in seriousness. All the tricks in the comedian's bag are used, especially unincremental repetition and immediate reversal. In the early chapters characters are only glimpsed, the world is wide and busy and complex, and scenes shift quickly before the reader's feelings become committed or his beliefs threatened. As the narrative wears on, however, a number of sober matters are being attended to within the comic framework. The first two-thirds of the story provides no clear present tense, but toward the end one becomes aware that the novel's clocks

Subsequent references to *Catch-22* appear in parentheses following the quotation.

have been the number of missions the men are forced to fly and the deaths of Yossarian's friends. As the missions are performed and as the men die, so the novel moves.

Carefully timed disclosures of the motivations accounting for crucial incidents and the slow release of information as the chronology of the novel's incidents comes into focus make it apparent that a deeply bitter vision is in control, a rational vision outraged at the world's lack of rationality. "Where are the Snowdens of yesteryear?" (p. 35), for example, a question initially funny simply as a pun since we know nothing of Snowden, becomes, with later knowledge, horrible. Yossarian's whole attitude toward the war and society, we learn near the end of the book, had come to him as he helplessly watched his dying comrade Snowden while on the mission to Avignon. "Man was matter. . . . The spirit gone, man is garbage. That was Snowden's secret. Ripeness was all" (pp. 429–30). In such a world values are inverted, and to set them right Yossarian insists that the good guys are the cowards and other men of principle, while the bad guys are the patriots and other opportunists. One by one Yossarian's friends meet death — by accident, or disease, or suicide, if not in battle. "They've got all my pals" (p. 425), he discovers as the war nears its end. Some, like Clevinger, disappear quite accountably, while others, like Dunbar, disappear because of mysterious forces; Doc Daneeka, still quite alive, is declared officially dead, while Mudd, killed on his first mission before checking into the squadron, is not acknowledged ever to have existed at all. Thus when the denouement comes, the inversion of values, the confusion of perceptions, the triumph of chaos and brutality make Yossarian's otherwise cowardly flight an admirable withdrawal, a deliberate choice not simply to survive but to act morally by refusing a world that is immoral. It is flight from the inhumanity of a situation where people are always "cashing in on every decent impulse and every human tragedy" (p. 435). He knows that to desert the squadron he must, in a sense, flee the whole world and that he will "always be alone," "in danger of betrayal" (p. 440), an outrider of the law. But the law, the rule of social order, is exactly what Yossarian is refusing, for the law is the rule of discontinuity, the rule of Catch-22.

The key to the novel's vision is in the title reference to Catch-22, the phrase used for the pandemic paradox of evil. Catch-22 is the catch by which an otherwise coherent and rational world is rendered absurd; it is an elliptical inner logic defeating all perception: "How can he see he's got flies in his eyes if he's got flies in his eyes?" This flippant formulation of the paradox, Yossarian feels, makes "as much sense as anything else" (p. 46), simply because the principle of Catch-22 means that ultimately all sense is frustrated. The contradictions enhancing the rule of stupidity and blindness and cruelty are shown to be operative in the military realm in the authority of expediency by which the commanding officer can set aside all demands of decency and justice. They are operative in the economic realm in the glowing success of Milo Minderbinder's international cartel which can contract for both bombing and defending the same target. The irrationality and brutality of the social order are highlighted when the meaning of Aarfy's boast, "I never paid for it in my life" (pp. 235, 408), becomes clear. M.P.'s burst into the officers' apartment in Rome, arrest Yossarian for not having a pass, and apologize for the intrusion to Aarfy, who has just raped and murdered the maid. And so on. Catch-22 is the principle that anyone has a right to do anything he can get away with doing.

On this premise Heller bases his whole novel. Because absurdity underlies every dramatic incident, the narrative abounds in false syllogisms, *non sequiturs*, paradoxes, and contradictions which Heller fully exploits for their comic possibilities. Subtly the novel builds to a symbolically potent climax. In "The Eternal City," a chapter much in debt to Joyce's "Ulysses in Nighttown," the story's considerable laughter turns to Dantesque groans of agony, as the bizarre, violent scene treated earlier with farce is given the metaphysical weight of an apocalyptic vision from Dostoyevsky or Kafka: "The tops of the sheer buildings slanted in weird, sur-

realistic perspective, and the street seemed tilted" (p. 402).
At the sight of an urchin on the streets of Rome,

> . . . Yossarian was moved by such intense pity for his
> poverty that he wanted to smash his pale, sad, sickly
> face with his fist and knock him out of existence. . . .
> He made Yossarian think of cripples and of cold and hun-
> gry men and women, and of all the dumb, passive, devout
> mothers with catatonic eyes nursing infants outdoors
> that same night with chilled animal udders bared insensi-
> bly to that same raw rain. Cows. Almost on cue, a nursing
> mother padded past holding an infant in black rags. . . .
> What a lousy earth! He wondered how many people were
> destitute that same night . . . how many husbands were
> drunk and wives socked, and how many children were
> bullied, abused or abandoned. . . . How many suicides
> would take place that same night, how many people
> would go insane? How many honest men were liars,
> brave men cowards, loyal men traitors, how many sainted
> men were corrupt, how many people in positions of trust
> had sold their souls. . . . The night was filled with hor-
> rors, and he thought he knew how Christ must have felt
> as he walked through the world, like a psychiatrist
> through a ward full of nuts, like a victim through a prison
> full of thieves. What a welcome sight a leper must have
> been! At the next corner a man was beating a small boy
> brutally in the midst of an immobile crowd of adult spec-
> tators. . . . Mobs with clubs were in control every-
> where [pp. 403–7].

So powerful is Yossarian's exposure to undisguised evil that
the reader begins to feel as Tappman the chaplain felt when
trying to find the human touch in a world governed by
Catch-22: "So many monstrous events were occurring that
he was no longer positive which events *were* monstrous and
which *were* really taking place" (p. 274). Something of this
is also felt by Yossarian, who concludes, with surprising
philosophical cogency about the ontological status of evil,
that Catch-22 is a legal fiction:

Catch-22 did not exist, he was positive of that, but it made no difference. What did matter was that everyone thought it existed, and that was much worse, for there was no object or text to ridicule or refute, to accuse, criticize, attack, amend, hate, revile, spit at, rip to shreds, trample upon or burn up [p. 400].

In fact, man himself — Mudd, Doc Daneeka, the soldier in white — is almost a legal fiction in this book. Since existential man bears the scars of the threat of non-being, it is appropriate for Heller to use the language of paradox to describe his condition.

Yossarian is no hero, not in the social sense, for he decides for self and against society. In context this is a decision for sanity as opposed to absurdity, for reason as opposed to chaos. Catch-22 defeats rational connections: *he* will make them; it disallows responsibility: *he* will be responsible. His is a decision to survive, because he judges both himself and life to be worth saving: "I've been fighting all along to save my country. Now I'm going to fight a little to save myself. The country's not in danger any more, but I am" (p. 435).

Heller's success in keeping the comic structure while projecting a bitter vision about the whole human enterprise is not a pure one. In order to qualify Yossarian for the comic role he must keep his background vague, leave his character undeveloped, and rest the burden of Yossarian's appeal upon his sense of the future. Ambiguity is also necessary about the new society into which Yossarian is to go, for if Catch-22 is a metaphysical principle of inbuilt chaos, certainly it obtains in Sweden as well as in Pianosa. Consequently there remains some confusion about just who the enemy is, about whether the obstacles which stand in the way of the comic hero are only social or also metaphysical. But of the quality of reality obtaining in this society — Pianosa, *our* world — there is no doubt: it is irrational, disconnected, incongruous; it provides no basis for moral action: it is, withal, absurd.

Elements of fantasy, therefore, are not incongruous. The fantastic becomes the norm. Heller joins here a long tradition of those who have written of the fantastic, but only with his contemporaries — Bellow, Malamud, Styron, Durrell, Beckett, Golding — does he share the distinctively modern way of treating it. In his book we do not feel, as we do in Edgar Allan Poe, for example, even where Poe's narrative seems methodical and dispassionate, that the events before us are really to be looked upon as special, rare, fantastic. Rather, the novel's atmosphere is such that what is taking place is *of course* what we all know to be true of our humdrum experience. It is the non-absurd world which strikes us as special and fantastic. By use of the comic structure, qualified in some of the ways I have indicated, Heller is able to take the surprise out of absurdity. With absurdity established as a premise rather than a conclusion, Heller can probe its moral implications as adroitly as a Camus or a Sartre and yet react with a completely different temperament; he can, with Kafka, employ the surrealistic archetypes of nightmare and yet avoid Kafka's malaise; and he is able to express a concern for the seriousness of evil that is very close to Dosteyevsky's, without ending in the utter philosophical skepticism which is sometimes Dostoyevsky's final position.

Thomas Pynchon's *V.* and *The Crying of Lot 49* are also, like *Catch-22*, novels in which an ultimate vision is forced from extreme situations and issues in various strategies of comic escape. Yet there the fundamental similarities end. For what is *seen* in Pynchon's novels is deliberately obscured rather than illuminated by the comic elements. Heller, one feels, has something to say and, in his own mode, makes it as clear as he can. Pynchon, one feels on the other hand, has something he is willing only tentatively to suggest, since the connections he sees mean too much if they are really there. Perhaps, his novels plead in desperation, we are wrong about it all. And it is in the way he goes about rendering his theme that Pynchon shows himself to be unusually inventive in technique, even if not wholly successful. For though his first two books are novels of quest for meaning, in each Pynchon has employed methods calculated to defeat his characters *lest* they succeed in seeing too clearly. We have had the novel of the anti-hero before; Pynchon has given us a form for the comic novel of anti-vision.

In *V*. Pynchon controls meaning, keeps obscure the connections apparently obtaining between events, by placing his narrator in competition with his characters. In their own right, the characters take an ambivalent attitude toward learning the meaning of their experience. They are at once yearning to make connections and afraid they might make them. "Approach and avoid"[9] — such is the strategy. Thus the novel is deeply involved in tension, not only within the characters but also between the characters who are reluctantly learning meanings by making connections and the narrator who, for the reader, is calling these meanings into question, not by denial but by comic multiplication of connections. Justification of this tension lies in the vision the novel is trying to suppress, and for that we must look closely at the structure of the novel.

Three story lines are developed in the novel. Two of them — Benny Profane's and Herbert Stencil's — are in the novel's present tense, 1955–56, while the third, focusing upon Victoria Wren, is over by 1942. Initially the two present-tense stories appear to have little to do with one another. The first traces Benny's meanderings from Norfolk to New York City and finally to Malta. Benny, an ex-Navy man, is an incorrigible *schlemihl* whose chief activity is yo-yoing up and down the East coast or between Times Square and Grand Central on the subway. He is not on an obvious quest, has no apparent direction, makes no effort either to seek out or to avoid a group of friends from his old Navy destroyer *The Scaffold* or another group known as the Whole Sick Crew who lounge about New York City, mostly at their bar, the Rusty Spoon. Roadwork, if anything, is his occupation, but he has no commitment to it and learns from it only that all streets lead simply to more streets. In the course of his yo-yoing he works underground shooting alligators in the sewers for New York

[9] Thomas Pynchon, *V*. (Philadelphia: J. B. Lippincott Co., 1963), p. 55. Subsequent references to *V*. appear in parentheses following the quotation.

99

City's Street Department and briefly holds a job as a night watchman for a company doing research on casualty kinesthetics and fallout effects. At the end of the novel he is on Malta, still man-on-a-string, vaguely planning to find roadwork there.

The action of the second present-tense story centers upon young Stencil's quest for the meaning of the letter "V," a reference to which he had found ten years earlier in his father's journal under the heading of Florence, 1899: "There is more behind and inside V. than any of us had suspected. No who, but what: what is she. God grant that I may never be called upon to write the answer, either here or in any official report" (p. 53). His discovery of this passage had roused young Stencil from the half-conscious inertness of regarding sleep as life's major blessing to a grim but strong sense of animateness. He hangs about with the Whole Sick Crew, hoping by serendipity to stumble across clues to his puzzle. He takes a special interest in a girl from Malta, Paola Maijstral, yet draws back, feeling that somehow Malta is his destiny as it was his father's, who disappeared there in 1919.

Both present-tense narratives seem to go nowhere, finally, although there is something of a dramatic shape to each. Benny starts on the streets and ends there, yet he is responsive to Paola, Fina, and Rachel and, in a crucial scene with Rachel, learns something about himself. In the course of his story, Stencil gathers a great deal of information about V., and he does go finally to Malta, taking Benny and Paola with him, but when it appears that he might discover the meaning he seeks, he goes off to Sweden on an apparently false lead.

The third narrative, Victoria Wren's, is woven into the novel mostly through Stencil's reconstructions of the various ways in which the evidence he has gathered can go together. Victoria, who appears in the narrative under a number of aliases and disguises, seems to be part, at least, of what was denoted by the letter "V" in old Stencil's journal entry. Her story spans the period from 1898 (when she turns up in Alexandria at the age of eighteen) to 1942 (when she dies in Malta), while young Stencil's quest for the meaning of V.

begins in 1945 and carries into the novel's present tense, 1955–56.

The sections of the novel in which Victoria's character is presented — and they are six in number, taking up half the book — vary greatly in reliability. In the first, young Stencil projects himself into the role of eight imaginary characters who witness V.'s appearance as Victoria in Alexandria and Cairo in 1898. It is an episode of espionage centering on the Fashoda affair and ending with the murder of one British spy and Victoria's seduction of another. In this first episode there is established the pattern whereby "V.'s natural habitat" is shown "to be the state of siege" (p. 62). The account of V.'s second appearance, which is told by Stencil, concerns Victoria's presence in Florence in 1899, where she seduces old Stencil on a couch in the British Consulate and then participates in a siege of the Venezuelan Consulate. The third episode is about the experience of Kurt Mondaugen, a young engineering student studying sferics, who was with V. in 1922 at a plantation in German South-West Africa while it was under siege for two and a half months during a revolt of the native Bondels. Kurt's story is retold by Stencil. V. appears in this section as Vera Meroving, and we learn that she had also been at Fiume in 1920 with D'Annunzio during the Christmas siege. The confessions of Fausto Maijstral, covering the years from his birth in 1919 to V.'s death in 1942 but focusing upon the war years, is the fourth major source on V.'s career. It is not edited by Stencil's imagination, but information about V. is only part of Fausto's story. Here she appears as the Bad Priest and is killed by a falling beam in an air raid during the siege of Malta. The fifth episode, the story of V.'s erotic love for the girl Mélanie in Paris in 1913, is told by the narrator but as if he were piecing the evidence together from Stencil's point of view. Finally, the last chapter of the book is given as an epilogue relating the encounter of old Stencil with V. — under the name of Veronica Manganese — on Malta in 1919. The narrator of this section is unambiguously omniscient, although he does not tell all he supposedly knows.

Now, it is the manner in which the three narrative strands are presented which gives *V.* its special character as a novel of comic discontinuity. Within the first few pages a special relationship between the reader and the narrator is established by the latter's mode of direct address. "Try to squeeze a watermelon into a small tumbler sometime when your reflexes are not so good," we are told. "It is next to impossible" (p. 18). Later passages present us with a rundown on the news of the day — actual events from the news media for 1956. At one point we are even directed to confirm the facts just presented: "Look in any yearly Almanac, under 'Disasters' — which is where the figures above come from" (pp. 290–91). Such passages indicate that what we are being given here is something in the nature of a report, an attempt to put data before us from any and all points of view by a narrator who refuses commitment to any specific meaning or set of meanings the material might suggest.

However, the narrator-reader relationship aside, it is the narrator's relationship to the three stories he is telling that gives the novel its comic character. Benny's story is fragmentary in its very nature — his movements are random, his character is passive — and with it the narrator has little difficulty in exploiting the comic possibilities. But Stencil's story is something else again, for of its own force it drives toward some coherence, some conclusion. As Stencil's quest begins to gain momentum, the narrator adopts a strategy of anti-narrative in order to achieve his end of anti-vision.

It is, of course, Stencil's pursuit of the background story of V. that makes all the difference, for V.'s story takes us into the deeper sources of the present-tense characters' experience. As V.'s story unfolds through Stencil's investigation, that is, as the novel becomes unambiguously devoted to historical interpretation, connections between contemporary events begin to be explained. Initially, indeed, the actions of the characters peopling Benny's story take much of their comic quality from the fact that they are presented as if *sui generis* — such as the scenes of thirsty sailors fighting for advantageous position at Suck Hour before the beer-spouting foam rubber

breasts ornamenting the Sailor's Grave bar in Norfolk; or of
Rachel making erotic passes at her M.G., paying special attention to the gearshift as she washes it; or of Benny heaving
mousetraps at the night watchman down the passageways of
the ship *Susanna Squaducci*; or of Da Conho, with his .30-
caliber machine gun, in imagination cutting down with a
"yibble, yibble, yibble" the smug American Jews in Hart
Schaffner and Marx suits who ought to be in Israel fighting
the Arabs, he feels, rather than stuffing themselves in the
restaurant where he is the chef.

These antics would not have the effect of implying any
serious definition of the human condition, were it not for the
introduction of Stencil's quest. But, in this context, they become dramatic images of an ominous logic in human events.
The incidents in Benny's story do, of course, imply all along
the conclusions to which Stencil is driven in his quest. Paola's
disguise as Ruby, Esther's nose operation, Fina Mendoza's
Jeanne d'Arc act with the Playboys which ends in her rape
by the whole gang, Benny's education by Rachel about his
"schlemihlhood" — these and other scenes cannot be taken
lightly. But, were it not for the fact that Stencil takes a quest-
journey, they would remain only so much "local" detail.

When Stencil is first introduced he knows (or imagines)
only the incidents in the V.-story centering in Egypt, Florence, and Paris, and the quest which gives shape to his movements appears to lead everywhere and to imply, ultimately,
everything. But by the time the evidence comes in from
South-West Africa in 1922 and from Malta during the Second
World War (he never learns what the reader learns about
Malta in 1919), the V.-story takes on a general meaning beyond his personal destiny. All the while, the narrator is pur-
suing his strategy of anti-vision by keeping sheer boundless
multiplicity of both event and meaning before the reader:
V. is Victoria, Vera, Veronica, but also Valletta on the island
of Malta, as well as Vesuvius and Venezuela; and the mysterious letter seems also to stand for the "V" of perspective lines
made by lights on a receding street, the "V" of spread thighs
or of migratory birds; it is the V-Note, where the Whole Sick

Crew listens to jazz, as well as Veronica the sewer rat, the
Venus of Botticelli, the Virgin Mother, and the *mons Veneris*.
There is even the suggestion, but no clear evidence, that V.
is Stencil's own mother. By functioning as historian-reporter,
finding the letter "V" everywhere, the narrator competes with
Stencil to defeat the meanings he is trying to build. It is the
narrator, not Stencil, who for the reader is making Stencil's
quest into a quest for a metaphysical absolute, and he does
this by forcing V. to mean everything and thus nothing. Stencil is trying to narrow V. down to something comprehensible –
though certainly not with any incisiveness, for he fears, and
with good reason, that real understanding will send him back
to half-consciousness.

As he sorts through the "grand Gothic pile of inferences"
(p. 226) he has gathered from the "rathouse of history's rags
and straws" (p. 225), Stencil sees the world about him explained as the product of an ominous and appalling force in
human affairs, a force that promises an ultimate annihilation
of the human world and its complete replacement by the
inanimate. It is not simply a vision of death and destruction,
but a ravaging of all meaning, an emptying of all significance
in the human enterprise, the coming of a Nameless Horror, a
horror not even bestial but insensible. It is, of course, in
Victoria's personal history that he sees this most clearly. Hers
is a "progression toward inanimateness" fitting "into a larger
scheme" (p. 411) of which she is both victim and priestess.
The scheme is literally present in her very flesh, for, as she
grows older, she becomes increasingly obsessed "with bodily
incorporating little bits of inert matter" (p. 488) – a glass eye
with a clock iris, a wig, false teeth, fabricated feet, a star sap-
phire sewn into her navel. Her love for Mélanie is, in Stencil's
mind, a desperate attempt to journey into a fetish world to
postpone her fate. Even Stencil, who bitterly thinks "let her
be a lesbian, let her turn to a fetish, let her die: she was a
beast of venery and he had no tears for her" (p. 412) –

> even Stencil couldn't remain all unstirred by the ironic
> failure her life was moving toward. . . . Victoria was

being gradually replaced by V.; something entirely different, for which the young century had as yet no name. We all get involved to an extent in the politics of slow dying, but poor Victoria had become intimate also with the Things in the Back Room [p. 410].

As Victoria evolves from a person of specific identity to a paradigm of political history, she becomes gradually desexed. Disguised as the Bad Priest on the island of Malta, she preaches not chastity, but sterility, and Stencil has a vision of her as mechanized in all functions, including "a complex system of pressure transducers located in a marvelous vagina of polyethylene; the variable arms of their Wheatstone bridges all leading to a single silver cable which fed pleasure-voltages direct to the correct register of the digital machine in her skull" (pp. 411–12).

Throughout V.'s story there are images of the female being ravished by the inanimate: the impalement of Mélanie at the crotch on a pointed pole "slowly raised by the entire male part of the company" (p. 413) of automatons at the Théâtre Vincent Castor; "Malta . . . a noun feminine" lying on her back, "an immemorial woman. Spread to the explosive orgasms of Mussolini bombs" (p. 318); Foppl with the Herero girl; Mélanie's self-ravishment with a mannequin beneath a mirror.

So long as these violent images have a human base, Stencil is able to maintain his pursuit of the V.-structure. But when the stories of Kurt Mondaugen and Fausto Maijstral give credibility to the existence of an "ultimate Plot Which Has No Name" (p. 226), Stencil begins to panic: "Events seem to be ordered into an ominous logic" (p. 449), he repeats over and again to himself, placing emphasis on different words. Do they *seem* to be ordered? Are they seemingly *ordered*? Is the logic *ominous*? As he nears the answer to his questions on Malta, he begins to sleep over long periods, to fall back again into the pre-1945 state. When the evidence about Father Fairing comes to Stencil, he is desperate: it is no longer by coincidence that he is learning these things, but by design. The logic *is* ominous, "something far more appalling" than history (p. 450). When Benny confirms the information about Fairing, Stencil rushes to Fausto, who says, "God knows how many Stencils have chased V. about the world." Stencil's last words in the novel then occur; about himself he asks, "Is it really his own extermination he's after?" (p. 451).

In *V.* Pynchon tells us that he does believe in history, if that means only that there are facts. But, if there is more than discrete fact, then we are at the bottom of a fold in history's fabric and cannot determine warp or woof or pattern:

> By virtue . . . of existing in one gather it is assumed there are others, compartmented off into sinuous cycles each of which come [*sic*] to assume greater importance than the weave itself and destroy any continuity. . . . We are accordingly lost to any sense of a continuous tradition [pp. 155–56].

History gilds, alters. As an act of social memory it is, to use Fausto's words, based "on the false assumption that identity is single, soul continuous" (p. 307); and thus it gives rise to "the fiction of a humanized history endowed with 'reason'" (p. 306). Since Pynchon implicitly rejects such history, he feels, at this time anyway, that we cannot, perhaps should not, see what the facts mean, for when we do they appear to mean too much: man's self-defeat, arising from overconfidence in his own *virtu*, at the hand of his own inanimate creations.

There is an ominous logic in all this — *maybe*. There are accidents: connections which do connect and connections which are only misleading. But what we do know is multiplicity, diversity, fragmentation, discontinuity. "The world is all that the case is" (pp. 278, 288) — this message, decoded from Kurt Mondaugen's sferics in 1922 (and which some readers will recognize as the opening sentence of Wittgenstein's *Tractatus Logico-Philosophicus*, published in 1922), is the message of the spheres, and to remain sane we should let it go at that and ask no questions. What one can most hope for any one individual is what Fausto hopes for his daughter — that she be "only Paola, one girl: a single given heart, a whole mind at peace" (p. 314) and not, like Stencil, "a repertoire of identities" (p. 62) or, like himself, a series of rejected personalities (p. 306). In the face of the ominous logic which seems to take shape "from events much lower than the merely human" (p. 483), Stencil is right to escape. Benny is also right to cling to his "schlemihlhood": he can survive, if he can believe what he tells Brenda when she asks what he has learned from "all these fabulous experiences." "Offhand," says Benny in his very last words in the novel, "I'd say I haven't learned a goddam thing" (p. 454).

One can trace in *The Crying of Lot 49* the same anti-vision and the same ambivalence within the questing character which distinguish *V.*, but its plot takes a different turn, for its questing character does make the connections and discover their meaning, though here a full disclosure is withheld from the reader. The angle of developing vision is always that of Oedipa Maas. But she herself is endowed with a lightness of touch, a humorous self-critical disposition, a *joie de vivre*, which saves her almost to the last from the insanity she comes desperately to hope explains the connections she sees. Not many characters on the last page of their story, awaiting final judgment, could whisper to their possible Enemy, "Your fly is open!"

It is in a strangely whimsical vein that the object of Oedipa's quest is conceived, the fantastic cabal of the Tristero system, a vast three-and-a-half-century-old private postal network, patronized now only by solitaries and social outcasts who live outside "the life of the Republic."[10] What sets her off on the quest is a responsibility imposed on her by her dead lover Inverarity to administer his estate. In one of the novel's controlling images, Oedipa thinks of herself as a Rapunzel-like character, encapsulated in a tower. While Inverarity was alive she had remained safe in her tower, knowing that the

[10] Thomas Pynchon, *The Crying of Lot 49* (Philadelphia: J. B. Lippincott Co., 1966), p. 124. Subsequent references to this novel appear in parentheses following the quotation.

price she paid was "an absence of an intensity" (p. 20) about life, a lack of surprise. At points and moments she had been aware of the narrowness of her prison; she knew she had settled for such a life because of "gut fear" (p. 21) that outside the tower was only void, only death, or what would pass for it — meanings which would destroy the limited sense she had made of life. Inverarity's will forces her out of the tower and into the void, to face whatever nameless and malignant magic had held her prisoner. Thus, in form, *Lot 49* is, like the Stencil narrative of *V.*, inquisitive, a cosmic detective story alternating between epistemology — how do I know what the facts are? — and metaphysics — what do these facts mean?

Oedipa responds in the spirit of a caper to early intimations that the Tristero exists. The Tristero is a sort of lewd dancer, a stripteaser on the stage of history, and she, in uncovering it, is attempting to see through "the breakaway gowns, net bras, jeweled garters and G-strings of historical figuration." Yet from the beginning she also wonders if what she is after is going to get her in too deeply: when its dance ends, when Tristero's "terrible nakedness" is revealed, would it "come back down the runway, . . . bend to her alone among the desolate rows of seats and begin to speak words she never wanted to hear?" (p. 54.)

Early in her inquiry into Inverarity's estate she experiences an "odd, religious instant" as she looks at the printed circuit board pattern made by the streets of San Narciso, the headquarters of Inverarity's activities. It is an instant in which she feels in the hieroglyphic pattern before her a "sense of concealed meaning, of an intent to communicate" (p. 24). This sense of some impending revelation, of words she both wants and fears to hear being spoken out of the void, increases steadily throughout the novel, as she moves amid signs and symbols of communication. The freeways also seem patterned like the printed circuits of a transistor radio; she finds herself living in a motel called Echo Courts; and she learns that the disc jockey to whom she is married thinks of himself, with the aid of LSD, as "an antenna, sending . . . [his] pattern

out across a million lives" (p. 144). Oedipa finds herself involved with a group of electronics scientists who hold Sinewave Jam Sessions on Saturday nights with "audio oscillators,
gunshot machines, contact mikes, everything man" (p. 48);
she tries for an ESP message from a profile photograph of
Clerk Maxwell on the Nefastis Machine; she seduces one man
before a TV set and is propositioned by another who likes to
engage in the sexual game while the news from China is on.
The largest metaphor of communication, however, is the
Tristero system whose possible existence lures Oedipa into
scholarly research for the true text of a seventeenth-century
play and leads her to wander aimlessly all night through San
Francisco, where she witnesses a nether world of secret communication.

As the coincidences blossom, suggesting another "separate,
silent, unsuspected world" (p. 125) intruding upon this one,
Oedipa becomes "anxious that her revelation not expand
beyond a certain point. Lest, possibly, it grow larger than she
and assume her to itself." Like Stencil of *V.*, near the end of
her inquiry she feels "reluctant about following up anything"
(p. 166). Her human contacts with the Tristero disappear or
change: her husband takes up LSD; Dr. Hilarius, her shrink,
goes mad; Metzger, her co-executor, elopes with a depraved
nymphet; her contact at The Greek Way grows mute; but,
most important of all, Driblette, the actor-director of the
Tristero play, walks into the Pacific, taking his own life.

Deliberately or by accident, Inverarity's will forces Oedipa
tentatively to acknowledge that outside of her tower there
may not be a void after all, that some "accommodation" may
have been "reached, in some kind of dignity, with the Angel
of Death." If the Tristero does exist, then there is "another
mode of meaning behind the obvious" (p. 182), a meaning
aligned, perhaps, with the numinous beauty of truth, with
justice, with reason. This is a meaning which others have
known and which she could have known "if only she'd looked"
(p. 179). If the Tristero does exist, however, the only way one
can "continue, and manage to be at all relevant" to the daily
world is "as an alien, unfurrowed, assumed full circle into

some paranoia." The other side of the proposition is, for her, equally terrifying. If there is no Tristero, she is already "in the orbiting ecstasy of a true paranoia"; the void is real and in it are "only death and the daily, tedious preparations for it" (p. 182).

Although Oedipa is allowed in the last scene of the novel to discover the truth, the reader never learns what this truth is. However, we are given all we need to know: if this world is not the fragmented, disconnected thing it appears to be— dull, out of focus, void of meaning, and leading to death— then its apparent discontinuity is actually held together by a secret, elusive, and transcendent meaning the knowledge of which leads to madness.

Joseph Heller and Thomas Pynchon have given us novels which show, in Ihab Hassan's phrase, "the deflection of laughter toward anguish."[11] Both have begun with the absurdity of our experience as a premise, and both have forced a vision from their characters at the point of extremity. But here the similarities end, for, in dramatizing the discontinuity which makes up our experience, they have come to highly individualized versions of the reality implied. In what I take to be a non-ominous coincidence, both Yossarian and Stencil flee to Sweden because of what they have seen, the one to fulfill his vision, the other to avoid his fate. Heller, more than Pynchon, realizes the ancient role of comedy in focusing attention upon our betrayals of our own values, while Pynchon probes more relentlessly into the nature of things, and into our modes of knowing, by comic excursions into history.

Pynchon's comedy calls us back not to the sanity and freedom for which Yossarian will save his life or die trying, but to an unblissful but tolerable ignorance in the midst of an absurdity which may be intelligible after all. For all the intellectual activity of his questing characters, Pynchon remains tentative about the value of the intellect. In the pursuance

[11] "Laughter in the Dark: The New Voice in American Fiction," *American Scholar*, 33 (Autumn, 1964): 637.

of his quest, Stencil acquires a fulfilling sense of animateness. But with the prospect of ending the quest, of making the connections, comes an apocalyptic vision of an absolute threat to life. The threat is not simply from death which, metaphorically, would be right enough, but from the take-over of the inanimate that promises to reduce the whole human enterprise to something utterly meaningless. While "the unnamable act, the recognition, the Word" (p. 180) of which Oedipa awaits sure knowledge at the end of her quest does not threaten absolutely, it does require, at least, an even more disjunctive, paranoid condition than has already characterized her experience. Thus Pynchon's two novels end in a peculiar kind of misologism, for the perception of rational connections in experience is rejected not because it does not tell us the truth, but because it does.

Through the comic mode Heller tries to identify the spiritually destructive features of our common life which we write into the human story through failure to live by the values that reason would commend. The bitterness in his vision is directed not so much at the nature of things as at a profound failure of intelligence. But his comic exposure of the murderous catch by which we reduce our common life to absurdity always finds its basic premise in the belief that there must be some meaningful way whereby our fractured lives may be made whole.

If there is more than an accidental relationship between insight and art, it may be that by reference to it we can explain why Joseph Heller's novel is more convincing than are the two novels by Thomas Pynchon. I do not mean in this way to argue with Pynchon about his conclusions, nor even about the perceptions on which he bases his peculiar misologism. But while both men have made the structures of their novels metaphors for the chaos with which they are dealing, Heller has at the same time given his novel a shape which counters the chaos. Pynchon has, however, taken more risks artistically, and perhaps only in this way will more be gained finally for those who are seeking in the modern novel new modes of moral and religious insight pertinent to our time.

So far, however, there has not yet occurred the deepening of perception to which he may be led by his technical innovations. His second book, though less ambitious, marks a certain advance over *V.*: not only is it funnier, but also its technical stratagems appear less labored. In *Lot 49* he exposes fragmentation in our experience and hints at meanings that may be humanly unacceptable, yet the shape of his book does not become itself a victim of his subject.

It is not merely their subject matter, however, which threatens poise and control in some of our new writers. For those writing in the comic mode face the further difficulty that in comedy there lies an innate tentativeness that may to some extent contravene or disable serious statements about the human condition. The suggestive thrusts of comedy threaten always to undercut themselves and, specifically in the case of Heller and Pynchon, to strain and crack the literary mold in which they are cast. Perhaps because he is less speculative than Pynchon, Heller has been able to keep the comic form intact. Indeed, Pynchon's tendency to obscure a clarity about the human situation he feels we cannot bear gains a kind of support in the very resistance that the comic mode itself offers to formal clarity. The blackness of his comedy and the darkness of his laughter want, in other words, to hide from the light of reason what he fears may be the essential truth.

4

J. D. Salinger: The Artist's Struggle to Stand on Holy Ground

JAMES T. LIVINGSTON

It was Seymour, of course, who said it: "All we do our whole lives is go from one little piece of Holy Ground to the next."[1] And it is just here that we get a splendidly concise statement of the thematic center of Salinger's fiction. The whole of his work constitutes an ever more intensive exploration of what Mircea Eliade has called "the two modalities of experience — sacred and profane,"[2] his later work most especially reflecting a search for ways of effectively rendering the life of man in a "sacralized cosmos."[3] That Salinger should have such pre-occupations ought not to be surprising to readers of his stories about the Glass family. Yet numerous critics have ignored (or deplored) the religious concerns in his fiction.

Salinger himself has joked a little about this in the "formal introduction" to his story "Zooey." Acknowledging that the facts of the narrative may speak a trifle too vulgarly for themselves, he has his narrator apologize in advance to any critics who might find the story unforgivably didactic because of its "too vividly apparent transcendent element."[4] In the end, we are told, such an objection does not apply because what we are being offered is not a short story but a "sort of prose

[1] J. D. Salinger, *Raise High the Roof Beam, Carpenters; and Seymour — An Introduction* (Boston: Little, Brown & Co., 1955), p. 248.
[2] Mircea Eliade, *The Sacred and the Profane* (New York: Harcourt, Brace & Co., 1959), p. 14.
[3] *Ibid.*, p. 17.
[4] J. D. Salinger, *Franny and Zooey* (Boston: Little, Brown & Co., 1961), p. 48.

home movie,"[5] and it is suggested that, though the plot may seem to hinge on mysticism or on some kind of religious mystification, it is only a "compound, or multiple, love story, pure and complicated."[6] And if Salinger's treatment of this subject involves some name-dropping (God, and Jesus Christ) of an unusual sort, it is because his subject requires it.

Taking their cue from these remarks, several critics, notably Arthur Mizener and Alfred Kazin, have argued that the power to love is in fact the basic subject of all Salinger's mature work.[7] Yet, though this is an integral part of his fiction, the more basic testimony being made, as we shall see, is that *agape* has its source and ground in a more fundamental reality — the experience of the Sacred.

In the first comprehensive monograph on his work, *The Fiction of J. D. Salinger*, by Frederick Gwynn and Joseph Blotner, it was suggested that the "high point of Salinger's art" is the story of 1950, "For Esmé — With Love and Squalor," and the terms *love* and *squalor* are said to designate the story's chief realities.

The story is divided into two parts. In the first part the narrator, who has just received an invitation to Esmé's wedding, recalls how when he was in England during the war, for pre-invasion training, he was rescued from loneliness and boredom in a brief encounter with the then thirteen-year-old Esmé and her five-year-old brother Charles, who had invited themselves to his table at a café. Learning that he was a writer, Esmé had asked the narrator to write her an "extremely squalid and moving story," and had added, "Are you at all acquainted with squalor?" "I said not exactly but that I was getting better acquainted with it, in one form or another, all the time, and that I'd do my best to come up to her specifications." Esmé's final words to him had been, "I hope that you return from the war with all your faculties intact."[8]

[5] *Ibid.*, p. 47.   [6] *Ibid.*, p. 49.
[7] Arthur Mizener, "The Good American," in *Salinger: A Critical and Personal Portrait*, ed. Henry Anatole Grunwald (New York: Harper & Bros., 1962), p. 30.
[8] J. D. Salinger, *Nine Stories* (New York: Modern Library, 1953), pp. 155–56.

J. D. Salinger

The second part of the story is narrated in the third person, suggesting how painful remain the events which it relates, in spite of the passage of some six years. Sergeant X, as he is called, is now in Bavaria at the end of the war, his faculties wrecked by the squalor he has come to know intimately through five violent and exhausting campaigns. He picks up a copy of Goebbel's book *Die Zeit Ohne Beispiel*, taken from a captured Nazi official, and finds a brief inscription on the flyleaf, "Dear God, life is hell," to which he adds a quotation from Dostoevski, "Fathers and teachers, I ponder, 'What is hell?' I maintain that it is the suffering of being unable to love."[9] That Sergeant X, like his German counterpart, is suffering such a hell is made clear in the conversation that follows with his only companion of the war, Corporal Z, an ignorant, vulgar, brutal man whose insensitivity makes Sergeant X physically ill. After the Corporal has awkwardly retreated, the Sergeant notices a package in his unopened mail. Indifferently he opens it and finds it to contain a letter from Esmé, together with a broken watch which had belonged to her father and which she had been wearing at the time of their encounter. Her father had been "s-l-a-i-n" in North Africa, she had spelled out to the Sergeant since her younger brother was present. The letter and the wristwatch, innocent and loving expressions of sanity, are sufficient to restore the Sergeant to peace. "Then suddenly, almost ecstatically, he felt sleepy. You take a really sleepy man, Esmé, and he *always* stands a chance of again becoming a man with all his fac - with all his f-a-c-u-l-t-i-e-s intact."[10] Although the watch functions as an emblem of love within the context of the story, it is an instance of the way in which Salinger endows simple objects with the power of a sacred presence. And, in Salinger's design, this presence is opposed to the profanity of Corporal Z and the German's inscription in Goebbel's book. Thus, love and squalor are but another form of the contrast between the sacred and the profane.

William Wiegand finds a key to Salinger's work in the form of spiritual sickness described by Seymour Glass as

[9] *Ibid.*, p. 160.   [10] *Ibid.*, p. 173.

"banana fever" in the first of the stories about the Glass family, "A Perfect Day for Bananafish." This spare and cryptic story, like several of Hemingway's early Nick Adams stories, can be fully understood only in the light of subsequent developments in the series. It, too, is divided into two distinct scenes. The first, set in a hotel room in Florida where Seymour and his wife Muriel are vacationing, consists mostly of an extended long-distance telephone conversation between Muriel and her mother. The tone is satiric, as the two middle-class women are revealed in all their intellectual and spiritual vacuousness. And the inanity of the wife is rendered so sharply as to suggest as least a partial explanation of Seymour's suicide, with which the story ends; but there are hints (confirmed in the later story about their wedding day, "Raise High the Roof Beam, Carpenters") that Seymour's "maladjustment," for which he has been undergoing psychoanalysis, is in fact more complicated. In the second scene, on the beach, we observe Seymour talking and swimming with a little girl, Sybil. It is to her that he recounts the "tragic life" of the bananafish who swim into holes where there are lots of bananas and eat until they are so fat that they can't get out of the hole. Then they get banana fever and die. Sybil accepts this tale, and immediately after, as they play in the water, she announces that she has seen a bananafish with six bananas in its mouth. This prompts Seymour to kiss the arch of her foot as she lies on a rubber float. Then, back in the hotel elevator, he angrily denounces a woman for staring at his feet. Walking into his room where Muriel lies sleeping he takes a gun from his suitcase and fires a bullet through his right temple. Obviously, Seymour, like the bananafish, is glutted with physical sensation, with "the overwhelming physicality of existence."[11] But Seymour does, in fact, see more. And his heightened consciousness results in his being "surfeited with the joy of life."[12] In "Raise High the Roof

[11] The phrase is James E. Miller, Jr.'s, *J. D. Salinger*, University of Minnesota Pamphlets on American Writers, No. 51 (Minneapolis: University of Minnesota Press, 1965), p. 28.

[12] Wiegand, "Seventy-eight Bananas," in *Salinger: A Critical and Personal Portrait*, p. 123.

Beam, Carpenters," Salinger furnishes several examples of this which are summarized in Seymour's entry in his journal, "Oh, God, if I'm anything by a clinical name, I'm a kind of paranoiac in reverse. I suspect people of plotting to make me happy."[13] What is crucial here is that Seymour's joy is a response to what he sees as holy, for banana fever, which is a characteristic illness of Salinger's major heroes, can be better understood and becomes even more convincing when it is placed within the more fundamental contrast of the sacred and the profane.

Warren French, who has written the only book-length study of Salinger's fiction, argues that "For Esmé" is too "triumphantly affirmative" to be typical of Salinger's work, just as "A Perfect Day for Bananafish" overstresses "the destruction of innocence."[14] French finds the story of 1948, "Uncle Wiggily in Connecticut," to be a more balanced work in its depiction of the two worlds which he sees as constituting the heart of Salinger's vision. French chooses the adjectives used by so many of Salinger's characters to describe those worlds — "phony" and "nice." These terms are particularly appropriate for analyzing the characters and conflict in "Uncle Wiggily in Connecticut." Eloise, a phony suburban housewife, spends a drunken afternoon with an old college chum, slowly revealing the emptiness and bitterness of her present life when set beside the memory of her lost lover Walt Glass, who had been senselessly killed in a freak accident in Japan after the end of World War II. Walt had once called her sprained ankle "Poor Uncle Wiggily," just as he had once said with his hand on her stomach while they had been riding together on a train that "her stomach was so beautiful he wished some officer would come up and order him to stick his other hand through the window."[15] Although nothing more is made of the incident, it is apparent that Walt, too, is given to something like the same sort of emotional

[13] Salinger, "Raise High the Roof Beam," p. 88.
[14] Warren French, *J. D. Salinger* (New Haven: College & University Press, 1963), p. 37.
[15] Salinger, *Nine Stories*, pp. 43–44.

sensitivity which distinguishes his brother Seymour. In the story, however, it is phoniness that is finally triumphant, as Eloise comes in the end to recognize the cruel bitch she has become. This recognition seems to entail no change in her character. She can only plead, sobbing, to her friend, "I was a nice girl, wasn't I?"[16] The clichés "phony" and "nice" may be adequate to describe Eloise's conflict; for the story is, as French believes, a dramatization of "the effects rather than the causes of the human predicament."[17] And the language of "phoniness" and "niceness" also suggests Salinger's alertness to distinctively American idiom, but such jargon is hardly sufficient to bear the weight of his more profound and complex vision in other stories, where, in fact, he wants to plunge beneath the surface of what is phony or nice to what is more radically sacred or profane.

The most recent of the comprehensive studies of Salinger's fiction is by James E. Miller, Jr., who explores the varied contexts of the theme of alienation:

> an alienation which may conclude in some kind of reconciliation or accommodation, but which may also result in distortion of the soul, bitterness, nausea, and the ultimate withdrawal into death. The causes of the alienation are frequently obscure but always complex. . . . Sometimes . . . the cause of alienation lies deeply within, in a turbulence of the spirit — plunging the individual into a dark night of the soul, or dazzling him in the ecstasy of a vision of mystical union — two radically different states that mystics have always found in close conjunction.[18]

Miller's final description of Salinger's work as "a cry of mystical joy transcendent over the modern wasteland and its agony"[19] is suggestive of the extent of Salinger's affirmation and of the necessity of such radical terms as I am proposing

[16] *Ibid.*, p. 56.
[17] French, *J. D. Salinger*, p. 41.
[18] Miller, *J. D. Salinger*, p. 20.
[19] *Ibid.*, p. 45.

for the understanding of his vision. But it is important, as I shall show, not to overemphasize the "mystical" element in Salinger's fiction.

Paul Levine and Ihab Hassan are the critics whose studies point most clearly in the direction of the sacred and the profane as terms for the central tension in Salinger's work. Levine traces through the stories the development of "the misfit hero," a designation that is convincing until he gets to the story "Zooey," where he sees that a "world of difference" separates Franny and Zooey from Salinger's earlier misfits.[20] It is true that "Zooey" is Salinger's most explicitly religious story, for it dramatizes Franny and Zooey's problem in clearly religious terms; but the story only treats explicitly what had been implicit in Salinger's fiction almost from the very beginning of his career. Levine also notices the special power of Salinger's style "to contain that off-center moral vision which allows the reader to discover the immensely significant in the apparently trivial and seemingly meaningless.[21]

Hassan's distinctive contribution to Salinger criticism is his definition of the "rare, quixotic gesture" made by the "responsive outsider" in his encounter with the "assertive vulgarian."

> The gesture . . . is the bright metaphor of Salinger's sensibility, the center from which meaning derives, and ultimately the reach of his commitment to past innocence and current guilt. It is a gesture at once of pure expression and of expectation, of protest and prayer, of aesthetic form and spiritual content. . . . There is often something prodigal and spontaneous about it, something humorous or whimsical, something that disrupts our habits of gray acquiescence and revives our faith in the willingness of the human spirit. But above all, it gives of itself as only a *religious* gesture can.[22]

[20] Paul Levine, "J. D. Salinger: The Development of the Misfit Hero," in *J. D. Salinger and the Critics*, ed. William F. Belcher and James W. Lee (Belmont, Calif.: Wadsworth Publishing Co., 1962), p. 114.
[21] *Ibid.*, p. 115.
[22] Ihab Hassan, "The Rare Quixotic Gesture," in *Salinger: A Critical and Personal Portrait*, pp. 140–41.

As Hassan goes on to say, this dramatic metaphor specifies the "limits of Salinger's language and the forms his fiction takes."

When the gesture aspires to pure religious expression — this is one pole — language reaches into silence. . . . When, on the other hand, the gesture reveals its purely satiric content — this is the other pole — language begins to lapse into sentimentality.[23]

It is between these two poles of silence and sentiment that Salinger the artist struggles, in his attempt to stand on Holy Ground. His experiments with language, point of view, theme and character are all part of that struggle which, judging from both the later texts and the slowness of his production, must be agonizing. The narrative manner of "Seymour: An Introduction" is primarily an exhibition of that agony, for, though the story is focused on Seymour, it is the narrator Buddy who is most fully revealed, in all his desperate imbalance. Many critics concluded from the story that it was Salinger who had lost all control, a reading that is doubtful, particularly in the light of Salinger's most recent story "Hapworth 16, 1924,"[24] where some measure of control is again in evidence, though only partially, since the story consists mostly of a long letter written by Seymour. In his concern to explore further the Glass family and the problem of Seymour's suicide, Salinger is willing to risk the difficulties of an unreliable narrator. But, as Hassan has noted, the risks Salinger has taken with his art are presupposed in his "religious view of things."[25]

Before the nature of Salinger's religious vision is described, some additional instances of his way of treating the sacred in his stories need also to be noticed. In his first long story, "The Inverted Forest," a talented poet (surely an early version of Seymour Glass) named Raymond Ford is shown in his movement toward tragic self-destruction. An awkwardly

[23] *Ibid.*, p. 141.
[24] *The New Yorker*, 41 (June 19, 1965): 32–113.
[25] Hassan, "Rare Quixotic Gesture," p. 142.

constructed story, with an incredible plot, it is only partially redeemed by Warren French's allegorical interpretation of it as the portrayal of the "idea that the artist does not have any social obligations."[26] Nevertheless, in one scene a young woman Bunny Croft, who is later to steal Raymond from his wife and contribute crucially to his destruction, brings him the manuscripts of some poems to criticize. And Raymond says,

> "I can't tell you you're a poet. Because you're not. . . .
> But you're inventive. . . . A poet doesn't invent his
> poetry — he finds it . . . . The place . . . where Alph,
> the sacred river ran — was found out, not invented. . . .
> I can't stand any kind of inventiveness."[27]

This revealing passage from an early work forecasts what was to become one of Salinger's major preoccupations — namely, the power of certain natural objects to body forth the presence of the sacred, so that it need not be invented but only found and recognized.

Salinger's most famous work *The Catcher in the Rye* is especially rich in profane images which are transformed into sacred presences by Holden Caulfield's deeply moral, though neurotic, sensibility. One of the most touching and humorous of these images occurs near the end of the novel, just after Holden has fled from the apartment of Mr. Antolini, the former English teacher with whom he had sought temporary refuge.

> I passed these two guys that were unloading this big
> Christmas tree off a truck. One guy kept saying to the
> other guy, "hold the sonuvabitch *up!* Hold it up, for
> Chrissake!" It certainly was a gorgeous way to talk
> about a Christmas tree. It was sort of funny, though, in
> an awful way, and I started to sort of laugh. It was about
> the worst thing I could've done, because the minute I
> started to laugh, I thought I was going to vomit. I really

[26] French, *J. D. Salinger*, pp. 68–71.
[27] J. D. Salinger, "The Inverted Forest," *Cosmopolitan*, 150 (March, 1961):124. This story was composed in 1947.

did, I even started to, but it went away. I don't know why."[28]

Much of the power of the novel is derived from the capacity of Holden, in his innocence and purity, to glimpse the holiness of things. But he is also "fallen," and thus a shocked participant in and witness of the world's profanity. The episodic structure of the novel is Salinger's means for portraying Holden in a sequence of increasingly profane experiences that momentarily destroy his equilibrium. But the strength of Holden's vision of Holy Ground is sufficient to make us hope that he will prevail in his struggle with the world's absurdity.

In "De Daumier-Smith's Blue Period," another of Salinger's more impressive stories, the sacred presence is rendered in a moment of mystical vision. The narrator has drifted into a job as instructor in a Canadian correspondence art school, where he is sparked into life by his only talented student, a nun, Sister Irma. When she withdraws from the course after receiving a long letter from him, he enters his "blue period." In the climax of the story he stops to look into the window of an orthopedic appliances shop. Earlier this "garden of enamel urinals and bed-pans, with a sightless, wooden dummy-deity standing by in a marked-down rupture truss," had served to remind him of his alienation.[29] This time, a "hefty girl" is changing the truss on the dummy, and, when she realizes that she is being watched, her embarrassment and confusion lead her to fall "heavily on her bottom," over a stack of irrigation basins. Reaching out to her, De Daumier-Smith's fingers hit the window glass. Then he has his "Experience."

> Suddenly . . . the sun came up and sped toward the bridge of my nose at the rate of ninety-three million miles a second. Blinded and very frightened — I had to put my hand on the glass to keep my balance. The thing

[28] J. D. Salinger, *The Catcher in the Rye* (New York: New American Library, 1954), p. 177.
[29] Salinger, *Nine Stories*, p. 241.

lasted for no more than a few seconds. When I got my sight back, the girl had gone from the window, leaving behind her a shimmering field of exquisite, twice-blessed, enamel flowers.[30]

The story is carefully wrought, but the Experience, with its transformation of the profane into the sacred, is still, dramatically, a *tour de force*.

"Zooey" is the story which renders Salinger's religious vision most fully. It dramatizes a spiritual crisis in the life of the youngest Glass daughter Franny, who is a college senior. The action involves her movement from despair and collapse to new faith and reconciliation through the persistent efforts of her brother Zooey (older than herself by five years) to help and guide her through a crisis that he shares. It is in Franny's cure that the tension of the sacred and the profane finds its resolution.

Salinger has experimented with many different therapies in his fiction in his search for ways of restoring his protagonists to health. William Wiegand has offered the following catalogue of Salinger's remedies for the sickness of modern man: suicide in "A Perfect Day for Bananafish"; forgetfulness in "Uncle Wiggily in Connecticut"; sublimation in art in "The Laughing Man"; the barefaced denial of pain in "Pretty Mouth and Green My Eyes"; the love and understanding of parents in "Down at the Dinghy"; the love and understanding of children in "For Esmé — with Love and Squalor" and *The Catcher in the Rye*; psychiatry in *The Catcher in the Rye*; a mystic vision in "De Daumier-Smith's Blue Period"; a mystic Buddhist faith in "Teddy"; and an Eastern mystic slogan in "Franny."[31] In "Zooey," Salinger shows that reconciliation with both society and God is possible only through the courageous practice of Christian love. In so doing, Salinger has Zooey explicitly reject each of the various alternatives enumerated above. Buddy points out that, although Zooey was the only member of the family who had been bitter

[30] *Ibid.*, p. 250.
[31] Wiegand, "Seventy-eight Bananas," pp. 128–29.

about Seymour's suicide, he had really forgiven him. The others had been "outwardly unbitter and inwardly unforgiving."[32] Zooey is scathing in his criticism of a psychoanalysis which seeks to adjust people to "the joys of television, and *Life* magazine every Wednesday, and European travel, and the H-bomb, and Presidential elections and the front page of the *Times*, and the responsibilities of the Westport and Oyster Bay Parent Teacher Association, and God knows what else that's gloriously normal" (pp. 107–8). Zooey similarly rejects as unrealistic any attempt to deny the existence of suffering and evil in the world or to sublimate it or to forget about it. Any mysticism characterized by escapism, piousness, or sentimentality he also objects to vehemently. To understand the solution offered in "Zooey," however, it is necessary to specify the nature of the malaise afflicting Salinger's heroes.

It might appear at first that this sickness is quite untypical of most modern Americans, and in a sense it is. Zooey and Franny are, as Zooey says, "freaks, with freakish standards" (pp. 138–39). The character of their particular freakishness, given to them through their extraordinary education as children at the hands of Buddy and Seymour, arises from their habit of experiencing the world in the dimension of the sacred. The "Introduction" to "Zooey" consists mostly of a long letter in which Buddy tries to explain to Zooey why he and Seymour had taken over his and Franny's education while they were quite small, conducting the home seminars in metaphysics which Franny and Zooey have come to resist. The inspiration for the letter is a supermarket conversation between Buddy and a little girl of whom he has inquired the names of her boyfriends, thus leading her to say in reply, "Bobby and Dorothy." And Buddy immediately recalls one of Seymour's remarks, that "all legitimate religious study must lead to unlearning the differences, the illusory differences, between boys and girls, animals and stones, day and night, heat and cold" (p. 67). Being deeply alarmed at the "statistics on child pedants and academic weisenheimers who grow up into fac-

[32] Salinger, *Franny and Zooey*, p. 68. Subsequent page references to this text will be noted parenthetically following the citation.

ulty recreation-room savants" (p. 65), Seymour and Buddy
had sought to commit their youngest brother and sister to a
quest for true knowledge. Drawing upon the idea of *satori* —
a state of pure consciousness which Dr. Suzuki says is "to be
with God before he said, 'Let there be light' " — they wished
to hold the children back from the light of knowledge, as
long as possible, until they were able to conceive of a state
of being where the mind knows the source of all light (p. 65).
So Franny and Zooey had received a rigorous training in the
concepts of Jesus, Gautama Buddha, Lao-tse, Sri Rama-
krishna, Meister Eckhart, and everyone else who seemed to
know something about this state of being, and this long
before they had had much else of formal education. This early
training has thrown Franny and Zooey out of gear with the
ordinary human reality, for, now, they are "Christians." And
though their religious nurture has been rather "unorthodox,"
it is, nevertheless, in the figure of Christ, in the Word made
flesh, that they have come to behold the primary fact of human life. The incident Franny relates of Zooey sharing a
glass of gingerale with Jesus in the kitchen when he was ten
years old suggests what is for them the true locus of the
mysterium tremendum. (It is significant, of course, that
Franny both dismisses this story and yet takes it quite seriously.) And, despite their enormous sophistication and all the
"light of knowledge" they have actually absorbed, they can
never throw off their perception of the spiritual realities
which are the source of that light.

In a way, Seymour functions ambiguously as a kind of
contemporary Christ-event for his brothers and sisters. For it
is he who has incarnated a goodness and wisdom that have
committed his brothers and sisters — or at least Franny and
Zooey and Buddy — to a human vocation in the world so near
to spiritual perfection that they can only rebel against it.
Many critics have complained that the Glass children exhibit
a kind of "clubbiness" which prompts them to love only each
other and only to judge the rest of the world. But, though
it is because of Seymour that the Glasses are set apart from
the world, it is also because of him that they know they must

find a way to live in the world. Yet his saintliness is something problematic, for in both "A Perfect Day for Bananafish" and "Raise High the Roof Beam, Carpenters" Seymour has become so detached from the "normal" world that he can hardly communicate. Though he is clearly attempting, through marriage and psychoanalysis, to re-establish the contact he knows is necessary for the sanctified life, he fails and does, in fact, finally destroy himself. And the same difficulties are faced by Franny, Zooey, and Buddy; but their struggle may be more significant, religiously, than Seymour's, for they do somehow manage more competently to deal with the world on its own terms.

Indeed, the measure of Franny's and Zooey's success may be helpfully taken by reference to Paul Tillich's concept of salvation. Tillich speaks of salvation as "healing" of the estrangement between God and man, through "participation in," "acceptance of," and "transformation by" the New Being.[33] This is the "three-fold character of salvation" as regeneration, justification, and sanctification. Now Franny and Zooey have known salvation as regeneration, as "Participation in the New Being." They have also experienced salvation as Justification, as "acceptance of the New Being." They live out of a sensitive awareness of Grace, and they affirm that it is the New Being in Jesus Christ that manifests this Grace. Their problem is at the level of salvation as sanctification, of "transformation by the New Being." They have the knowledge and the perception of saints, but they have not been empowered to live out that knowledge in the world, and, as a consequence, they tend to be proud and judgmental rather than humble and loving. But the hard fact is that, in addition to having knowledge, the true saint must be "transformed by the New Being." Salinger's central vision, in other words, is of a world suffused with Grace, but it is a Grace, as in the case of Franny and Zooey, that at once judges us into despair and repentance and beckons us to wholeness and reconciliation.

In "Raise High the Roof Beam, Carpenters," Seymour

[33] Paul Tillich, *Systematic Theology* (Chicago: University of Chicago Press, 1957), 2: 166.

speaks of the experience of Grace as being an intense awareness of "the main current of poetry which flows through
things, all things."[34] Anyone deprived of understanding or
taste for this current of poetry in life might just as well be
dead. "Poetry" is for Salinger an "implacable, demanding
kind of wisdom";[35] it is this wisdom, as the source and end
of education, that Franny finds so crucially absent in college.
And this is a part of the meaning of Grace.

But the idea of Grace also involves the notion of all "classi-
fications" as illusory, and the notion of a unity of essence
beneath all factitious distinctions. Buddy's letter to Zooey was
prompted by his being reminded of this unity by the little
girl who told him her boyfriends' names were Bobby and
Dorothy. And though Salinger never denies the existence of
such distinctions (the Many), he is primarily concerned with
the Many under their identity in the One.

This concern with the One shades boundlessly into a third
aspect of the experience of Grace in Salinger's characters,
namely, that of Incarnation, or the embodiment and revelation of spirit in matter. Indeed, one of Salinger's special
powers is his ability to juxtapose the august and the mundane
in such a way that the latter is mysteriously infused by the
former, yet all the while retaining its distinct identity. Thus
it is that chicken soup becomes "consecrated."

Out of this deep awareness of Grace come three impulses
discernible in all the Glass children. First, there is the impulse
of gratitude. As Zooey tells Bessie:

> "For a psychoanalyst to be any good with Franny at all,
> he'd have to be a pretty peculiar type. I don't know. He'd
> have to believe that it's through the grace of God that he
> has the native intelligence to be able to help his goddam
> patients at *all* . . . if she got somebody . . . who didn't
> even have any crazy, mysterious, *grat*itude for his insight

[34] Salinger, *Franny and Zooey*, p. 84.
[35] The phrase is Josephine Jacobsen's, and it is her study of Salinger
which has helped me to define two of what I set forth as the three
aspects of Grace in his fiction. See her essay "Beatific Signals" in
Salinger: A Critical and Personal Portrait, pp. 165–70.

and intelligence — she'd come out of an analysis in even worse shape than Seymour did" [pp. 108–9].

Second, there is the impulse toward joy, the mood so evident in Zooey during the first scene and in Franny at the end of the story when "for joy . . . it was all [she] could do to hold the phone, even with both hands" (p. 200). We have already observed Seymour's tendency to think himself a "kind of paranoic in reverse" because he suspects "people of plotting to make me happy." And Buddy speaks of his own joy in "Seymour: An Introduction" and carefully differentiates it from any kind of superficial jocularity. Finally, the third impulse prompted by the experience of Grace is the impulse toward love. Buddy is right in calling "Zooey" a "compound, or multiple, love story, pure and complicated." Zooey's dogged persistence in trying to help Franny is an expression of this love, and she recognizes this, just as Bessie understands that this is what is behind Zooey's "high-spirited bullying" of herself. And all the quotations from literature and the Bible and Eastern philosophers are attempts to explain and deepen this impulse toward love.

In summary, then, Franny and Zooey are indeed freaks, because of their extraordinary sensitivity to the presence of Grace in the world and because of their consequent impulses toward gratitude, joy and love. Their problem is not one of knowledge or ignorance. It is the problem of living out what they already know. Situated as they are in the profane urban "jungle" of our time, they find themselves continuously appalled by the superficiality and blindness in which the other denizens of the jungle live. Worst of all, not only does their immersion in this jungle of darkness constantly frustrate their better impulses, but they see within themselves equally appalling distortions of what they know they should be and do in the light of their sense of Grace.

At least six major perversions of the Christian faith are set forth in the story. There is, first of all, the attempt to make Christianity into something so "gloriously normal" that it is no more than a "hobby." This is the tendency to identify the faith with what is generally acceptable and important in the culture. Second, there is the attempt to turn the Christian faith into a series of intellectual or moral or dietary propositions, the acceptance of which precisely delineates the faithful. Third is the attempt to use the faith for the selfish piling up of "negotiable" treasure, be it earthly or heavenly. Then the fourth perversion involves the attempt to make the faith an escape from either the harsh realities of life or the "doing of whatever the hell [one's] duty is in life, or just one's daily duty" (p. 168). A fifth distortion entails the attempt to reduce the faith to sentiment, to transform Jesus into a merely endearing and loveable figure. Finally, there is the perversion of pride which transforms the Christian into a judge and the faith into a platform for handing down verdicts on others. The final three distortions are, of course, those to which Franny is most prone, while the sixth and perhaps the fourth are particularly Zooey's problems. But the essential problem common to them both is that of how the genuine and sensitive Christian is to live on Holy Ground, in a world constantly asserting its profanity. Their ever-present danger is that of being so overborne by the profane that they lose the virtue which Paul Tillich calls "courage."

Salinger's solution to this problem is two-sided. Half of the solution is action. It is appropriate that the protagonists are an actor and would-be actress by profession. Zooey is also by nature a man of action. His final advice to Franny is: "The only thing you can do now, the only *religious* thing you can do, is *act*. Act for God, if you want to. Be God's actress — what could be prettier? You can at least try to, if you want to — there's nothing wrong in trying" (p. 197). James Miller has pointed out Holden's constant vacillation in *The Catcher in the Rye* between "the imperative of involvement and revulsion at involvement."[36] Reconciliation can come only through the practice of Christian love. This must be done, as Buddy says in his letter, "with all your might," and, as Seymour suggests, it must be done for the Fat Lady. "There isn't anyone out there who isn't Seymour's Fat Lady. That includes your

[36] Miller, *J. D. Salinger*, p. 13.

Professor Tupper, buddy. And all his goddam cousins by the dozens" (p. 200). If Seymour is a kind of Christ-event for Franny and Zooey, then the Fat Lady represents Seymour's, or Christ's, resurrection.

The other half of the solution to Franny and Zooey's problem is "detachment—the only thing that counts in the religious life" (p. 196). Although Salinger, in this area of his thought, is dependent on the religions of the East, and though the very word *detachment* may suggest the impractical and the escapist, it would appear that what he really means is closely akin to, if not identical with, what Tillich calls the "Protestant principle"—that critical element of doubt inherent in the act of faith. Here the "latitude of private conscience," as Martin Green calls it, comes into view.[37] "An artist's only concern," Zooey tells Franny, "is to shoot for some kind of perfection, and *on his own terms*, not anyone else's" (p. 198). And the religious man aims at something similar. "What I don't like," says Zooey to Franny, "and what I don't think either Seymour or Buddy would like either, as a matter of fact—is the way you talk about all these people. I mean you just don't despise what they represent—you despise them. It's too damn personal, Franny. I mean it" (p. 161). Until Franny achieves the proper detachment she is incapable of acting in Christian love. The quotation adduced by Salinger from the Bhagavad Gita is to the point in this respect:

> You have the right to work, but for the work's sake only. You have no right to the fruits of work. Desire for the fruits of work must never be your motive in working. . . . [P. 176.]

Franny is "finished with the theatre forever" (p. 196) because the fruits of her labor do not correspond to her expectations. She is incapacitated in her duty by her despair over this fact. In this way, detachment and action, the two halves to Salin-

---

[37] Martin Green, "Amis and Salinger: The Latitude of Private Conscience," *Chicago Review*, 2, no. 4 (Winter, 1958): 20.

ger's solution, go together to form a whole, each being necessary to the other.

Franny is intelligent and sensitive enough to suspect her own idolatry, and this is the cause of her physical collapse. Zooey shows her that she is attempting to play God in judging what we as men cannot judge. He does this by asserting the sovereignty of God: "This is God's universe, buddy, not yours, and he has the final say about what's ego and what isn't" (p. 166). It is significant, though, that Zooey is unable to help Franny in face-to-face conversation. As he observes, she takes personally everything he says; and this, together with her knowledge of his own problems and failures, makes any real communication impossible. Franny is brought to understanding only by talking to Zooey on the telephone, where this threat is more removed. From this distance, Zooey is able to point Franny to the figure of Christ. Moreover, he enables Franny to see beyond her counterfeit Christ, a composite of "Jesus and St. Francis and Seymour and Heidi's grandfather," to the real Christ who threw tables around in the temple and thought people were more important than birds of the air, in short the Christ who was made flesh. Zooey does this through the pathetic image of the Fat Lady. The theme of incarnation recurs. Because of this image Franny's moment of recognition and reversal sternly satisfies the mind, while it stirs the heart and implements the will. "This is no maudlin positive thinking about . . . ugliness. Nor is it sentimental evasion. The sordidness [of the image] is not compromised with; it is destroyed."[38] Through detachment Zooey and Franny are able to become aware of the life of Grace within the life of Nature. Or, as Zooey expresses it, they can recognize the Kingdom of God that all the pathetic Fat Ladies and Professor Tuppers are carrying around with them, inside, "where we're all too goddam stupid and sentimental and unimaginative to look" (p. 170). Then reconciliation and the practice of Christian love become possible.

The measure of Salinger's success in his struggle to stand

[38] Jacobsen, "Beatific Signals," p. 166.

on Holy Ground is, inevitably, a matter of dispute, since both the question of transcendence and the delineations of its nature are at stake. We must remember that Salinger is an artist, not a systematic theologian. And, further, as Buddy says, we are all "limping men" and should be "courteous and kind to each other" (p. 69). What is surely most significant for our time is that the artist's struggle itself should be directed toward so high a goal. The extent of Salinger's affirmation and its dramatic power are striking, quite apart from any final assessment of its "truth." R. P. Blackmur observed once that "an age of faith comes about when religious convictions are part of — incarnate in — secular experience."[39] Salinger's work dramatizes that kind of faith. His is a remarkable and desperate effort to "free himself of the surface of things and to penetrate into matter in order to lay bare its ultimate structures."[40] And to the degree that he manages to make us see beyond the natural object — the enamel basins, the broken watch, Holden's red hunting hat, the chicken soup, the Fat Lady — to sacred presences, Salinger has indeed "found out — not invented" his poetry, and we are helped by it.

[39] R. P. Blackmur, "Religion and the Intellectuals," *Partisan Review*, 17, no. 3 (Spring, 1950): 227.

[40] Mircea Eliade, "The Sacred and the Modern Artist," *Criterion*, 4, no. 2 (Spring, 1965): 23.

5

Flannery O'Connor and the Grotesque Recovery of the Holy

PRESTON M. BROWNING, JR.

In contemporary American letters, Mary Flannery O'Connor is something of an anomaly. A Roman Catholic who wrote about Protestant fundamentalists, a "Southern lady" whose stories are filled with sex, crime and violence, an orthodox Christian whose work has been read and admired by the cultured despisers of religion, and a profoundly religious writer whose books were often mistaken for nihilistic tracts, Flannery O'Connor defies every attempt to place her (even tentatively) in any school or tradition. Moreover, it is impossible to fit her into the pat critical stereotypes of the "young American writer." She did not write a great first novel, her stories are not patently autobiographical, and, while her work does contain recurring images, motifs and character types, she did not, as so many other young American writers are alleged to have done, work a single fictional vein and rewrite the same novel several times over. There are adolescents aplenty in her novels and stories, but there is no trace of that seemingly narcissistic preoccupation with adolescence which marks, and some would say mars, the writing of a Salinger or an Updike. She shunned the modish, avant-garde literary circles of New York and did not publish in *The New Yorker*, yet she won during her lifetime significant critical acclaim and managed to establish, in little more than a decade of writing, a reputation which continues to grow and which may eventually rival that of some of our most respected twentieth-century authors. And when she died in 1964 at the age of thirty-nine, it was with her imaginative powers at floodtide, as the stories in the posthumously published volume, *Everything That Rises Must Converge*, amply indicate. She continued to write as long as she was physically able, and the finest thing that can be said of her last stories is that they rival in excellence her first. It is futile to predict what she might have accomplished had she been granted a longer life, but every evidence afforded by her final work suggests that she might well have become that rarest of literary specimens — an American novelist capable of sustained excellence and productivity into middle age and after. In a sense of the word which she, I think, would have appreciated, Flannery O'Connor was a freak.

But if Flannery O'Connor may not yet have given expression to the full amplitude of her creative genius at the time of her death, what sense is to be made of a statement such as Warren Coffey's, that "when she died at thirty-nine . . . it was with her work done . . ."?[1] This, assuredly, is a startling assertion to make of any young author, and especially of one whose legacy consists principally of two slender novels and two collections of stories. But, startling though it may be, Coffey's judgment does possess a certain cogency, for I suspect that Flannery O'Connor was a writer with something very special she wanted to say — call it a "message" if you like — and that in the score of short pieces and the two novels she managed to write, before her career was ended by the disease which plagued the last fourteen years of her life, she succeeded in saying it, and in saying it definitively. The marvel is that the "message" became art— at times, art of the highest quality — and not propaganda.

What Flannery O'Connor considered her fiction to be about she herself made plain in a comment repeated by her fellow novelist John Hawkes: "I don't think you should write something as long as a novel around anything that is not of the gravest concern to you and everybody else and for me this is always the conflict between an attraction for the Holy and the disbelief in it that we breathe in with the air of the

[1] Warren Coffey, "Flannery O'Connor," *Commentary*, 40 (November, 1965): 94.

times."[2] "The times," as she indicated elsewhere, embraced for her a good deal more than merely mid-twentieth-century America; but, in a special sense, it was the ethos of the 1950's, "the complacent years," against which Miss O'Connor's stories were directed. I use "against" deliberately, for Miss O'Connor was a satirist of extraordinary potency, and, in a decade when "positive thinking" was as much a part of the American way of life as cookouts and rock-and-roll, Flannery O'Connor turned out a magnificent assortment of stories each of which might well have been entitled "The Power of Negative Thinking."

Gifted with an imagination peculiarly sensitive to all the nuances of manners and folkways, what Lionel Trilling has characterized as the "hum and buzz" of a culture, Flannery O'Connor discerned in the manners of the 1950's an imperturbable smugness, a flatulent optimism, and a crass self-righteousness so deeply entrenched as to be movable only by the harshest kind of attack. She also perceived, at the root of this shallow complacency, what she felt to be an utterly fatuous belief in the omnipotence of a highly rationalized, technological society whose manipulation of human beings is calculated to turn out, as an end product, persons like a character in *Wise Blood* who is said to be "so well adjusted that she didn't have to think anymore." The attitudes which Flannery O'Connor satirizes through her often brilliantly original characterizations are those of an age in which the intellectuals are positivists and the nonintellectuals are "positive thinkers." But these attitudes, whether they are found in an inveterate rationalist such as the teacher Rayber in *The Violent Bear It Away* or in such absurdly self-righteous snobs as Mrs. Turpin in the story "Revelation," bespoke to Flannery O'Connor a deathly incapacity for existence in depth which she considered to be the besetting affliction of the contemporary world. This secularism — as virulent in the conventionally religious as in the atheistic — is her peculiar bête noire, and, like a latter-day Joshua, made sardonic and caustic by the

[2] Quoted in John Hawkes, "Flannery O'Connor's Devil," *Sewanee Review*, 70 (Summer, 1962): 397.

ingrained spiritual dullness of her adversary, she sallies forth, in story after story, to do battle for the Lord.

But, in addition to the positivists and the positive thinkers, one finds in her stories a third character type which might be designated the "criminal-compulsive" — the twisted, the neurotic, the guilt-ridden and the God-haunted protagonists who have earned Flannery O'Connor a reputation for gratuitous grotesquerie and violence and which have led some critics to the unflattering conclusion that she is merely a "Roman Catholic Erskine Caldwell." But such a response is plainly wrongheaded, for in her exploration of that "conflict between an attraction for the Holy and the disbelief in it" which is so deeply a part of our age, these violent and flawed beings play an indispensable role: it is they who serve as spiritual catalysts, administering the shock which awakens the positivists and the positive thinkers from their dream of a world made secure by shallow goodness or superficial rationality.

In the story called "Good Country People," for example, which is found in her first collection, *A Good Man Is Hard To Find*,[3] there appears a minor specimen of the criminal-compulsive, as well as a family relationship involving a positivist and a positive thinker — a relationship developed in numerous variations in later stories. Joy and her mother, Mrs. Hopewell, offer the paradigm situation: the disaffected young rebel, more often than not cynical but in any case intellectual and typically alienated from the world of the smug, uncritical parent; the parent, self-satisfied, optimistic, spouting platitudes of a moral or religious cast, but in fact dedicated to a philistine value system and the profit motive. Mrs. Hopewell (the name is obviously symbolic) is a steady subscriber to the "life can be beautiful" philosophy. In contrast to her daughter Joy, whose distinguishing characteristics are an extremely sour disposition and a wooden leg, Mrs. Hopewell staunchly maintains that "people who looked on the bright side of things would be beautiful even if they were not." Joy, though decidedly not beautiful, is brilliant but cyn-

[3] *A Good Man Is Hard To Find* (New York: Harcourt, Brace & Co., 1955).

ical, and takes a perverse pleasure in affronting her mother's flaccid optimism with a look of "constant outrage." Joy's perversity, having its genesis partly in her intolerance for her mother's mediocre mind and cliché-ridden speech, leads her to change her name to Hulga, the most unpleasant sound she can think of; and she complements the ugliness of her adopted name by a sullen rudeness of behavior to her mother and the latter's "companion," Mrs. Freeman. A self-styled atheist, with a Ph.D. in philosophy, Hulga feels nothing but contempt for the stupidity and banality of the world inhabited by her mother who appears incapable of thought more profound than the sentiment that "good country people" — of whom Mrs. Freeman is, in her view, a notable example — are the "salt of the earth."

Into this world there suddenly intrudes another representative of good country people (or so Mrs. Hopewell assumes), in the person of one Manley Pointer, an itinerant Bible salesman. Young and, as it seems, quite innocent, Pointer manages to ingratiate himself with Mrs. Hopewell, matching her clichés with unctuous platitudes about "Chrustian [*sic*] service" and "real honest people" who nowadays are to be found only "way out in the country." Hulga's response to the uninvited guest is at first that of impatience and revulsion, but she soon begins to see in the situation possibilities congenial to her bent of mind. After promising Pointer on a certain day to go on a picnic with him the following morning, Hulga lies in bed contemplating how, by seducing this young man, she can lead him into realms of awareness undreamt of by his innocence.

> She imagined that the two of them walked on the place until they came to the storage barn beyond the two back fields and there, she imagined, that things came to such a pass that she very easily seduced him and that then, of course, she had to reckon with his remorse. True genius can get an idea across even to an inferior mind. She imagined that she took his remorse in hand and changed it into a deeper understanding of life. She took all his shame away and turned it into something useful.

Hulga, it seems, had as a child "sometimes been subject to feelings of shame but education," the reader is told, "had removed the last traces of that as a good surgeon scrapes for cancer." Now the emancipated Hulga will liberate this victim of backwoods ignorance and superstition and permit him to nibble some of the crumbs from the banquet table of reality at which she has long since sated herself. As the condescending Eve, she will lead him into knowledge — not, however, knowledge of good and evil, but a more austere perception that both good and evil are illusions. "I'm one of those people who see *through* to nothing," she tells him, "We are all damned . . . but some of us have taken off our blindfolds and see that there's nothing to see. It's a kind of salvation."

The dénouement of the story is at once pathetic and ironically comic. Hulga and the salesman do indeed enter the storage barn and climb to the loft, but, here, Hulga's coldly calculating intelligence forsakes her completely. Earlier, while walking in the woods, she had allowed Pointer to kiss her, and at that time her mind was described as "clear and detached and ironic . . . regarding him from a great distance, with amusement but with pity." In the barn she kisses him with seeming passion, although "her mind" all the while "never stopped or lost itself for a second to her feelings." Pointer declares his love for Hulga and demands that she permit him to remove her artificial leg as proof of her love for him. This she refuses to do until he announces that it is her artificial leg which fascinates him: "It's what makes you different. You ain't like anybody else." And this, of course, is Hulga's undoing, literally and figuratively. Allowing her secret pride in her "difference" and her submerged self-pity to becloud her "clear and detached and ironic" vision, Hulga gives Pointer her leg and immediately loses that mastery over him on which her entire scheme depends. Feeling himself now in command, Pointer takes from his valise a hollowed-out Bible containing a small whiskey flask, a pack of pornographic cards, and a box of condoms. Hulga the cynic, the believer in nothing, is at first too startled to speak; when at last she does respond, it is in a voice described as "almost pleading": "'Aren't you,' she murmured, 'aren't you just good country people?'" Pointer answers with a surly "Yeah. . . . but it ain't held me back none"; and when Hulga complains furiously that he's "a perfect Christian," i.e., a thoroughly hypocritical one, this young man whom she has assumed to be the epitome of "real innocence" disabuses her once and for all of *her* illusions: "'I hope you don't think,' he said in a lofty indignant tone, 'that I believe in that crap! I may sell Bibles but I know which end is up and I wasn't born yester-day. . . .'" As he disappears out of the loft, with Hulga's leg safely ensconced in his valise, along with souvenirs of other, similar escapades, Pointer delivers his *coup de grâce*: "'And I'll tell you another thing Hulga . . . you ain't so smart. I been believing in nothing since I was born.'" While Hulga remains in the barn, her face "churning" with anger, Mrs. Hopewell and Mrs. Freeman watch Pointer crossing over the meadow to the highway. Mrs. Hopewell refers to the Bible salesman as "so simple" and adds, typically, "but I guess the world would be better off if we were all that sim-ple." To which Mrs. Freeman, who takes pride in her reputa-tion of having "always been quick," replies, "Some can't be that simple . . . I know I never could!"

The tale should end, so Stanley Edgar Hyman insists, at the moment of the "'symbolic defloration,'"[4] but this, of course, is to miss half the story's point, for what is being satirized is Mrs. Hopewell's optimism and gullibility and Mrs. Freeman's self-satisfaction, no less than Hulga's arti-ficially induced cynicism.

Viewed thematically, this is one of Flannery O'Connor's most interesting early stories, since what is involved in the encounter between Hulga and Pointer is a confrontation be-tween a facile, superficial and finally sentimental nihilism and a nihilism which, while completely nonintellectual, is none-theless real and implacable. Hulga's mean-spirited perversity proves merely a façade, behind which lives a secret self

[4] Stanley Edgar Hyman, *Flannery O'Connor*, University of Minnesota Pamphlets on American Writers, no. 54 (Minneapolis: University of Minnesota Press, 1966), p. 17.

wrapped in naiveté, superciliousness, and petty self-indulgence; and when she is forced to acknowledge the existence of perversity profounder than her own — more a part of the scheme of things, because partaking more fully of evil as a metaphysical reality — she responds with incredulity, shock and impotent outrage. The shock of evil is, recurrently, a central event in Flannery O'Connor's work, and in each case the initiate into what Hawthorne called "the sinful brotherhood of mankind" experiences a sense of utter helplessness as he is made to confront a dimension of reality whose very existence his positivism or his positive thinking has prompted him to deny or ignore.

Mrs. Cope in "A Circle in the Fire," another of the early stories, is one born to just such a destiny. As her name suggests, Mrs. Cope possesses inordinate confidence in her ability to deal with contingencies, to cope. Although she pays lip service to some vague notion of divine providence ("We have a lot to be thankful for," she says. "Every day we should say a prayer of thanksgiving."), her real religion consists of faith in her own resourcefulness and perseverance: "I have the best kept place in the county," she declares to Mrs. Pritchard, the hired hand's wife, "and do you know why? Because I work. I've had to work to save this place and work to keep it." *"I don't let anything get ahead of me* and I'm not always looking for trouble. I take it as it comes" (my italics). Mrs. Pritchard, who, in the economy of this story serves a function not unlike that of the Greek chorus, begins a reply: "If it all comes at oncet sometimes" but is cut short by Mrs. Cope's self-assured retort, "It doesn't all come at once." To which Mrs. Pritchard, not sharing Mrs. Cope's sanguine faith in the predictability of the human situation, answers: "Well, if it ever did . . . it wouldn't be nothing you could do but fling up your hands."

Appropriately, it is precisely at this moment that Mrs. Cope begins to learn the truth of this homely wisdom for which she has formerly felt nothing but mild contempt. For down the road to her farm come three teenage boys from Atlanta, one of whom, a bespectacled and hollow-chested youth named Powell, had lived on her place as a child. Powell and his companions are the very incarnation of unprovoked, irrational malignity, as Mrs. Pritchard is quick to discern. ("You take a boy thirteen year old is equal in meanness to a man twict his age. It's no telling what he'll think up to do. You never know where he'll strike next.") But Mrs. Cope is too blinded by her positive view of human nature and her unshakable confidence in her own competence to take Mrs. Pritchard's warning seriously. When one of the boys tells her that Powell once locked a small brother in a box and set fire to it, the only response she is capable of is a cheerful and incredulous inanity: "I'm sure Powell wouldn't do a thing like that." Later, when she learns that, contrary to her explicit instructions, the boys have been riding her horses and smoking in her barn, and that, instead of staying for one night as she had initially thought, they intend to stay indefinitely, Mrs. Cope begins to understand, but dimly, that she has been overmatched. And as these young delinquents gratuitously commit first one and then another act of destruction or perversity, she comes ever closer to realizing the truth of Mrs. Pritchard's oft-repeated litany, "There ain't a thing you can do about it." But still she insists on responding with sweet reasonableness and persuasion rather than in the terms of the direct action which her twelve-year-old daughter urges. Finally, having discovered that the young hoodlums whom she had earlier admonished to "act like gentlemen" have drained the oil from her tractor and let the bull out of its pen, Mrs. Cope drives off to town after warning her unwelcome guests that, if they have not left by the time she returns, she will call the sheriff.

Even at this juncture, however, Mrs. Cope is incapable of recognizing either the extent of the boys' maliciousness or the limitations of her capacity to manage a situation which, as is obvious to everyone but herself, is already well out of hand. To Mrs. Pritchard's ominous anticipations of what the boys may do now that they have been threatened, Mrs. Cope omnisciently replies: "Ridiculous. . . . I've scared them and they've gone and now we can forget them." Mrs. Pritchard continues to predict ("I look for them to strike just after dark"), and Mrs. Cope just as insistently maintains that the "poor things" have left. Condescending to what she considers Mrs. Pritchard's superstitious mind and proud of her own rationality, Mrs. Cope goes bindly to her tryst with fate. For, on the next morning, Powell and his friends set fire to Mrs. Cope's most treasured possession — her woods. As the fire licks its way among the trees and the boys whoopingly skip out a war dance, Mrs. Cope, for once stunned and impotent, stands silent before the reality of evil, at last utterly incontrovertible. Even the child, who is portrayed throughout the story as a good deal wiser than her mother and who has witnessed the firing of the woods, feels "weighed down with some new unplaced misery. . . ." And, as she stands beside her mother, staring "up at her face as if she had never seen it before," she beholds there the image of that new misery which she herself has just experienced, "but on her mother it looked old and it looked as if it might have belonged to anybody, a Negro or a European or to Powell himself."

The beautiful irony of this final description of Mrs. Cope resides in the fact that, much in the manner of the Pharisee in the parable, Mrs. Cope has for years been saying, in effect, I thank thee that I am not as other men are. True, her pride is not as much in her moral perfection as in what she calls her "blessings," but for her the distinction hardly exists. "Lord, we have everything," she exclaims at one point, and, on the afternoon before her great moment of recognition, she had enumerated to the child the things for which they should be thankful, exclaiming that "they might have had to live in a development themselves [Powell's fate] or they might have been Negroes . . . or they might have been Europeans ridden in box-cars like cattle. . . ." So, believing herself immune to those ills which plague the generality of men and placing excessive confidence in the potency of her own intelligence and will, Mrs. Cope is totally unprepared for the shattering discovery that finally comes, that there is no escaping "the human condition." As in that ancient story of a protagonist whose superb self-confidence makes him believe that he is

not only the "first among men," but, more than this, the
favored child of Fortune, Mrs. Cope, like Oedipus, discovers
that to be human is to stand in a field bounded by fallibility,
finitude, suffering and fate. And only by means of the shock
of evil, the inescapable confrontation with an irrational and
intractable malignancy, is she brought to this awareness. For
the child the recognition seems to bring its own moment
of grace, for, as she stands "taut, listening," she hears faintly
"in the distance a few wild high shrieks of joy, as if the
prophets were dancing in the fiery furnace, in the circle the
angel had cleared for them." Literally, of course, she hears
only the war whoops of Powell and his fellow incendiaries,
but the figure has the effect of suggesting that the child's
imagination, being more ingenious and freer of self-delusion
than her mother's, is able to apprehend something redemptive even in the heart of catastrophe. But, before the mystery
of human depravity, Mrs. Cope is simply stunned, "as if she
had had a search light thrown upon her in the middle of the
night."

In the title story of *A Good Man Is Hard to Find* the shock
is even more dramatic and more terrifying. In this tale a
young father is about to take his wife and children and the
children's grandmother from their home in Georgia on a
vacation trip to Florida. The entire family is portrayed as
vapid and thoroughly philistine, but the grandmother especially displays a soul so empty that it seems to reverberate
with the echoes of her own incessant and aimless chatter.
Smug, self-willed and obsessed with breeding and "good
blood," she is determined that the family go to East Tennessee
to visit relatives, rather than to Florida. When attempts to
persuade her son to alter his plans prove unavailing, she insists that at least they turn off the highway to investigate an
old mansion she had visited as a child. And, in a deliberate
effort to excite the children, she fabricates a story of a hidden
panel and lost treasure. So successful is her strategy that the
son, Bailey, acquiesces, with reservations whose unconscious
irony lends chilling poignancy to the horror consequent upon
their taking this detour: "All right," Bailey said, "but get

this. This is the only time we're going to stop for anything like this. *This is the one and only time*" (my italics).

Minutes later, as the impatient Bailey drives rapidly along a bumpy country road, the old lady remembers with a start that the house they are searching for is in Tennessee rather than in Georgia. Utterly disoriented by her discovery, she kicks over a valise, thus allowing her cat — hidden in a basket beneath — to spring onto Bailey's shoulder. In the ensuing commotion, Bailey loses control of the car, which bounces off the road and overturns. No one is seriously injured, but, as they extricate themselves from the wreck, they see, on the road above, another automobile from which three escaped convicts suddenly emerge. The grandmother, with her unerring instinct for trouble, blurts out the identity of the group's leader, "the Misfit," whose picture she has seen in a newspaper.

From here the story moves with Sophoclean swiftness to its catastrophe: first Bailey and the boy, then the mother and her daughter, are led off to the woods and shot. Only the grandmother, rendered almost insane by fear, is left to confront the philosophical psychopath, "the Misfit," a man who finds no pleasure in life but "meanness" and who claims that "Jesus thown everything off balance." Like Mrs. Hopewell in her habitual refusal to recognize that there is more to life than "the bright side of things," the grandmother faces the Misfit with nothing more than a mouthful of banalities ("You're not a bit common!" "I just know you're a good man.") which serve to reinforce our already established impression that, for her, goodness and gentility are merely social counters to be employed whenever expediency demands it. When the Misfit declares that he has assumed his name because he cannot make "what all I done wrong fit what all I gone through in punishment," she responds by suggesting that perhaps he was only mistakenly committed to the penitentiary. But, like her other vacuous remarks, this statement demonstrates how unable she is to comprehend either the Misfit's belief that everything was once "thown off balance" or the mystery of evil which he himself ambiguously em-

144

bodies. That the world itself might be awry, that injustice might be a permanent and irreducible component of human existence, that sham gentility offers no "safe conduct" through this life — all of these intimations, as they flood her consciousness, leave her traumatized and panting, in a swoon of disbelief.

At last, faced with imminent death, the old lady grasps at the only supports available to her: conventional piety, her faith in good breeding, and the commercial ideals of the society she so pathetically represents. Indeed, her very way of pleading for mercy indicates how meretricious are the values that have sustained her life. Having tried to tell the Misfit that he must pray and having succeeded only in speaking the name of Jesus more as a curse than as a prayer, she makes one last attempt: "Jesus! . . . You've got good blood! I know you wouldn't shoot a lady! I know you come from nice people! Pray! Jesus, you ought not to shoot a lady. I'll give you all the money I've got." To which the Misfit sardonically replies, "Lady . . . there never was a body that give the undertaker a tip" and proceeds to shoot her three times through the chest.

The Misfit's honesty and spirituality (perverse though they be), are, of course, being opposed to the "bad faith" of the old woman. As the title suggests, the theme of this story is the question, What constitutes a good man; and the grandmother's insistence that the Misfit is an example of this rare species is both ironically appropriate and grotesquely inappropriate. The Misfit has no illusions about himself and responds to her desperate flattery with the matter-of-fact answer: "Nome, I ain't a good man." What is significant here, I think, is that the Misfit, like Haze Motes in *Wise Blood* and Tarwater in *The Violent Bear It Away*, and unlike both the positivists and the positive thinkers, takes the question of good and evil seriously. While his self-appropriated name connects him, with superb irony, to the world of popular psychology and textbook sociology in which he is merely a deviant from society's norms, the Misfit himself sees his problem religiously and metaphysically. His final speech to the old lady constitutes his radical vision of man's state:

"Jesus was the only One that ever raised the dead. . . . and He shouldn't have done it. He thown everything off balance. If he did what he said, then it's nothing for you to do but thow away everything and follow Him, and if He didn't, then it's nothing for you to do but enjoy the few minutes you got left the best way you can — by killing somebody or burning down his house or doing some other meanness to him. No pleasure but meanness."

A Southern "poor white" cousin of Dostoevsky's tortured agnostics, the Misfit decides that either Jesus told the truth about Himself, in which case one should stake his entire existence on Him, or else He was deluded, the logical inference of this being "God is dead." And since the latter seems to be the case, signifying that good is not the determinative principle of the universe, the Misfit concludes, much like the Dostoevskian hero, that "everything is permissible."

The point which this story decisively makes is that, while a good man is indeed hard to find, a truly evil one is just as rare. The Misfit, in his frustrated search for some assurance of the reality and permanence of good, turns to evil as a not-very-satisfactory but logical alternative to the wholly specious "good" offered him by contemporary society and best exemplified in the selfish, self-indulgent, easy-conscienced grandmother of the story. To society, the Misfit is a psychopathic killer; to Flannery O'Connor he would seem to be a kind of saint *manqué*, cutting through the cliché-ridden, heedless lives of the people he murders to radical questions of depth, of spirit, of the reality of good and evil as ontological entities. In his terrifyingly perverted lucidity, the Misfit implies that, if evil is defined as mere maladjustment, the concept of good then becomes meaningless. By insisting that he himself is *not* a good man, the Misfit evinces a rudimentary awareness of goodness as a possibility, even if not a possibility for himself. Moreover, to be truly human, the Misfit seems to say, man must be committed to either good or evil and must *do* good or evil; and since there appears to be no sanction for goodness — and such a sanction is precisely what the Misfit longs for and cannot find — he must, therefore, commit himself to evil. The Misfit reminds us of Dostoevsky's conviction that "crime does not indicate any natural amorality" but is rather a negative testimony to a good, apart from which man can scarcely live;[5] and, in his final comment that there is no real pleasure in life, this Christ-haunted criminal from the backwoods of Georgia intimates just how deep is his intuitive penetration into the mystery of good and evil which so tormented Dostoevsky.

The Violent Bear It Away, Flannery O'Connor's second novel and to my mind her most impressive achievement, has been characterized by Stanley Hyman as "wholly and centrally about Vocation and the prophet's necessary stage of resistance to Vocation."[6] Hyman likens the struggle of the fourteen-year-old protagonist to avoid his calling to that of Moses and Jonah and proposes that, in Tarwater's final acceptance of his burden to be "both vessel and instrument of divine purpose," there is to be found the story's deepest meaning: "Divine purpose is not answerable to human reason."[7] As far as it goes, this interpretation is certainly defensible: Tarwater *is* a reluctant prophet, he does in time come to feel that it is his inexorable destiny to trudge "into the distance in the bleeding stinking mad shadow of Jesus,"[8] and his ultimate realization that there is no escaping this fate does suggest that divine purpose will have its way with man, even though man's reason or his will would have it otherwise. But, while Hyman's reading of the novel is defensible, it seems to me hardly adequate; for it might just as plausibly be argued that, rather than being "wholly and centrally about Vocation," the novel concerns itself in large part with the difference between two ways of interpreting reality, and that the

[5] V. V. Zerkovsky, "Dostoevsky's Religious and Philosophical Views," in *Dostoevsky*, ed. Rene Wellek, in "Twentieth Century Views" series (Englewood Cliffs, N.J.: Prentice-Hall, Inc., 1962), p. 136.

[6] Hyman, *Flannery O'Connor*, p. 24.

[7] *Ibid.*, p. 25.

[8] Flannery O'Connor, *The Violent Bear It Away* (New York: Signet Books, 1961; originally published by Farrar, Straus & Cudahy in 1960), p. 66.

story of Tarwater's efforts to flee the call of the Lord provides the necessary fictional context within which this difference may be examined and defined.

More specifically, I would submit that there are in the novel two more or less parallel lines of action which occasionally touch each other and which do at last decisively intersect, in one of the two major climaxes of the story—the baptismal drowning of the idiot child Bishop late in Chapter Nine. There is, on the one hand, the struggle which takes place within Tarwater to throw off the influence of his great uncle Mason Tarwater, a wild-eyed, half-mad backwoods prophet, who had kidnapped the boy when he was a baby and had raised him up to be, like himself, a prophet of the Lord. In this effort Tarwater is aided by a friendly "stranger," who appears in various disguises, real and fancied, and who is actually both Tarwater's alter ego and the Devil. The stranger taunts Tarwater with the observation that true prophets receive from the Lord an unmistakable sign of their election and mutters sarcastically: "Lemme hear you prophesy something. The truth is the Lord ain't studying about you. You ain't entered His Head." Then, by way of further dissauding Tarwater from taking up his vocation, the stranger must discredit the boy's great uncle, whom he accuses of having been crazy, or practically so, since he was a "one-notion man" who, year in and year out, talked of nothing but Jesus and salvation: "Ain't you in all your fourteen years of supporting his foolishness fed up and sick to the roof of your mouth with Jesus? My Lord and Saviour," the stranger sighed, "I am if you ain't." In the voice of the stranger one can hear that latent skepticism and cynicism, that egocentric appeal to moderation and common sense with which, it seems, every truly dedicated prophet must at one time or another struggle. When Tarwater suggests that the choice he must make is between Jesus and the devil, the stranger's prompt reply is that, rather, the choice is between Jesus and self: "No no no," the stranger said, "there ain't no such thing as a devil. I can tell you that from my own self-experience. . . . It ain't Jesus or the devil. It's Jesus or *you*."

There is another distinctly different, but related voice in the novel, that of Tarwater's uncle, the schoolteacher Rayber, who also attempts to persuade the boy that to accept the mission bequeathed him by his great uncle is the sheerest madness. Here, in the confrontation between the fiercely independent, "primitive," uncouth boy and the superficially educated and stubbornly determined rationalist Rayber, we may discern a fundamental clash between two radically opposed modes of sensibility, between two different views of the world; and the collision between the two makes for a second line of action. Of course, the two struggles are inseparable parts of the one unified dramatic movement, but it is essential in reading this work to keep clearly in mind that Rayber represents not merely an added exacerbation of Tarwater's internal conflict but that in his own right he stands for an understanding of human existence which clashes violently with that of the old prophet and which is finally judged, found wanting, and rejected by Tarwater himself.

The son of old Mason Tarwater's sister and an insurance salesman who replied to his brother-in-law's questions regarding the salvation of his soul with the mocking assertion that he sold policies against all contingencies, Rayber is himself haunted by childhood memories of a pastoral paradise where he first learned that his life counted because of the love of a Saviour. Having been reared by parents who taught him nothing more than not to wet the bed (so the old prophet tells Tarwater), Rayber had come, when a lad of seven, to old Tarwater's place Powderhead, there listening to the old man talk of his redemption and then submitting to baptism. The impression left by this experience is so indelible that Rayber can never entirely shake off the prophet's influence, though in time he comes to believe that his uncle's religious fanaticism has done more to scar his life than to save it. Years later, as the two confront each other over the baby Francis Marion Tarwater, the illegitimate son of Rayber's sister and grandnephew to the old man, Rayber accuses his uncle of pushing him "out of the real world" by filling him with such "idiot hopes" that at last he "didn't know which was which."

At this point the battle for the soul of the baby is joined, as Rayber tells his uncle that he will not permit him to "ruin another child's life. This one is going to be brought up to live in the real world," he declares. "He's going to be *his own saviour. He's going to be free!*" (my italics). The old man's determination is more than Rayber has counted on, however, and at the first opportunity he baptizes the baby (Rayber, to prove how free of superstition he is, proceeds to turn the child over and irreverently pours water on his bottom) and, shortly afterwards, kidnaps the child and returns to Powderhead with him. Rayber's one attempt to retrieve the child results in ignominious defeat when a blast from the old prophet's shotgun carries away part of one ear, leaving him permanently disfigured and partially deaf.

Fearing for his own sanity, Rayber imposes upon himself the strictest kind of discipline, countering the old man's religious fanaticism with an emotional asceticism and a rationalistic fanaticism of his own, by means of which he hopes to control the irrational side of his nature. ("What we understand we can control," he tells Tarwater.) But what Rayber cannot understand and can control only with the greatest difficulty is an impulse which is, to him, "completely irrational and abnormal": "a morbid surge of love that terrified him — powerful enough to throw him to the ground in an act of idiot praise." Significantly, this "morbid surge of love" is particularly associated with Rayber's mentally defective child, Bishop, and would seem to connote (as the image of being thrown to the ground in praise suggests) a kind of mystical enthrallment with Creation, including even its deformities (Bishop). Equally significant is the association in Rayber's mind of this overwhelming love with the old prophet: "It began with Bishop and then like an avalanche *covered everything his reason hated.* He always felt with it a rush of longing to have the old man's eyes— insane, fish-coloured, violent with their impossible vision of a world transfigured — turned on him once again. The longing was like an undertow in his blood dragging him backwards to what he knew to be madness" (my italics). Good positivist

that he is, Rayber understands love clinically and thera-
peutically and, as such, considers it to be valuable and useful.
What frightens him is a love that man cannot manipulate or
control, cannot put to use for his own or someone else's "im-
provement." It is the mystery of a love which seems to transcend human need and initiation that Rayber abhors — "love
without reason . . . love that appeared to exist only to be
itself, imperious and all demanding."

As the novel opens, Tarwater, now fourteen, is preparing a
grave for the body of his great uncle who has just died. Instead of completing his task, however, he goes off to his
uncle's still, gets thoroughly drunk and returns to the cabin
after dark, setting fire to the structure as a kind of declaration
of independence from the old man and as a final act of defiance of the father figure toward whom he has long felt both
love and resentment. Much of his antagonism grows out of
Tarwater's suspicion that his great uncle may, after all, have
been crazy and that, in bringing him to this wild spot with
only himself for tutor, the old man may have robbed him of
valuable knowledge of the real world and of fourteen years
of life in the city. Then, too, there is the old man's constant
reference to Tarwater's freedom as "the freedom of the Lord
Jesus Christ," and the boy, by nature extremely independent,
finds the suggestion that his freedom is not self-generated a
source of nagging irritation. However, the old prophet's years
of labor have not been wasted, for no matter how ambivalent
young Tarwater may be toward his great uncle's command
that he accomplish a task which the old man left unfinished
(the baptizing of the idiot child Bishop), the boy's unwaver-
ing response to his uncle Rayber, to whose home he flees after
the episode just described, is one of smouldering antipathy.
Having for years heard the old man tell of how Rayber had
once written an article about him, declaring him a "type that
was almost extinct," and of how, when he realized that it was
he, Mason Tarwater, to whom his nephew was referring, the
old man "felt he was tied hand and foot inside the schoolteacher's head, a space as bare and neat as the cell in the
asylum, and was shrinking, drying up to fit it," — remembering

all this the boy approaches his uncle with a mixture of wonder and dread. For the old man's warning that, with Rayber, his very selfhood would be in jeopardy has been too often repeated to be ignored:

> "And if you were to go there, the first thing he would do would be to test your head and tell you what you were thinking and how come you were thinking it and what you ought to be thinking instead. And before long you wouldn't belong to your self no more you would belong to him."

The old man's prediction proves disturbingly accurate, for Tarwater finds, upon entering his uncle's house, that he is scrutinized by "two small drill-like eyes," seemingly intent upon boring to the very depths of his soul. Instinctively, young Tarwater draws away from this creature who strikes him as being a kind of mechanical man, with his "black-rimmed glasses" and his electrical hearing aid — a device increasingly referred to in the novel as "the machine." After an exchange in which Tarwater, bent on asserting his independence from the start, facetiously asks the teacher if his "head light[s] up," Rayber begins to try to win the boy's confidence and to free him from what he considers the bondage of "false guilt" and ignorance in which the old prophet had left him. Rayber himself suffers feelings of guilt for not having made a greater effort to save Tarwater, while still a baby, from the warping influence of the old man; and, frustrated in his efforts to apply his advanced educational theories to his idiot son, he sees in his young nephew a chance both to redeem the past and to shape a human life after a pattern of his own design. In his arrogant assurance that he can at last best the old man by undoing the work of fourteen years, Rayber tries to establish an intimate relationship with the boy, calling him Frankie and assuring him that he at last has a friend. "You have more than a friend now," he declares; "you have a father." Tarwater's reply — immediate, scornful, defiant — marks him as irredeemably the child of the old prophet: "I ain't ast for no father," he twice repeats. "I'm out of the womb of a whore. . . . And my name ain't Frankie."

From this point forward, while Tarwater fights his inner battle to resolve the conflict between that part of himself which is repelled by the call to prophecy and that part which cannot deny the old man's commission, another battle takes place in which Tarwater's will is pitted against Rayber's (the second line of action). And here, I think, we come close to the heart of Flannery O'Connor's vision. For what is most centrally involved in *this* struggle are two radically divergent concepts of freedom. As we have already seen, old Tarwater had believed that in Rayber the power of mind, of the Idea, was grown so rampant as made it inevitable that he should entrap and shrink to nothingness the selfhood of anyone on whom he might chance to fasten. Rayber is, in fact, presented as a kind of monster of abstract intellect, capable of peering "through the actual *insignificant* boy . . . to an image of him that he held fully developed in his head" (my italics). And young Tarwater is determined that no one, and especially not his uncle, shall rob him of his freedom. Thus, when Rayber attempts to give the boy an intelligence test, Tarwater remembers the old man's warning and hisses at the schoolteacher: "I'm free. I'm outside your head. I ain't in it. I ain't in it and I ain't about to be." The schoolteacher, certain that the boy is a victim of a compulsive neurosis, a consequence of years spent with the old prophet, responds predictably: "You don't know what freedom is." To Rayber the boy's every action exhibits an independence which could only have been acquired from the old man — "not a constructive independence but one that was irrational, backwoods, and ignorant."

Yet, for all his talk of freedom and constructive independence, Rayber himself is anything but free. Thinking of himself as an emancipated modern man, totally divested of religious belief, and capable, through the most rigorous application of will power, of controlling what seems to him an irrational psychic undertow, Rayber is, in fact, a victim of his own intellectual habits which cause him to substitute thought for life. This was the old man's most perceptive observation regarding his nephew, that he lives, as Rayber himself admits, with his "guts in [his] head," and that this condition renders him incapable of acting: "'It was me could act,' the prophet says, 'not him. He could only get everything inside his head and grind it to nothing.'" And so, when, late in the novel, Rayber resolves to confront Tarwater with his analysis of the boy's difficulty and announces that, while they are both plagued by compulsive tendencies, he (Rayber) at least has no compulsion to baptize Bishop, we can hear the old man's voice, distinct and filled with contempt, in Tarwater's retort:

> "It ain't the same. . . . I can pull it up by the roots, once and for all. I can do something. I ain't like you. All you can do is think what you would have done if you had done it. Not me. I can do it. I can act. . . . It's nothing about me like you."

When Tarwater does finally decide to act, his prophecy is fulfilled: he acts decisively, drowning the idiot boy in a lake where the three of them have gone for an outing, while Rayber, who had himself once attempted to drown the child and had discovered that he was incapable of the deed, lies in bed, silently acquiescing in the death of his son. Moments before, he had been struck with the realization that all he desires is for the world to be consumed, and at the thought of his own destruction he feels utter indifference. Discovering at last his true self, Rayber wishes only to be a passive "observer" of the final holocaust, thinking that "this indifference was the most that human dignity could achieve. . . . To feel nothing was peace." The absolute desolation of Rayber's soul could hardly be more graphically portrayed than in Flannery O'Connor's final description of him as he stands at the window overlooking the lake, his heart beating with a "dull *mechanical* beat" (my italics):

> He stood waiting for the raging pain, the intolerable hurt that was his due, to begin, so that he could ignore it, but he continued to feel nothing. He stood light-headed at

the window and it was not until he realized there would be no pain that he collapsed.

Rayber's ruthless control of his emotions brings him at last that freedom from the irrational undertow for which he has so long striven; but, to his dismay, he discovers that to feel nothing is not peace but horror. Having trod for years the razor's edge between madness and emptiness, he finds at last that the old man (through Tarwater) has beaten him again — not by plunging him into a frenzy of "idiot praise" but by constantly presenting him with an option which, in his steadfast refusal, leaves him finally alone in an utter void. Rayber achieves his freedom — freedom from Bishop whom he looks upon as a mere mistake of nature; freedom from Tarwater, whom he has gradually come to hate; and freedom from the "morbid surge of love" which, terrifyingly, has long lurked in his dark subconsciousness. But the price he must pay for this freedom is high indeed, for in achieving it he sacrifices, or so it would seem, an essential part of his humanity.

And what of Tarwater's freedom? If he remains outside the schoolteacher's head, is he not still a victim of the old man's monomania? For, when he drowns Bishop as an ostensible act of defiance and a final repudiation of his calling (with the stranger, now his "faithful friend," standing alongside, urging him to the deed), Tarwater utters involuntarily the words of baptism. Of course, he explains to himself that this was simply an accident and that his drowning the child far outweighs his baptizing him. Confident that his act does constitute an irrevocable "No!," Tarwater starts out for Powderhead, thinking that it was not as a boy "that he returned. He returned tried in the fire of his refusal, with all the old man's fancies burnt out of him, with all the old man's madness smothered for good, so that there was never any chance it would break out in him. He had saved himself forever. . . ." But before reaching his destination he accepts a ride with a stranger whom we recognize as Tarwater's faithful friend the Devil, now in the guise of a city slicker homosexual. The stranger drugs Tarwater and rapes him, and, when the boy awakens, he is so repelled by the whole incident that he sets fire to the bushes about him, in an effort to burn clean the "evil ground" wherever touched by the stranger. That the experience will prove decisive in determining Tarwater's destiny is made clear when the ground upon which he stands, known to him since childhood, is described as "look[ing] like strange and alien country." Tarwater moves forward to Powderhead, no longer believing that there he will live out his refusal but rather knowing that it is his fate to discover there a "final revelation." His eyes, the reader is told, "no longer looked . . . as if they were meant only to guide him forward. They looked as if, touched with a coal like the lips of the prophet, they would never be used for ordinary sights again."

The rest, one might say, is epilogue. Tarwater returns to Powderhead, where he finds his great uncle's grave marked by a rude cross (the old man had been dragged by a local Negro from the shack and given a Christian burial while the boy was off getting drunk). And, here, he is indeed granted an ultimate revelation. On the entire journey from the lake to Powderhead, Tarwater has been beset by a raging thirst and an insatiable hunger, and, as the boy reaches what was once his home, he feels the hunger attack him with renewed force. Standing motionless before the piercing, judging eyes of the Negro Buford, and recognizing in the grave with its cross a sign of the faith he has, unconsciously, held all his life, Tarwater undergoes a transforming mystical experience — that "final revelation" in which he sees a multitude, among whom is the old man, being fed from a "single basket." The old prophet seems to lean forward and the boy repeats his motion, "aware at last of the object of his hunger, aware that it was the same as the old man's and that nothing on earth would fill him." Turning toward the encircling forest, Tarwater sees "a red-gold tree of fire ascend[ing] as if it would consume the darkness in one tremendous burst of flame." Knowing that at last he has received his sign, his own burning bush, Tarwater throws himself upon the grave of the old prophet and hears the long-awaited command: GO

WARN THE CHILDREN OF GOD OF THE TERRIBLE SPEED OF MERCY.

It can be argued, of course, that Tarwater is simply what Rayber takes him to be — a victim of a neurotic compulsion by which he is finally overborne. In this interpretation, Tarwater's freedom is no more a reality than is Rayber's. But, in the economy of the story itself, it is evident that Tarwater, as he so often boasts, makes things happen and is empowered to act. Furthermore, I think it safe to assume that it was Flannery O'Connor's conviction that, to be genuine, freedom must be grounded in commitment of some sort and must have a definite object, otherwise it becomes what Francis Fergusson in his discussion of Ibsen's *Ghosts* characterized as "the anomalous 'freedom' of undefined and uninformed aspiration" — *Unendlichkeit.*[9] Naturally, that commitment need not be a Christian commitment, but it is clear that Flannery O'Connor took a very skeptical view of what is achievable in the way of freedom, on the basis of a secularist ordering of human life. So it is not strange that those characters in her fiction whom she expected us to discern as exemplifying an authentic freedom are so often people who are warped and grotesque and obsessive. For, as she remarked on one occasion in a lecture, with such persons in mind: "Those who, like Amos and Jeremiah, embrace a neglected truth will be seen to be the most grotesque of all."[10] And because she considered the Christian Gospel a sorely "neglected truth" in our day, she peopled her fictional world with grotesques like old Mason Tarwater the "mad" prophet, who was indeed a "one-notion" man but whose one notion she deemed so essential for human health and wholeness that, apart from it, all talk of freedom is meaningless. Hence, she appeared to affirm the apparent paradox that commitment to the fundamental truth about mankind — no matter how passionate, violent, and

[9] Francis Fergusson, *The Idea of a Theater* (Garden City, N.Y.: Doubleday Anchor, 1953; originally published by Princeton University Press, 1949), p. 174.
[10] Quoted in Bob Dowell, "The Moment of Grace in the Fiction of Flannery O'Connor," *College English*, 27 (December, 1965): 239.

seemingly compulsive that commitment might be — makes for a greater freedom, ultimately, than anything achievable by the positivists and the positive thinkers. Convinced that a mind such as Rayber's, shaped by the assumptions of scientism and positivist philosophy, could never engender a freedom of the whole man but only a wasteland of the self haunted by lifeless abstractions, Flannery O'Connor wanted very much to create, in this story as in others, a protagonist whose very commitment to a seemingly irrational and perverse freedom manifests a depth of being undreamt of in the positivist philosophy.

Just here we may have an explanation of why it was that, though not herself a Protestant, Flannery O'Connor was attracted to and was able to use so powerfully materials drawn from the culture of Southern Protestantism. Being a Roman Catholic she felt no compunction, as does the average educated Protestant, to dissociate herself from Southern Protestantism in its more aberrant and exotic forms; and, while she satirizes certain aspects of sectarian fundamentalism, she never satirizes the fervor of fundamentalist belief nor its passionate concern for salvation. Moreover, her own brand of Catholicism having more in common with the thought of Pascal than with that of Thomas Aquinas,[11] she was predisposed to see in the fundamentalist's assertion of the utter corruption of man's heart (apart from radical commitment to Jesus Christ) a truth too often blinked at both in the churches of the respectable and in the highly secularized society by whose norms those churches seem increasingly to live. More than anything else, however, I think it was the Southern fundamentalist's belief in the mystery surrounding human existence which appealed to Flannery O'Connor and which, together with these other features of Southern folk religion, provided her with a ready-to-hand and indigenous frame of reference within which her own vision could be given artistic form.

But that vision, in my opinion, was a good deal more com-

---

[11] For a perceptive discussion of the Jansenist strain in Flannery O'Connor's Catholicism, see Coffey, "Flannery O'Connor," pp. 96–98.

plicated and ambiguous than the orthodox Christianity she professed in her several statements about the bearing of her faith upon her art: if it was Christian orthodoxy to which she subscribed, her work is manifest proof that it was orthodoxy with a difference. For her persistent habit of finding the human reality in the extreme, the perverse, and the violent calls for a closer examination than it has been possible for me here to attempt. In one of her frequently quoted comments concerning the Christian writer's predilection for the grotesque, she said it was her feeling

> that writers who see by the light of their Christian faith will have, in these times, the sharpest eyes for the grotesque, for the perverse, and for the unacceptable. . . . Redemption is meaningless unless there is cause for it in the actual life we live, and for the last few centuries there has been operating in our culture the secular belief that there is no such cause.
>
> The novelist with Christian concerns will find in modern life distortions which are repugnant to him, and his problem will be to make these appear as distortions to an audience which is used to seeing them as natural; and he may well be forced to take ever more violent means to get his vision across to this hostile audience . . . to the hard of hearing you shout, and for the almost blind you draw large and startling figures.[12]

Without implying any intentional misrepresentation on her part, I believe it can be argued that, while this explanation tells the truth about her use of the grotesque, it fails to tell the whole truth. For it seems to me that in her fiction Flannery O'Connor reveals a penchant for the twisted, the abnormal, and the grotesque which surpasses their usefulness as technical devices and which suggests that she believed, with Thomas Mann, that "certain attainments of the soul and the intellect are impossible without disease, without insanity,

[12] Flannery O'Connor, "The Fiction Writer and His Country," in *The Living Novel, a Symposium*, ed. Granville Hicks (New York: Collier Books, 1962; originally published by Macmillan in 1957), pp. 162–63.

159

without spiritual crime."[13] Presumably for this reason so many of her protagonists are violent, neurotic, oftentimes criminal beings, and, without glorifying criminality per se, she more than once implies that the criminality and the spirituality (actual or potential) of these people are correlative qualities.

In his perceptive essay entitled "Flannery O'Connor's Devil," John Hawkes proffers the interesting suggestion that the Devil of *The Violent Bear It Away*, "in giving voice to his dry country-cadenced nihilism and in laying out the pure deflated truth of mere existence . . . is speaking not only for himself but for the author."[14] It is Mr. Hawkes's view that, perhaps without being fully aware of it, "as writer [Flannery O'Connor] was on the devil's side,"[15] and that, in much of her work, disbelief in the Holy "emerges fully as two-sided or complex as 'attraction for the Holy.'"[16] Granted, there is in her authorial voice a measure of the "diabolical" and, in her stories and novels, a preoccupation with evil amounting almost to an obsession. But one can grant this without necessarily coming to Mr. Hawkes's conclusion that Flannery O'Connor was "on the devil's side." For if the notion of spiritual crime is taken seriously, it becomes possible to argue that it is precisely by way of evil itself that the Devil's nihilism is overcome. Only by committing murder, for example, are Haze Motes and Tarwater brought to a point where they can receive a "final revelation" of the truth of their existence. "The dialectic of good," Dostoevsky believed, "is set in motion through suffering — and often through sin";[17] the same, I think, can be said of Flannery O'Connor. Her vision as a writer, which bears a striking resemblance to that of Dostoevsky, is founded upon a similar dialectic: just as Haze Motes

[13] Quoted in Ihab Hassan, *Radical Innocence: Studies in the Contemporary American Novel* (Princeton, N.J.: Princeton University Press), p. 26.

[14] Hawkes, "Flannery O'Connor's Devil," p. 402.

[15] *Ibid.*, p. 400.

[16] *Ibid.*, p. 401.

[17] Zerkovsky, "Dostoevsky's Religious and Philosophical Views," p. 136.

proclaims that "the only way to the truth is through blasphemy," Miss O'Connor seems to say that, in an age so well adjusted to its own tawdry norms that the very idea of Good becomes precarious, the only way to the Holy is through evil.

Thus I maintain that Flannery O'Connor indeed took crime and evil seriously and gave them a positive valuation in her attempt to validate the reality of the sacred. For one of her profoundest preceptions appears to have been that man is a creature of depth, and that modern secularism, in robbing man of that depth, deprives him of his capacity for genuine evil as well as for true good. Perhaps what she sensed finally was the absolute necessity of the recovery of depth if life is to have any truly *human* meaning; and she seems also to have sensed the inevitability of this recovery involving a plunge into the radically profane as a way to the Holy.

6

J. F. Powers and Secularity
MAYNARD KAUFMAN

Few contemporary writers have pursued a single subject so relentlessly as J. F. Powers. The Roman Catholic parish priest is his favorite character, and the tension between the priest's religious vocation and the secular culture in which that vocation is exercised provides the dramatic center of his fiction. Powers has published two collections of short stories, *Prince of Darkness* in 1947 and *The Presence of Grace* in 1956, and a novel. Twelve of the twenty stories in the books of 1947 and 1956 are concerned directly with the priest and his problems. Some of the particular characters and settings from these stories reappear in the novel, *Morte D'Urban*, one of the more important works of recent American fiction and winner of the National Book Award in 1963. It is obvious that Powers' preoccupation with priestcraft has provided him with a formula for good fiction, and one suspects that he has his finger on a significant issue in the life of our time. Certainly the sensitivity and skill with which he handles this issue indicate that he is a writer who is seriously exploring what is implied in the tension between the religious and the secular.

One of the more problematic aspects of Powers' fiction, however, concerns its status as "religious" literature. For many of the stories in his first collection are without any distinctively Catholic theme. And, even when he is working with explicitly Catholic material, he frequently treats religion itself as a secular phenomenon. The contrast between the secular setting and the religious theme or moral insight is thereby lost. Thus the reader is made to question whether religion is

163

really a separable phenomenon within the secular world. Indeed, the reader is invited to consider religion as in many respects simply one particular phase of a generally secularized culture. So it may in part be true, as Peter De Vries has argued, that Powers is not a religious writer, that he is not writing about souls agonizing over belief or unbelief but about egos in conflict with each other, and that he is not concerned with "Faith" but with the "Household of Faith." [1] These distinctions are helpful in specifying the general tone of Powers' stories, but it would be a mistake to infer that he is incapable of handling an emphatically religious theme. "Lions, Harts, Leaping Does" is a powerfully written story in this mode. We are made to feel the making of a saint in a fairly conventional manner, even though — or because — the dying friar is too humble to be sure of it himself. But one of Powers' principal concerns is with the Household of Faith rather than with Faith itself, and his perspective on this Household is that of a sympathetic initiate. He does not undertake to resolve all the perplexing issues of its inner life: many of them remain to irk and nag the characters, but they are not ultimately disruptive. Father Fabre, the young curate in "A Losing Game," wants little more than a decent piece of furniture from the junk in the church basement but fails to get even that from his taciturn pastor. But in "The Presence of Grace" Father Fabre sees the pastor exercising his pastoral function as shepherd of the flock, healing their petty schisms, and he learns to respect the pastor's wisdom. Another of the ever-present problems in the Household of Faith is the housekeeper in the rectory, and "The Valiant Woman" is focused on a priest who would like to get rid of his housekeeper but is unable to find a decent way of doing it.

A second issue with which Powers deals in several stories concerns the business of priestcraft. And, here, one will recall most especially the Father Burner stories: "Prince of Darkness," "Death of a Favorite," and "Defection of a Favorite."

[1] Peter De Vries, "Introduction," in J. F. Powers, Lions, Harts, Leaping Does, and Other Stories (New York: Time Reading Program, 1963), pp. xv–xx.

J. F. Powers and Secularity

Father Burner is not a humble, God-fearing priest but one who burns with ambition, and he is nicknamed "Prince of Darkness." But, though he has failed to advance from the position of assistant to that of full pastor in seventeen years of parish work, his ambition to become pastor of his own parish seems modest enough. Though he does not whitewash Father Burner's sins—which are seven, and deadly—Powers invites from his readers a certain sympathy, for this obscure cleric is aware of his own sins and failures, and he knows that the true mark of the priest is not on himself as it is on his colleagues: "They, the others, were stained. . . indelibly, as indeed Holy Orders by its sacramental nature must stain, for keeps in this world and the one to come. . . . With him, however, it was something else and less, a mask or badge which he could and did remove at will, a temporal part to be played, almost only a doctor's or lawyer's."[2] Father Burner is the prototype of Powers' priests who, unlike those of Graham Greene, are portrayed in a non-sacerdotal way which reveals that the secularism of modern culture has penetrated into the very heart of the priest's own self-understanding. But there is much in Powers' fiction which suggests that he is wanting not merely to satirize the worldliness of priests but to explore the possibility that the process of secularization itself may be something not simply to be lamented but to be Christianly accepted and appropriated. Indeed, his basic perspective appears to be something like that of Gabriel Vahanian, when Mr. Vahanian remarks that modern religiosity "looks like a curious mixture of Christianity, secularity, and secularism."[3]

The attempt to appropriate modern secularism as itself a form of Christian secularity is, then, one of the major motives guiding Powers' short stories. "By secularity," says Vahanian, "is meant the sphere of man's action. This means temporality in contrast to the divine eternity; and it means finitude in contrast to God's infinitude."[4] Secularism, on the other hand,

[2] J. F. Powers, *Prince of Darkness and Other Stories* (Garden City, N.Y.: Doubleday Image Books, 1958), pp. 177–78.

[3] Gabriel Vahanian, *The Death of God* (New York: George Braziller, 1961), p. 67.

[4] *Ibid.*, p. 66.

is a form of religiosity. In "The Forks," for example, secularism is represented by the Monsignor who rails against people
who seemed to think "that Catholicity and capitalism were
incompatible"; he complains about all the laymen and princes
of the Church who are "talking atheistic communism," and
then he proceeds to invest his opinions with divine sanction
by appealing to "the Mind of the Church."[5] Against this Monsignor, Powers places an assistant with a sensitive social conscience, Father Eudox. The major issue between them is what
Father Eudox should do with the annual check of one hundred dollars which he receives, along with other clergymen,
from the Rival Tractor Company. Father Eudox wants to
endorse his check over to the strikers' relief fund, and, of
course, the Monsignor objects to this. The issue is resolved
after Father Eudox counsels a woman whom he mistakenly
assumes had wanted to bequeath her estate to the Church.
When he realizes that she had only wanted a broker's tip
on how to invest her money, he tears up his check in disgust
and flushes it down the toilet. Then, in the final paragraph,
the motif of stewardship is introduced, and Father Eudox is
implicitly condemned as the steward who, though he had
received but one talent, yet buried that one (Matt. 25:14–30).

The secular world is symbolized, in many of these stories,
by the obsession with money. In "The Lord's Day" the nuns
have to count and sort the coins from the morning collections
on Sunday afternoon, and they refer to their pastor as Father
O'Mammon rather than O'Hannon. The obsessive preoccupation with money is, as Norman O. Brown has pointed out,
dialectically related to the realm of the sacred: "The money
complex is the demonic, and the demonic is God's ape; the
money complex is therefore the heir to and substitute for the
religious complex, an attempt to find God in things."[6] Secularism, as the desire for money or material things, thus invariably
turns into a form of religiosity which does not help man genuinely to affirm the natural or the given world any more than

[5] Powers, *Prince of Darkness*, pp. 90–91, 98.
[6] Norman O. Brown, *Life Against Death* (New York: Vintage Books,
1959), p. 240.

does a conventional religious attitude. So the secularized priest who is consumed by worldly ambition is the Prince of Darkness. Or Mr. McMaster, the smooth operator in "The Devil was the Joker," is an impersonation of the Devil in his serpentine form. Mac, as he is called, sells religious paraphernalia to priests and parishoners in the church itself and represents the Devil's insinuation of himself (money) into the very heart of parish life. Or, again, Myles Flynn, a very religious young man who had been expelled from the seminary he attended, probably because he was too unworldly, agrees to travel with Mac in the hope of finding a bishop willing to sponsor him for the priesthood. Myles is continually complaining about "greed" in the "modern world" and would like to think of humanity as "the Mystical Body of Christ," while Mac, "allied with the modern world for better or worse, defended the indefensible and fought back."[7] At one point Myles remembers the advice which the disciples received as they went out into the world: "Be ye therefore wise as serpents and simple as doves" (Matt. 10:16). Such an attitude would be characteristic of secularity, but it is Mac who is wise as a serpent, while Myles is simple as a dove; and they are split apart. Thus the worldly and the unworldly are in juxtaposition, and neither can be affirmed. The secular man can only affirm the world as the Devil's, and, as such, it is indefensible. The religious man can never affirm the real world, this modern world, with the categories of the sacred, and is thereby unable to recognize it as God's world.

In discussing secularity or, as he puts it, "secular Christianity," Ronald Gregor Smith argues that it is "very different both from an undialectical assertion of the triumph of God in the world and an equally undialectical assertion of the maturity of the world."[8] When these two positions are opposed to each other as religion and secularism, as they are in the short stories, they are adulterously related in a kind of divine-

[7] J. F. Powers, *The Presence of Grace* (New York: Atheneum, 1962), p. 129.
[8] Ronald Gregor Smith, *Secular Christianity* (New York: Harper & Row, 1966), p. 204.

demonic dialectic. Secularity, in this context, would be the attempt to transcend this dialectic, to get off the horns of this dilemma. Although the norm of Christian secularity is implicit in the short stories and provides a perspective for judgment on both secularism and excessively spiritual or otherworldly religiousness, the stories provide no adequate dramatic embodiment of secularity as a uniquely Christian posture in the modern world. It is in the character and action of Father Urban that Powers finally comes very close to achieving a dramatic representation of secularity, and for this reason the theological significance of *Morte D'Urban* is immense.

As his name implies, Father Urban Roche is an urbane and secular city man who likes to remind his listeners that for many years he traveled out of Chicago. Chicago is the home of the fictional Order of St. Clement, and Urban is a Clementine priest, frustrated because it seems to him that the Order labors under the curse of mediocrity. At the point of the story's beginning, the Order has just been given a valuable piece of Chicago real estate for their downtown headquarters. This was a gift from Billy Cosgrove, one of Urban's rich and worldly friends. But the gift seems to be unappreciated by Father Boniface, the Provincial; and Urban is disappointed by the Provincial's religious and unworldly attitude. "Father Urban knew, none better, that the Order wasn't up to the job of being an effective influence for good on the near North Side or anywhere else in this fast-changing world of today, and it never would be, he knew, with men of Father Boniface's stamp calling the shots" (p. 16).[9] But, although Urban complains, he continues to work hard for the Order, directing retreats and parish missions. In addition, we are told, "he found time and energy to make friends, as enjoined by Scripture, with the mammon of iniquity" (p. 16). This is an allusion to Luke 16:9, the Parable of the Unjust Steward, which provides a thematic context for the interpretation of the novel as a whole. This parable is a fitting vehicle for the idea of secularity because it deals with the secular use of

[9] Parenthetical page references in the text are to the Popular Library edition of *Morte D'Urban* (New York, 1963).

secular money without assuming that the user is either a saint or a sinner. Such a use of money is firmly related to Urban at the outset of the book. As a Clementine Urban is supposed to possess nothing, and the cassock he wears is supposed to be pocketless: "St. Clement of Blois, the Holy Founder of the Order . . . regarded pockets rather than money as the root of evil—but Father Urban was away from the Novitiate most of the time, and while he was away his pockets filled up" (p. 11). In spite of this, however, we are told that Father Urban was true to his vow of poverty—to the spirit rather than to the letter.

The novel not only asks us to consider Urban as the Unjust Steward, it also asks us to consider why the unjust steward was commended for his prudence rather than simply condemned. The Parable of the Unjust Steward comes up specifically for discussion in a later chapter, "Twenty-Four Hours in a Strange Diocese." Although Urban has preached on the text he does not seem to understand it very well and acknowledges that it presents difficulties of interpretation. His private opinions on the text also manifest his confusion, as well as the possibility that he understands it better than he knows.

> Our Lord, in Father Urban's opinion, had been dealing with some pretty rough customers out there in the Middle East, the kind of people who wouldn't have been at all distressed by the steward's conduct—either that or people had been a whole lot brighter in biblical times, able to grasp a distinction then. It had even entered Father Urban's mind that Our Lord, who, after all, knew what people were like, may have been a little tired on the day he spoke this parable [p. 186].

This quotation not only serves to illustrate how fully Urban's attitude toward the figure of Christ comports with the non-sacerdotal attitude of the novel toward priests; it also indicates how much the point of view in the novel is essentially ironic, in that it is generally sympathetic to Urban yet limits his moral consciousness, so that he can remain partially oblivious to the moral quandaries which the reader perceives. This is a subtle and very light irony which places Urban in a moral perspective and yet by no means disparages him for his worldliness or secularity. For example, is it possible that Urban, wondering whether people in biblical times were brighter, "able to grasp a distinction then," is referring to a distinction like that between secularity and secularism? Urban's thoughts here are not clarified further. But now it is necessary to review the total dramatic action in order to perceive how the novel's irony qualifies Urban with reference to his ambiguous situation in a religious order which has become superfluous because it has come to be infected with the secular religiosity of conventional Christendom.

Through Father Urban's mediation the Clementine Order had received the office building from Billy Cosgrove for its new Chicago headquarters. But, shortly after this, Urban, who had been doing the "flying" for the Order as a very successful preacher, is grounded. He receives orders from Father Boniface that he is to be transferred to Duesterhaus, Minnesota, a dismal place somewhere beyond the Twin Cities. Duesterhaus is the location of one of the Order's white elephants, an abandoned sanitarium which it is trying to remodel into a retreat house; and it is here that much of the action in the novel occurs.

The staff at the retreat house in Duesterhaus (eventually named St. Clement's Hill) includes Father Wilfrid Bestudik the Rector, Brother Harold the cook, and the two new transferees, Father Urban and Father John Kelleher, known as Jack. The characterization of Father Wilfrid, though unobtrusive, is most successful in providing a contrast or foil against which Father Urban emerges as an engaging, intelligent, and sympathetic character. Whereas Urban consciously and deliberately cultivates his secularity and "makes friends with the mammon of iniquity," Wilf, owing to his lack of vision and purpose, has been more totally and unconsciously secularized. He is completely dominated by trivial material concerns; he calls station-to-station rather than person-to-person to save thirty cents on a telephone call; he prefers to order paint for remodeling from discount houses rather than buy it locally. Hard cash is more important to him than intangibles like good will, and, although he does not make any money for the Order, he is an expert at saving, stretching, and conserving it.

Father Urban's tenure at St Clement's Hill can be divided into three phases. First there is the difficult period of adjustment to a rural ethos, then come several worldly successes for Urban as he finally finds his métier even in Duesterhaus and its environs. Finally there is a series of failures culminating in what could once have been called "the making of a saint." Perhaps this final phase ought not to be so designated, however, because the traditional distinction between saint and sinner, religious and secular, is something the novel wants to blur.

The humiliation of manual labor, especially under Wilf's direction, makes Urban's assignment at St. Clement's Hill especially onerous. He tries gallantly to keep his grievances to himself and to work along with the rest, but his heart is not in it. So he does only what he is asked to do until he has the opportunity to address the annual Poinsetta Smorgasbord in the neighboring town of Great Plains. Sponsored by the Commercial Club, it is the kind of affair in which Urban feels most at home. After his presentation, he is asked what he thinks of Wilf's campaign to put Christ back into Christmas. Urban, at his diplomatic best, answers: "As I see it, merchants — to mention only one group — are paying homage in the way best suited to them and their real talents" (p. 77). Having thus discredited Wilf and dissociated St. Clement's Hill from the Christmas Crusade, he goes on to disparage the infallibility of the Pope and receives a tremendous ovation from his non-sectarian audience.

After Christmas Urban receives several invitations to speak but turns them down to spite Wilf. Urban's morale is very low during this period; he spends a good part of his working day wandering back and forth between the lavatory and the job. Eventually he is relieved of his drudgery when he is sent to St. Monica's in Great Plains to replace the pastor during his Florida vacation. From this point on Urban begins to operate in his usually efficient manner. The pastor dies of a heart attack, and Urban hopes to remain at St. Monica's to direct the building of a new church, but the Bishop squelches his plans. So he must return to St. Clement's Hill.

Though retreatants are now beginning to be numerous at the Hill, Urban wants to go after a different breed, the more successful people. Very soon, with Billy Cosgrove's help and money, more land is acquired, a golf course is laid out, and the Hill becomes a popular resort center, so popular indeed that the Bishop begins to covet it as the location for a diocesan seminary, and it appears that the Clementines may be in danger of losing it entirely. Urban has been overextending himself in several ways, and this is made obvious by the insertion of a highly symbolic chapter at this point: "Twenty-Four Hours in a Strange Diocese." Urban has gone to preach in the neighboring diocese of Ostergothenburg, a place which seems to be hostile to the Clementines. He finds the curates dull and inhospitable and the people indifferent, but, in spite of this, he pursues the one promising contact he has made. He sets out in his borrowed car, a little Barracuda S-X 2, to find Mr. Zimmerman of Zim's Beer, disregarding the little warning voice inside which keeps saying "Turn back! Turn back!"

Several motifs in this chapter have the effect of emphasizing that Urban is going too far into the world for the aggrandizement of his Order and himself. At the Zimmerman place the conversation turns to the Parable of the Unjust Steward which had been the text of Urban's sermon that morning in Ostergothenburg. Mr. Studley, a secular man who calls no man "Father," takes over Urban's part in the discussion and seems to make more sense of the text with his socialistic interpretation than Urban had been able to make. "Mr. Studley not only made it seem that he and Father Urban were together but that he, Mr. Studley, was, of the two of them, the sounder man" (p. 185). Mr. Studley and Father Urban seem to feel with each other; Studley sits in Urban's Barracuda, and Urban goes over to Studley's place and sits in his World War I airplane. Mr. Studley emerges as Urban's *Dop-*

pelgänger who, in his refusal to call a priest "Father," makes explicit Urban's own disregard for the sacredness of his office. The futility of Urban's aggrandizing movement from the church to the world is symbolized when Urban, finally leaving in a fit of pique, signs the guest book: "Pope John XXIII" (p. 188).

Like Joyce's *Ulysses*, *Morte D'Urban* is a comic novel in which the more serious thematic elements are established through the use of symbolic allusions and mythic parallels. The legendary material which provides both comic comparisons and a sense of dignity to Urban is of course the Arthurian material. Urban's colleague at the Hill, Jack, has been rewriting the story of King Arthur as a children's classic with a Catholic twist, and, when Urban persuades the Order to accept the idea of the golf course, he also proposes that the Order publish this and other books under the editorship of Mrs. Thwaites's son Dickie. Urban explains that "Sir Lancelot is the real hero of the King Arthur story. Well, in the end Sir Lancelot lays aside his sword and becomes a priest" (p. 162). And, indeed, the novel does identify Urban himself with Sir Lancelot. For example, when the Bishop comes to the golf course again he brings with him Father Feld, just the type of young scholar to head up a seminary. In the round of golf they play Urban is paired against Father Feld, the Bishop's champion, and Urban feels that "the match between him and Father Feld took on the appearance of a judicial duel" (p. 196). Although Urban knows that winning at golf will not assure the survival of St. Clement's Hill, he plays to win anyway, for the sake of the psychological advantage. And he is in fact about to win, when his head is struck at the No. 9 hole by a golf ball which just happens to have been driven by the Bishop. The Bishop is sorely embarrassed and thereafter abandons his plans to take over St. Clement's Hill. So Urban does win the tournament, for his golf course is saved. His triumph is referred to, perhaps not just ironically, as "an act of God" (p. 202). But, as a consequence of this blow on the head, Urban begins to be troubled intermittently with headaches which slow his pace. And from this point onward the action moves into its third phase, as his deepening involvement in the world for the sake of the Order leads him from one compromising situation to another.

The first of his failures is with the wealthy Mrs. Thwaites, who had invited him to recuperate at her house. In spite of the fact that Mrs. Thwaites is a daily communicant, Urban makes little impact on her spiritual life. After communion or confession she simply turns up the volume on the TV sets she is constantly watching. Next to TV she seems to like dominoes best and has been winning the wages away from Katie, her maid. Urban, champion of damsels in distress, speaks to Mrs. Thwaites in Katie's behalf. But Mrs. Thwaites ignores him, and for his pains he merely succeeds in losing her friendship. The result is the Order's loss of further benefactions from this lady.

Then, shortly after his return to St. Clement's Hill, Urban accepts an invitation to go fishing with Billy Cosgrove at a resort in northern Minnesota. Although Urban knows that Billy is a cruel and callow business man, he has tolerated him for the sake of his donations to the Order. But now, in the course of their brief holiday together, as he is treated with scant respect by Billy for two days and nights, Urban begins to chafe under the coarseness of Billy's condescension. Finallly, when the fish don't bite, the worst side of Billy's character comes out, as he tries to drown a deer they encounter in the water. Urban, feeling cheap as an accomplice in such unsportsmanlike behavior, throws the motor into high gear and dumps Billy into the water. After Billy is picked up, he again takes over the controls and then dumps Urban, who is eventually rescued by the resort operator and placed on a bus headed for the Hill, wet shoes and all, while Billy departs in the station wagon he had purchased for the Order.

It is worth noting that Urban fails with Billy, as with Mrs. Thwaites, because of his human sensitivity and concern, choosing to side with a deer or a helpless girl and thus losing favor with powerful people. There comes a time when he finds the ways of the world degrading and withdraws, and at this point his usefulness to the Order is diminished.

J. F. Powers and Secularity

Urban's final humiliation occurs even before he gets home. While waiting for the bus to Duesterhaus he is picked up (there is no other term for it) by Sally Hopwood, Mrs. Thwaites's daughter. She invites him to join her for a drink in her childhood playhouse, a "castle" on one of the islands of Mrs. Thwaites's lake. Sally lures Urban to this secluded spot on the pretense that her husband will also join them. But the husband fails to appear, and Urban and Sally continue to drink their Scotch and to listen to records. Finally Sally wants to go swimming, and Urban, fearing that the situation will become compromising, tries to dissuade her. Their talk becomes more intimate, and she convinces Urban that, although he is a successful operator, he has no real friends. Sally, more than willing herself to be his "friend," eventually takes off her clothes to go swimming and says "try and stop me." Urban does not, of course, and she exasperatedly throws her shoes at him and leaves with the boat. Once again Urban has to swim for shore, and this time he has to abandon his shoes. He walks to a filling station and phones his friend Monsignor Renton, who, after he has heard the parts of the story Urban thinks he can tell, concludes that "the moral, if any, is stay away from people" (p. 251).

In the following weeks Urban does stay away from people, neglecting not only his associates but even his golf. Jack is working on his version of *Morte D'Arthur*, and his hardest problem is the characterization of Sir Lancelot. It is obvious that Lancelot was a bastard (born out of wedlock), but whether he was guilty of "sinful love" or, as Jack and Urban decide to put it, "high treason" (p. 255) with Queen Guenever is more difficult to ascertain. They finally decide he was not guilty — at least not guilty when charged — and Jack can proceed to the point where Lancelot "died to the world," did penance in prayers and fasting, took no regard of worldly riches, and was so abstinent that "he waxed full lean" (p. 256). And when Urban's barber tells him "You've lost some weight," the parallel between Urban and Lancelot is firmly established; all that remains to be told is Urban's death.

Urban's "death" occurs after he has achieved what would

175

normally have been the pinnacle of success for him. He is elected to the office of Provincial of the Order and returns to Chicago. The Order has been losing everything it had gained through Urban's earlier activity. Billy Cosgrove does not renew their lease on his Chicago office building and offers it to a rival religious order instead. But, contrary to everyone's expectation, Urban does nothing about it. His headaches become more frequent and severe, "arriving and departing like sections of the Twentieth Century Limited," but he suffers them in silence, opening his breviary and closing his eyes, saying "I'll be with you in a minute, Father." Thus, we are told, "without wishing to he gained a reputation for piety he hadn't had before, which, however, was not entirely unwarranted now" (p. 268). Urban withdraws from his former friends and sees as few people as possible. There is one exception: he does entertain Mr. Studley from Ostergothenburg, who arrives one day just as Urban contracts another headache. To the secular man who calls no man "Father" he says in his usual way, "I'll be with you in a minute, Father." But so far as the Order of St. Clement and its many problems are concerned, he is no longer capable of the alacritous response.

In the "Dirge" with which the book concludes the point of view shifts from a position sympathetic to Urban to a more objective and impersonal narration. The reader, no longer privy to Urban's thoughts and feelings and unable to find any joy in his "piety," is thus made to feel that Urban has in fact been overtaken by a kind of death. Indeed, if we follow the late William Van O'Connor in regarding the novel as focused on a "man's desire to achieve the pure act of success,"[10] it must then be accounted as the story of one who almost succeeded but who ultimately failed. For Urban, because he saves a deer from drowning, loses his most generous patron, suffers a series of absurd reversals, and finally loses not only his spiritual vitality but even his physical health. This inter-

[10] William Van O'Connor, "John Updike and William Styron: The Burden of Talent," in *Contemporary American Novelists*, ed. Harry T. Moore (Carbondale, Ill.: Southern Illinois University Press, 1964), p. 206.

pretation, however, fails to consider the "religious" counter-movement implied by the Arthurian parallel, and it attributes a final pathos to the novel which is simply incongruent with its predominantly comic tone.

On the other hand, if *Morte D'Urban* is read primarily in terms of the Arthurian parallel, a serious pattern of religious implication emerges. This interpretation has been interestingly worked out by Marie J. Henault.[11] Urban's spiritual discipline includes a couple of blows on the head, his failures with Mrs. Thwaites and Billy Cosgrove, and the two dunkings in the lake which purify him. When Monsignor Renton gives him another pair of shoes and dry clothes, he becomes a new man. The Old Adam then dies and a more pious Urban seems to emerge at the end. But there are problems with this reading, too, not least the fact that the worldly Urban, who had made friends with the mammon of iniquity like the Unjust Steward, should have been commended for his prudence rather than saved from such secularity, for he was working to bridge the gap between religion and culture, while the other Clementine Fathers were retreating from the secular world to the religious realm, without recognizing that it, too, had been secularized and had therefore become superfluous.

Indeed, in the terms of the Arthurian story itself, both Urban and Jack decide that Lancelot was falsely accused of "sinful love" or "high treason." So Urban the operator is not simply condemned, any more than Urban is saved by his piety at the end — a piety actually occasioned by his headaches. Furthermore, the parallel with the Arthurian legend is not simple but complex. Lancelot began as a knight in the secular world and then became a priest, while Urban begins as a priest in the secular world and then becomes — what? — religious in a quietistic sense? It is not quite that simple. To be sure, Lancelot becomes pious and dies, as Urban becomes "pious" and "dies." But in *Morte D'Arthur* the knights of the Round Table are dissolved after the passing of Arthur. Is there a parallel to Arthur's death in *Morte D'Urban*? May we

[11] Marie J. Henault, "The Saving of Father Urban," *America*, 108 (March 2, 1963): 290–92.

propose that the passing of Arthur has its analogy in the growing secularism within the Church? And why is Lancelot's "sinful love" translated as "high treason?" Is it because Guenever, with whom Lancelot's loyalty is compromised, is equivalent to the priest-seducing Sally or, since she is not in the Church, to the world in general? We may find evidence for these suggestions in Urban's final action in the book.

> The biggest change was in the physical appearance of the Novitiate. *Ceratocystis* had reached into the tribe of elm trees on the grounds, and by order of the new Provincial the infected members were cut down. For this he was roundly blamed. What men did not know, and what he did not tell them, was that the slaughter should have been carried out immediately after the examination, which had taken place during the previous spring. Father Boniface, that hard man, had been too soft to order the job done while the trees were in leaf, it seemed, and later had feared the effect it might have on his chances for a second term [pp. 267–68].

This action is significant, partly because of Urban's reflections on it.

> About these things, and others, he had little to say, but reading the speeches of Winston Churchill, and coming to "I have not become the King's first minister in order to preside over the liquidation of the British Empire," he thought, "No, nor did Mr. (as he was then) Atlee consider himself so called, but such was his fate" [p. 268].

Obviously Urban here finds in Clement Attlee an analogy to himself. We must also not fail to notice that *Ceratocystis* is not simply a disease of elms. Elms die of Dutch elm disease or phloem necrosis. "Cerato" may also refer to the cornea: cysts of the cornea: lack of vision. And we may say that Urban presides over the liquidation of the Order, as he cuts down the elms, because he perceives its lack of vision.

The "Dirge" which concludes the book is not for Urban

only but for the death of the Church. Urban does act decisively enough in having the Avenue of the Elms cut down,
and he does have the energy to entertain Mr. Studley. Moreover, his last worry in the book is for St. Clement's Hill, which
the Bishop has visited again. The final sentence in the book —
"Oddly enough, although for many years he'd traveled out of
Chicago, he seemed to think of the Hill as home." — seems to
relate Urban's quietism to Christ's kenotic action on the Hill
of Calvary. In any case, it must be acknowledged that Urban
has been undone by the ironies and ambiguities of historical
existence. His mobility as an operator is symbolized throughout the book by the mechanical speed and motion of the
trains which he uses and appreciates so much; but, at the
end, these trains are identified with his headaches. As Provincial of the Order he is dead, because the Order, moving
mechanically without a sense of vision and purpose, is superfluous, unconsciously secularized already and therefore per-
petuating a false duality between religion and secular culture.
But, chastened by the spiritual discipline which his ordeals
have entailed, Urban recognizes this and does something
about it.

True secularity would be found in a Church which accepts
its death as a *kenosis*, emptying itself of its temporal power,
and affirming this age without presuming to represent another
reality, more "authentic" or "religious." Protestant thinkers,
especially those influenced by neo-orthodox theology, have
long argued that a movement from church to world is true
to the Hebraic understanding of worldly existence in faith.[12]
Since Vatican II the spirit of *aggiornamento* pervades much
Catholic thinking, especially in Europe, and promotes a new
acknowledgment in Roman circles also of the maturity of the
secular world. So J. F. Powers, as a Catholic novelist on the
American scene, is not alone in his desire for a more positive
estimate, religiously, of modern secularity.

[12] Ronald Gregor Smith provides an excellent summary of the theological background of secularity in *Secular Christianity*. Harvey Cox
presents a programmatic essay on secularity in his book *The Secular
City* (New York: Macmillan Co., 1965).

In *Morte D'Urban* the logic of the movement from church to world is worked out dramatically, on a concrete human level, rather than in terms of abstract theological or sociological theories. And this movement may be more radical than theologians would like to think. Powers is no longer primarily interested, as Catholics have usually been, in the religious aspect of Christianity, or in the sacramental transformation of ordinary reality. Indeed, the basic emphasis of his fiction is associable with the tendency of many Christian thinkers today to become increasingly iconoclastic in their attitude toward religion, regarding it as a product of human culture which can easily become a subtle form of idolatry. The young American theologian Harvey Cox, for example, inveighs against the kind of religiousness which engages in endless quests for a succession of holy grails, and he asserts that "in Jesus of Nazareth, the religious quest is ended for good and man is freed to serve and love his neighbor."[13] And it is against the background of such a dichotomization as this between religion and Christianity that we may take the measure of J. F. Powers as a Christian writer who wants to discover the presence of Grace in a profane world. His non-sacerdotal Christian secularity does not require that things or occasions be sacramentally transformed into a "religious" pseudo-reality in order to manifest the presence of Grace, but only that the Church open its stained glass windows to the ordinary world.

The death of the Church as a "religious" institution is also a central motif in a story Powers has published since *Morte D'Urban*. The story, called "Keystone,"[14] takes us back to that "strange diocese," Ostergothenburg. On one level "Keystone" is the story of a shift of power in the diocese as Father Gau, the chancellor, gradually takes on the authority vested in Bishop Dullinger. Gau is a younger and more secular man, like Urban. Unlike Urban, however, his worldly success is more complete, and he does not have Urban's measure of self-

[13] Cox, *The Secular City*, p. 265.
[14] J. F. Powers, "Keystone," *The New Yorker*, 39 (May 18, 1963): 42–81.

understanding. Gau gets the Bishop to move a cemetery to
the site of an abandoned airport and to build a new church
on the deconsecrated ground. Land is bought from the ad-
joining Gun Club for an exclusive development to be called
Cathedral Heights. Here we see the Church moving into the
suburbs, and the new church is a heavy, earth-bound, hori-
zontal structure. In place of keystones in the arches above
the windows the architects have placed two stones with a
crack between them to give the illusion of verticality. The
Bishop had wanted the keystones, as he had wanted a church
built of field stone, but the architects assure him that it is the
steel that counts in a building, and that a building reinforced
with steel will last a long time — fifty to a hundred years. And
thus the new edifice is to be a truly secular church, built for
this present age only.

"Keystone" has been sensitively analyzed by John J. Kirvan, and he concludes that Powers is writing primarily not
to expose the unremarkable faults of the clergy but the counterfeit status of a secularized Church in urban America.[15]
Father Kirvan is certainly correct about "Keystone," but the
story, published in the wake of *Morte D'Urban*, can also be
read as a "keystone" to the interpretation of the novel. It
shows that Powers is ultimately concerned with the status of
a secular Church which still blindly thinks of itself as a "religious" institution. Indeed, the Church described in "Keystone" is, largely, a monument to what Harvey Cox has called
"technopolis"[16] — but, even as such, it is superfluous, for a
secular religion is simply secular*ism*. True faith, however, in
the sense of a man's fully responsible acceptance of the reality
of his historical situation, need not be dependent on the
Church as a cultic body or institution. And it is such a secular
faith, it is such a secular Christianity, that *Morte D'Urban*
holds out as a human possibility in our time.

[15] John J. Kirvan, "Ostergothenburg Revisited," *Catholic World*, 198
(February, 1964): 312.
[16] Cox, *The Secular City*, p. 5.

7

The Voices of Tragedy in the
Novels of William Styron

GUNNAR URANG

William Styron's novels are haunted by two possibilities which have come to seem largely irrelevant to the concerns of "post-modern" men. The first is the possibility of tragedy. In *Set This House on Fire*,[1] Styron's voice is heard behind the drunken ranting of the protagonist Cass Kinsolving as he proclaims:

We'll bring back tragedy to the land of the Pepsi-Cola and the peanut brittle and the Modess Because. . . . *Tradegy*, by God, that's what we'll give 'em! Something to stiffen their spines and firm up their joints and clean out their tiny souls [pp. 118–19].

Touching this page is the shadow of a presence that looms over the entire novel as well as over the earlier novel *Lie Down in Darkness*.[2] It is the spirit of high tragedy: of Sophocles, whose lines Cass has been declaiming moments before this outburst; of Marlowe and Shakespeare; even — if one may make such a leap — of William Faulkner, whose work, Richard Sewall asserts, "has gone farthest toward restoring to fiction the full dimensions and the true dialectical tension of tragedy."[3]

[1] William Styron, *Set This House on Fire* (New York, 1960).
[2] William Styron, *Lie Down in Darkness* (Indianapolis, 1951). For my purposes the novelette *The Long March*, published in 1952, will not be taken into account here.
[3] Richard B. Sewall, *The Vision of Tragedy* (New Haven, 1962), p. 133. For a detailed listing of actual parallels between Styron's novels and Greek plays, see L. Hugh Moore, "Robert Penn Warren, William

183

Styron's novels, first of all, are "serious"; they confront us with real suffering and compel us to feel that anguish as our own. Styron thus commits himself to an old-fashioned enthusiasm about "character" and "story." As he said in a *Paris Review* interview some years ago,

> Story as such has been neglected by today's introverted writers. Story and character should grow together; . . . They must, to give an impression of life being lived, just because each man's life is a story. . . . I used to spend a lot of time worrying over word order, trying to create beautiful passages. . . . I guess I just get more and more interested in people. And story.[4]

When we read a novel by Styron, in other words, we are not first of all meant to become conscious of a pattern of meaning to which the happenings refer; we are rather meant to become involved with the fate of those who do and suffer these things. And these agents and sufferers will not primarily be "figures." As Styron maintains, "All characters are 'round.'"[5]

We meet people, that is, who are convinced that they have something to lose and who have learned, in the "boundary-situation," that they stand to lose not less than everything. They begin to break down in the face of the forces menacing their existence, so that in descriptive imagery and in the intensifying rhythms of monologue and dialogue we hear something of the ancient recklessness, the heedless passion or rage which heightens our fear as it speeds them toward destruction.

What prompts them to such rage rather than to resignation? Their nobility, the tradition would tell us. Styron's people, however, must be judged insignificant rather than noble. But they are painfully aware of the human signifi-

Styron, and the Use of Greek Myth," *Critique*, 8 (Winter, 1965–66): esp. pp. 80–87.
⁴ Malcolm Cowley, ed., *Writers at Work: The Paris Review Interviews* (New York, 1958), p. 276.
⁵ *Ibid.*

cance that once was and of the conditions that have rendered
it problematical today. Milton Loftis, Styron tells us at one
point in *Lie Down in Darkness,* "thrust his head into his hands
and thought of war and time, of headland fires and of great
men, and of the shame of being born to such dishonor"
(p. 188). Cass Kinsolving, in the second novel, rages like an
Orestes or a Lear against his fate and at the same time, as a
"modern," mocks his own rage. Both men cry out against a
society whose leanness of soul makes their genuine agony
seem ridiculous. Milton remembers his father's ramblings:

> My son, . . . we stand at the back door of glory. Now
> in this setting part of time we are only relics of van-
> quished grandeur more sweet than God himself might
> have imagined: we are the driblet turds of angels, not
> men but a race of toads, vile mutations who have lost
> our lovewords [pp. 184–85].

This is not the cold irony of T. S. Eliot's juxtaposition of
heroic past and enervated present. It has, rather, the passion
of Hamlet's despairing self-mockery in "O what a rogue and
peasant slave am I."

But having committed himself to the presentation of character and suffering in these terms, Styron must then — like
the great tragedians — wrestle with the vexing questions of
fate, freedom, and responsibility. There are in these novels
dark forces menacing the self and crescendoing toward madness. Styron seeks to create real selves for the world of his
fiction; but he must also make the forces of evil real and
specify their nature.

The happenings in *Lie Down in Darkness* which are directly represented (rather than coming to us through someone's memories) cover a few hours of one weekday in August,
1945. That day is judgment day for Milton Loftis. As he sits
in the funeral director's limousine on the station dock at Port
Warwick, Virginia, "awaiting the symbol of his doom," the
shattered, self-destroyed body of his daughter Peyton, his

thoughts find words for this realization: "Life tends toward a moment" (p. 15).

The narrative technique reinforces this sense of impending judgment. A small segment of each chapter serves to advance the foreground movement; the rest is memory, little by little supplying the past which is relevant to this present. When all the memories have been sketched in and given color and texture, there remains bare only the one point in the foreground. We reach this moment early in the afternoon, just after the funeral. Milton, his estranged wife Helen, and their minister Carey Carr, have been driven back into the chapel by a sudden downpour. There Milton tries once more for reconciliation with his wife. When Helen remains unmoved by his desperate sincerity, he suddenly seizes her and begins choking her, in "one red flash of violence spread out like momentary lightning against the storm." Then, just as abruptly, he relaxes his grip and runs — out of the chapel into the rain, past the limousine where his mistress Dolly Bonner has been waiting, "bounding past wreaths and boxwood and over tombstones, toward the highway" (pp. 388–89).

In *Lie Down in Darkness* the forces tending toward this moment are felt to be, to some extent, dynastic and historical. As Louis D. Rubin, Jr. has pointed out, however, this feeling is not nearly so strong here as in some of the novels of Styron's model William Faulkner.[6] "'Son,'" Milton's father had said, "'you don't have to be a camp-follower of reaction but always remember where you came from, the ground is bloody and full of guilt where you were born and you must tread a long narrow path toward your destiny'" (p. 74). But Styron's concern is more with that "long narrow path toward your destiny," with the tragedy of individuals, not the community, and in psychological, not historical, terms.

Is it a kind of Freudian fate, then, which is in view? Much of the furniture of the novel is out of Freud: the memories of parental rigidity and perfectionism, the dream images of wingless birds, and the rest. Peyton's problem (and Milton's

[6] Louis D. Rubin, Jr., *The Farway Country: Writers of the Modern South* (Seattle, 1963), p. 198.

too) is distorted family relationships. Peyton recognizes the fact that she and her father have what she calls "a Freudian attachment," and she thinks: "I would tell Albert Berger a misery: behold we have not been brought up right" (p. 383).

The strong probability of failure was already present when Milton and Helen were married. It was increased when their first child Maudie was born physically and mentally defective. Disappointed in Milton and unable to re-make him in the image of her moralistic, authoritarian father, Helen began to turn her own self-pity into a sickly parody of love toward Maudie. Milton gradually developed an equally unhealthy feeling for their younger daughter Peyton, along with a sense of guilt for his neglect of Maudie. All this caused Helen to despise her husband more and made her increasingly resentful of the beautiful, spoiled Peyton.

In the scenes which Styron stages for us, we see Helen turn what should have been a festive Christmas dinner into an hour of intolerable tension. Then we see Milton in Charlottesville, lost in an alcoholic haze, stumbling from a football game to a fraternity celebration as he looks for Peyton, while Helen waits in a nearby hospital to find out whether Maudie will live or die. We see Peyton's wedding, at home in Port Warwick, ruined for her by Milton's overaffectionateness and Helen's jealousy and hate. Finally, in a lengthy stream-of-consciousness passage, we live with Peyton the last hours of her life — the torment of memories, the obsessive images of wingless birds, the search through their New York haunts for her husband Harry, the futile attempt to win him back, and then the climb and the plunge.

Marvin Mudrick has called this plot "mere fate, a bloated India rubber spider in the toils of which the characters are . . . crippled buzzing flies."[7] But Styron sounds with some persistence the note of responsibility. There had been moments of openness, when Milton came to the very edge of self-knowledge and when Helen knew that "by one word — Yes or Forgive or Love — she might have affirmed all, released

[7] Marvin Mudrick, "Mailer and Styron: Guests of the Establishment," *Hudson Review*, 17 (Autumn, 1964): 351.

all of the false and vengeful and troubling demons right up into the encompassing air of night" (p. 82). Milton recalled a specific moment which "had expressed for the last time the tenderness that existed between them," and wondered:

> Why hadn't something important happened, then? It was as if he — yes, she, too; how could he tell? — had just tried too hard. No one knows when the heart's eye opens; theirs had opened wide for a moment and had gazed each at the other, then blinked shut as quickly" [p. 159].

Each had chosen instead one particular way to "lie down in darkness." For Helen it was first a sickbed, in a darkened room smelling of medicine, and later a sick mind darkened by obsessive sexual images and bad dreams of vengeance. For Peyton it was promiscuity, lying down "with all the hostile men," and then the final darkness of self-destruction. For Milton it was a tawdry little affair with Dolly Bonner, whom he never really loved, and the deranged slumber of drunkenness. And the burden of guilt rests on Milton more than on the others, for contriving the net of failure in which they are all enmeshed. In Peyton's words, "He's never been beyond redemption, like Helen. . . . He's had so much that was good in him, but it was all wasted. He wasn't man enough to stand up like a man and make decisions and all the rest" (p. 317). On that last day, as he waits for the train bearing his dead daughter, he is slowly brought to the fearful realization that Dolly, the whisky, and Peyton have been for him "props and crutches . . . which supported him against the unthinkable notion that life was not rich and purposeful and full of rewards" (p. 43).

Responsibility, guilt, judgment. The theme of judgment emerges powerfully in other ways as well. There are patterns of imagery: whistles and horns, signals of judgment which become even more insistent in the second novel; the sultriness and then the breaking storm; Milton's guilty dreams of fire and the "dreaming blue vapor of defilement." There is the apocalyptic imagery associated with Peyton's sexual "fall": the pictures which her boyfriend Dick Cartwright remembers from his Presbyterian grandmother's Bible-reading—"pictures . . . of heaven and hell, of the seven-headed beast, the vials of wrath, the woman, full of abominations and the filthiness of her fornications, who was called the mother of harlots" (p. 228) — and the description of the lovers' bodies as "painted with fire, like those fallen children who live and breathe and soundlessly scream, and whose souls blaze forever" (p. 236).

Insofar as the novel exemplifies the tragic vision, it is in the tradition that W. H. Auden has called "Christian tragedy." The distinctions he made in an interesting essay of 1945 may have been too bold; yet they are distinctions that remain indispensable. Greek tragedy, Mr. Auden argues, is the tragedy of necessity. At the end of a Greek tragedy we say, "What a pity it had to be this way." Christian tragedy on the other hand, is the tragedy of possibility and makes us say, "What a pity it was this way when it might have been otherwise."[8] The pattern I find in Styron's *Lie Down in Darkness,* in short, is one which somehow combines the modern equivalent of Greek objective necessity with Christian subjective responsibility.

But another possibility haunts this novel. There is a note other than that of tragic judgment. We hear it to some extent in Peyton's wandering thoughts. Obsessed though she is with anticipation of death, some incredible hope of resurrection keeps breaking through. "Perhaps I shall rise at another time, though I lie down in darkness and have my light in ashes." This note is also apparent in an event that follows Milton's despairing flight. While Peyton's coffin has been transported to the chapel, something else has been going on by the seashore. Hundreds of Negroes in the community — including the servants in the Loftis household — have been getting ready to welcome Daddy Faith, who drives down once a year from Baltimore to preach and to baptize. His preaching is of judgment, of tragedy worldwide:

[8] W. H. Auden, "The Christian Tragic Hero," *New York Times Book Review,* December 16, 1945.

"Now de people done gone off to war and dey sent down de atom bomb on de Land of de Risin' Sun and de sojers come home wid glory in dey th'oats and wid timbrels and de clashin' of bells." He paused again; his eyes grew sad, caressing the throng. "Well, my people, it do seem to me dat we got a long way yet. De hand of de Lawd is against de sinful and de unjust, and de candle of the wicked is put out. But mo' time to pass yet and de eyes of de people shall see His destruction and dey shall drink of de wrath of d' Almighty. And dey shall see a time of war, like de preacher said, and dey shall hear the sound of battle in de land and de great destruction. . . .

"Dey gonna holler'O God, de proud are risen against me, and de assemblies of vi'lent men done sought after my soul! How long, Lawd, wilt Thou be angry fo'ever, shall Thy jealousy *burn like fire?*" [P. 398].

But he brings the cleansing of baptism, and another of his texts is "Comfort ye," a message of hope and renewal.

Are we, then, taken "beyond tragedy" in this book? A cynical reader might dismiss Peyton's affirmations as merely another manifestation of a residual Bible-belt religion which was also responsible for her (equally baseless) guilt feelings. As for Daddy Faith—we recall that the more sophisticated Carey Carr has substantially the same message but simply cannot believe in it deeply enough himself to proclaim it with conviction to his people. Perhaps Daddy Faith's words of hope, acceptable only to the childlike Ella and LaRuth, are for us merely an ironic underscoring of tragic hopelessness.

Because of the position of this scene, its length, and its style and tone, however, I cannot take it as simply ironic; neither is it convincingly redemptive, at least in its own terms. And the same is true of Peyton's resurrection texts. If they cannot be dismissed as mockery, they bring no sure comfort either. At best, they speak, in traditional symbols, of a Grace which somehow seems to be available and for which one feels paradoxically responsible; not understood and not responded to, it only adds an additional weight of lost possibility to an already insupportable load of tragic failure. Nearing her plunge, Peyton half-thinks, half-prays:

Have I through some evil inherited in a sad century cut myself off from You forever, and thus only by dying must take the fatal chance: to walk into a dark closet and lie down there and dream away my sins, hoping to wake in another land, in a far, fantastic dawn? [P. 382.]

And then, a few moments later:

I thought, oh Christ, have mercy on your Peyton this evening not because she hasn't believed but because she. No one. had a chance to. ever [p. 384].

In *Set This House on Fire*, too, "life tends toward a moment." Both novels remind us of what Faulkner said about his method: "There's always a moment in experience — a thought — an incident — that's there. Then all I do is work up to that moment. I figure what must have happened before to lead people to that particular moment, and I work away from it, finding out how people act after that moment."[9] Again, this moment for Styron is one of judgment, heavy with the accumulation of happenings which have led to the crisis it brings.

But the narrative technique is different, and this signals a decisive difference in thematic emphasis. For one thing, although it incorporates vast amounts of reminiscence by the protagonist Cass Kinsolving, the story is told through the consciousness of a minor participant, Peter Leverett. Cass is the "existentialist" hero, *our* representative on the brink. His harrowing experience of suffering imparts meaning to our less major hurts. But it is as the more "normal" Peter Leverett finds himself caught up in the torment which Cass is undergoing that Cass's experience really becomes ours. In a way, Peter is to Cass as Milton is to Peyton. But, whereas Peyton's sufferings come to us directly in only one chapter and are

---

[9] Sewall, *Vision of Tragedy*, p. 133.

meant to contribute primarily to our sense of Milton's tragic failure, in this novel Kinsolving's sufferings are the center of our attention, and what Leverett does and feels is peripheral. It is as if Peyton has come back — slightly older and now male, but cursed with the same corrosive past and approaching the same catastrophe — to challenge her destiny again.

Another difference becomes apparent. The story has been called up from the memories of these men two years after the climactic events, which took place in the southern Italian village of Sambuco. To continue the comparison, it is as if Peyton has survived and has even, somehow, triumphed. The question, then, is not only what happened to lead Cass to that moment two years before but also how he acted after that moment, what he found in the moment by way of openness toward a new future. Here is the story, as they remember it.

Peter Leverett, a Virginia-born lawyer, has spent some time in Europe with a government relief agency. Just before his return to America he is invited to Sambuco by Mason Flagg, a friend from school days. Peter knows, from their early association and from a later encounter in New York, that everything about Mason is phony: his writing, his views on sex, his friendships — everything except his money. Yet Peter, still attracted to him, accepts the invitation. At Sambuco he meets Cass.

Cass Kinsolving has come to Sambuco by a long route: an insecure boyhood in the South; World War II and a psychiatric ward in a naval hospital; marriage to a scatterbrained Roman Catholic, Poppy; and his failure, even in Europe, as a painter, the chagrin of which he seeks to escape in alcoholic excesses. He has become acquainted with Mason, only because Mason mistook him for a fashionable expatriate painter, and he has moved into the palace Mason Flagg has rented which is now being used also by a nondescript assortment of movie people for the filming of a third-rate picture. He has found two friends, the "intellectual" police officer Luigi Migliore and a beautiful peasant girl named Francesca. But he has also fallen into a degrading dependence on Mason, chiefly for that indispensable crutch, his whisky. At the same time, as part of his lust for domination, Mason has begun to want Francesca.

During Peter's first night in Sambuco, while the "flicker creeps," as Cass calls them, are partying in the large salon of the palace, Mason rapes Francesca. Cass learns of it and drunkenly vows to "stomp his face in." Later in that long night, however, Cass hears that Francesca has been found horribly beaten and near death. Convinced that Mason has done this too, Cass in a cold fury finds him, pursues him up the side of the mountain above the palace, bashes his head in with a large stone, and heaves his body over the edge of the cliff. Still later, Cass discovers that the mutilation of Francesca has been the act not of Mason Flagg but of the idiot Saverio. Luigi, from whom Cass learns this, is the only other person who knows it. In order to save Cass, Luigi alters the evidence, making it look as if Francesca's death has been a case of rape and murder followed by (Mason's) suicide. Shaken by these horrors, the movie crowd scatters, and a few days later first Peter and then Cass and his family go back to America.

Lie Down in Darkness led us to see that unrealized redemptive possibilities sharpen the pain of judgment and destruction. *Set This House on Fire* also has much to say of guilt. The personal dimension of responsibility and guilt is just as prominent here as in the earlier novel. This is true particularly in Cass's life, of course. His is the despair arising out of insupportable guilt, Kierkegaard's "sickness unto death." But even Peter carries a share of that burden, through the accident on the way from Rome to Sambuco in which he brings injury to a young man named di Lieto and through his growing awareness of his own bondage to all that Mason represents.

In *Lie Down in Darkness* Styron sought also to give a sociological, as well as a psychological, dimension to the fate of Milton and Peyton Loftis. There are, for instance, references to the evils of the Byrd dynasty in the politics of Virginia and uncomplimentary allusions to the White House and the State Department. The action of the novel is carefully shown as paralleling the progress of World War II, and Peyton's suicide comes on the day after Hiroshima. Daddy Faith's sermon sets both the war and the bomb in the context of national judgment.

In the second novel even more is done to broaden the context for the theme of judgment. American society is indicted for its mistreatment of the Negro, its indifference to poverty in other parts of the world, and its smug and vulgar affluence. The Italian setting enables Styron to "break away a little from all them magnolias" (as he put it in the *Paris Review* conversation) and to put American society and its politics in a larger frame. Much of this criticism is expressed in numerous conversations and arguments concerning the (peculiarly American) disease which Cripps, the movie director, describes as "a general wasting away of quality, a kind of sleazy common prostration of the human spirit" (p. 116). It is pretty well summed up in the lengthy diatribe (too lengthy, for its position early in the book) by Peter's father.

> What this country needs, . . . what this great land of our needs is something to happen to it. Something ferocious and tragic, like what happened to Jericho or the cities of the plain — something terrible, I mean, son, so that when the people have been through hellfire and the crucible, and have suffered agony enough and grief, they'll be men again, human beings, not a bunch of smug contented hogs rooting at the trough" [p. 15].

His indictment includes topical references ("He spat on his nigro brother and wore out his eyes looking at TV and fornicated with his best friend's wife at the country club") and biblical allusions ("Come Judgment Day . . . the good Lord's going to take one look at this empty husk, and He's going to say, 'How do *you* lay claim to salvation, my friend?' Then He's going to heave him out the back door and He's going to holler after him: 'That's what you get, friend, for selling out to Mammon!'") (p. 16).

Certain patterns of imagery suggest still another dimension of meaning. Voices on a hillbilly record which Cass is playing

194

on that night in Sambuco ask "Wha-a-at's the matter with this world?" and then reply:

Now this rumor we hear: another war we fear,
Revelations is being fulfilled . . .
. . . .
Your soul's on sinking sand, the end is drawing
near:
That's what the matter with this world. . . . [P. 121.]

Indeed, the symbols from the Book of Revelation and apocalyptic material in general become very prominent in the novel. It would not be excessive to say that each chapter seems to have its own symbol of judgment. There are sounds — even, for example, the ear-splitting Rebel yell that Cass howls at Mason's command, which is, Peter says, like "some ferocious horn or whistle running wild" and as a result of which, "like a churchyard transfigured by the trump of Judgment Day, the palace began to disgorge its slumberers, who with dressing gowns and bathrobes wound around them came forth squinting, barefooted, and with the aspects of those who foresee unspeakable horror" (p. 188). And there are visions — both nightmares and hallucinations — of such things as storms, waterspouts, torrential rains, and volcanoes erupting fire.

> The sea was placid, held in momentary abeyance, but the sun had grown hotter still, hung in the sky fiery, huge and, like some dead weight, oppressively heavy and near. The bugger is exploding, Cass thought as he edged back into a shadowed place, it's going to swell up and shrivel us like a bunch of gnats in a flame [p. 483].

Jonathan Baumbach notes that the "swelling sun is a projection of Cass's exploding guilt, but no less a real spectre of contemporary (hydrogen bomb) reality."[10]

These images of upheaval which, like the biblical symbol of earthquake, suggest human panic in the face of the visitations of a holy God and the sudden shattering of man-made

[10] Jonathan Baumbach, *The Landscape of Nightmare: Studies in the Contemporary American Novel* (New York, 1965), p. 136.

systems of security, and these "trumpet" blasts which accompany the tremendous supernatural warfare and betoken the defeat of evil and the rescue of the faithful — all these serve to impart a kind of cosmic magnitude to the theme of judgment.

Styron's way of handling the figure of Mason Flagg is also very much a part of this design. Mason is at the center of the experience of guilt and judgment for both Cass and Peter. He represents much that they, in a perfectly normal way, desire — sex, money, art. But he also represents a perversion, a parody, of each of these good things. Peter met him at St. Andrew's, the Episcopalian boys' school in Virginia, into which Mason "burst like some debauched cheer in the midst of worship, confounding and fascinating us all" (pp. 73–74). He was a liar from the beginning, sexually corrupt and a blasphemer. St. Andrew's expelled him when he was caught in the chapel basement "stark naked with the weak-minded daughter of a local oysterman, both of them clutching bottles of sacramental wine" (p. 78). In New York, some years later, Peter discovered other sinister things about his friend: his cult of sex, his penchant for gaining possession of persons. And in Sambuco we are merely seeing the full expression of all that Mason has always been.

But what does Mason become for the novel? Styron labors, on the one hand, to give psychological verisimilitude to the character. But he also includes the details I have mentioned and passages such as this:

> It was as if he was hardly a man at all, but a creature from a different race who had taken on the disguise of a man. . . . For him there was no history, or, if there was, it began on the day he was born. Before that there was nothing, and out of that nothing sprang this creature, committed to nothingness [p. 446].

When, after the murder, the investigator says of Mason, "The man was a devil," and Peter replies, "Untrue. He was no devil," he immediately adds, "But I didn't know" (p. 228). Mason Flagg, I am suggesting, is another fragment in the apocalyptic pattern. Mason as symbol—like such symbols from the book of Revelation as the Beast and the Antichrist—results from "the individualizing of opposition in the figure of a monster of iniquity, who will treacherously attack his weak and unsuspecting neighbors, but who will be smitten and destroyed by the power of God in a resounding disaster."[11] The "story" is given symbolic overtones resonant of allegory, so that the figure of Mason and the event of his overthrow parallel the figure of the "Beast" and his abrupt descent into the "lake of fire that burns with brimstone."

What happens to Cass under the influence of Mason Flagg is "something ferocious and tragic," in the words of Peter's father, something like the torment suggested in the symbolic imaginings of Revelation 14:

> If any one worships the beast and its image, and receives a mark on his forehead or on his hand, he also shall drink the wine of God's wrath, poured unmixed into the cup of his anger, and he shall be tormented with fire and brimstone in the presence of the holy angels and in the presence of the Lamb.

For Cass, however, unlike Milton or Peyton Loftis, it is not too late. His suffering has not been purely tragic, but redemptive. The house has been set on fire, but he has come to see that the fire of torment can become the fire of purgation, that, in T. S. Eliot's words:

> The only hope, or else despair,
> Lies in the choice of pyre or pyre—
> To be redeemed from fire by fire.[12]

Cass staggers down various wrong roads in quest of salvation before he finds the right way. One avenue leads toward darkness, nothingness, the "wild Manichean dreams" which draw him toward suicide and inspire nightmare impulses to wipe out his family, "to remove from this earth . . . all mark

[11] H. H. Rowley, *The Relevance of Apocalyptic* (London, 1944), p. 32.
[12] T. S. Eliot, "Four Quartets," in *The Complete Poems and Plays: 1909–1950* (New York, 1958), p. 144.

and sign and stain of himself, his love and his vain hopes and his pathetic creations and his guilt" (p. 485). And he sees the other side of the Gnostic or Manichean coin as well, the paradisaic vision of perfect goodness and beauty. If human existence is conceived of as only evil, salvation must consist in the release of the inner man from the bonds of the world and his return to his native realms of light. This comes through *gnosis*, divine revelation borne by a messenger from the world of light. Francesca brings him, he feels, such a vision of the other world. In the secluded grove where she poses for him, it seems as if they are under a spell, "untouched by anything except this momentary, fabulous, bountiful peace" (p. 440). But he is never allowed more than moments of this beatific existence. It is too good for this world and too good for Cass. He is plunged deeper into darkness and has to make his way into a salvation which contains both light and darkness and can be lived in this world.

Reformation through sheer will power fails, too, although he feels that even his temporary "will power vis-à-vis the murderous grape" is the "first dim sign of regeneration" (p. 292). But still Cass has failed to touch his real need, what Captain Slotkin, the Navy psychiatrist, had called the need of every man: to be freed into the condition of love.

For Cass that liberation comes gradually, by way of a series of relationships. Peter and Alonzo Cripps simply "stand by," to save the essential dignity of this tormented human being from the ultimate degradation. The relationship with Francesca brings Cass a glimpse of "paradise," of a love which is the supreme fulfillment of all eros. And she must be violated in order for him to see the enormity of evil. In the relationship with Poppy Cass learns what it is to be consistently loved and forgiven. In his journal he writes, "She gives & loves & I take & thats that" (p. 295). The police officer Luigi pronounces the words of forgiveness and acceptance for Cass: first the rebuke, "*Te pecchi nell' avere tanto senso di colpa!* You sin in this guilt of yours!" (p. 490), and then the exhortation, "For the love of God, Cass, ... consider the *good* in yourself! Consider hope! Consider joy!" (p. 499). More than this, Luigi also conceals the damning evidence against Cass, risking his own freedom thereby.

Through these relationships there begins to take place in Cass a process which he himself calls "regeneration." The first sign is the access of power which finally enables him to exorcise Mason, who has become for him the embodiment of the evil that you "have to stomp on like you would a flea carrying bubonic plague, getting rid of the disease and the carrier all at once" (p. 129). Meanwhile, he has also been able for a time to forget his own misery and spend himself with the recklessness of love for the dying peasant Michele. This takes the shape of an act of expiation, when we notice Cass's reflections on the smell of that peasant hut. "It is niggers. The same thing, by God. It is the smell of a black sharecropper's cabin in Sussex County, Virginia" (p. 416). Having once, as he tells Peter, assisted in an act of cruelty against a Virginia sharecropper, he now does what he can to lighten the dying agonies of an Italian peasant.

There are other signs, too. He returns to Poppy and the children. The bliss with Francesca was never anything more than a glimpse of an ultimate vision; and it is in the routinized life of everyday, with Poppy and his children, that he must learn what love really is. And he goes off the bottle. At the time Peter makes contact with him again, he has not had a drop of beer even, in nearly two years. This represents, of course, not some "moral" about the evils of drinking; it is symbolic of Cass's liberation from bondage to self and from his refusal to face others and himself.

As a last redemptive note, and one which affects Peter rather than Cass, there is—in the epistolary "Epilogue"—a kind of resurrection. Luciano di Lieto, the injured man who has been the reminder of Peter's share in guilt, has been two years in a coma. Suddenly—"like the Phoenix risen from the ashes of his own affliction" (p. 506)—he recovers consciousness and health.

The ending of *Lie Down in Darkness* is rich with traditional Christian imagery and allusions. But, because nothing clearly redemptive happens, we are left unsure whether this imagery points to real grounds for hope or merely heightens ironically the sense of irreversible doom. In *Set This House on Fire*, however, we see the redemptive possibility "beyond tragedy" worked out in character and action, but the Christian terms are explicitly rejected. He has not found Grace, Cass insists, "some belief, some rock [where] . . . anything might prevail." What he has done is to choose being over nothingness, without any very resonant hope (p. 500).

On the face of it, then, this is an "existentialist" novel. Man's situation, as seen in Cass, is one of absurdity and precariousness. Luigi attributes this to the absence of God, a God who at best is a riddle; so that

> this existence itself is an imprisonment. . . . We are serving our sentences in solitary confinement, unable to speak. All of us. Once we were at least able to talk with our Jailer, but now even He has gone away, leaving us alone with the knowledge of insufferable loss. . . . We can only leave notes to Him — unread notes, notes that mean nothing. I do not know why this has happened, but it has happened, that is our condition. In the meantime we do what we can [p. 497].

Yet, as we have seen, this "salvation" is actually something that *happens* to Cass, in certain relationships. And the pattern is unmistakably Christian. It is a liberation from a threat or danger, from the dark, destructive forces — of sin, guilt, and death — which constantly menace the self. Yet it is not escapism. Man is not removed to a place in existence where danger cannot overtake him; rather, he finds an unexpected and undeserved power to stand fast and not be shaken in the midst of danger. This power or freedom, furthermore, is inseparable from the recognition and acceptance of a forgiving, restoring work of "grace." [13] There is also what we might call the "texture" of the novel. Over against a handful of passages containing existentialist language can be placed an overwhelming accumulation of biblical-Christian images and allusions.

[13] I have made use of the convenient summary by Roger Hazelton in *A Handbook of Christian Theology* (New York, 1958), pp. 336–39.

The authentic Cass is not the one who — in somewhat stilted rhetoric — affirms being over nothingness, but the one who cries out, in biblical images and sermonic rhythms, his sense of imminent judgment and his raging thirst for salvation.

In his *Hudson Review* article "Mailer and Styron: Guests of the Establishment," Marvin Mudrick dismisses *Set This House on Fire* as "a bad ambitious novel, anxious to inflame and impress, full of cardboard wolves with grinning teeth." Styron himself, Mudrick declares,

> defeated as a novelist, has coldly chosen the garden path to the drawingrooms of the Establishment. One may suspect that he knew all along where he was heading and what it took to get there: talent, but not too vigorously exhibited; style, without bite or intelligence; supine moralities momentarily illuminated by sulphur and brimstone.[14]

Now it is true that certain signs of strain are inescapably present in Styron's fiction. But Mr. Mudrick's mudslinging, with its loose imputation of corrupt motive and cynical opportunism, can hardly be taken seriously. He finds, it is true, good things in the style of *Lie Down in Darkness*. "Styron's prose is open, scrupulous, limber, unplagued by echoes . . . : it modulates easily between plain narrative and lyric evocation, it can even accommodate itself to the pyrotechnic and ominous lightnings of Peyton Loftis's conclusive monologue."[15] But here, for once, he may be excessively generous, for Peyton's monologue seems at times too calculated, too intent on its "meanings." The allusions are too numerous and too literary, the references to wingless birds, clocks, and lying down in darkness too frequent. At other points in Styron's first novel one detects a different tendency — the bane of every "rhetorical" style — toward a relaxing of intelligence and a slackening of control, toward sentimentality. Adjectives are the symptoms: "swollen, mysterious scents," "swollen

[14] Mudrick, "Mailer and Styron," p. 366.
[15] *Ibid.*, p. 350.

notes," "immemorial descending dusks," "far fantastic dawn." There are a few lapses of this sort in Set This House on Fire, too. Sometimes, as in the previous novel, they tend toward false pathos, and more often toward a forced intensity, as in the passage where we are told that Cass "was carried swift as memory back to the very light of his own beginning, and there in some slumberous southern noon heard his first baby-squall in the cradle, and knew it to be the sound of history itself, all error, dream, and madness" (p. 464).

The "voice" of Cass Kinsolving is for some critics an even greater problem. One reviewer characterized his speech as ranging from semiliterate colloquialism to "the dreary impassioned rant of Faulkner's Nobel Prize speech." He went on to say that neither Cass nor Peter "manages to escape a kind of Humanities-course lecturing tone that comes too directly from the author's own paradigm of the book's tragic movement." [16]

But then we remember all that Cass has to exemplify in the novel. He must be ordinary yet capable of tragic passion, contemporary yet aware of the literary past, a pathetic victim yet striving for freedom to act. Milton and Peyton Loftis face less rigorous demands. They are almost entirely victims, and the tone for them is one of pathos. They recognize and acknowledge, and mourn, their part in the fateful accumulation of the past; but they do not act in passionate affirmation. Much of the sense of tragic stature comes by way of literary allusions in Peyton's monologue and through Milton's memories of his father's musings.

Cass, however, is still fighting—for his essential human dignity and for his creative powers. Styron makes him a Southern preacher's son with an artistic temperament, a man short on formal education but partially self-educated (in Sophocles, Montaigne, and a few other "classics"), a psychological casualty of the war, drunkenly teetering on the brink of disintegration. "Occasionally," Peter says of him,

> that gentle and easygoing thread would seem to snap within him, and he was abruptly all tension, recrimina-

[16] John Hollander, in Yale Review (Autumn, 1960), pp. 152–53.

tions, gloom. Even his diction changed. In the oddest way I was reminded of some red-necked Baptist preacher, garrulous and thick on the sidewalk with informal folksy good humor, who, ascending into the pulpit, turns into a tower of glittering fire and passion [p. 54].

Much of Part Two is couched in this preacher-rhetoric — crude and often ungrammatical, full of biblical phrases and rhythms, always passionate and at times almost hysterical.

Often Cass's passionateness is not so much that of tragic suffering as of savage indignation. Which suggests perhaps another element of vulnerability in the novel — namely, the large amount of explicit social criticism it contains. Indeed, some of Styron's critics have simply declared that it contains too much. And it is true, I think, that this novel tries — perhaps too hard — to "get it all in," to tell the whole truth about America in the late fifties.

In this connection, Irving Howe offers some useful observations about the larger issue posed by Styron's work. Mr. Howe reminds us that, whereas the basic problem for the "modern" novelist was the search for fundamental values, in the last few decades the novelist's problem has become that of devising a strategy for confronting not merely "the chronic confusion of values" but the additional fact that our *society* no longer lends itself to assured definition. The significant change is signalized by the use we make of the term "mass society." "By the mass society," says Mr. Howe,

we mean a relatively comfortable, half welfare and half garrison society in which the population grows passive, indifferent, and atomized; in which traditional loyalties, ties and associations become lax or dissolve entirely; in which coherent publics based on definite interests and opinions gradually fall apart; and in which man becomes a consumer, himself mass-produced like the products, diversions and values that he absorbs.[17]

[17] Irving Howe, *A World More Attractive* (New York, 1963), pp. 84–85.

Faced with these changes, most of the postwar novelists, Mr. Howe says, have preferred the way of indirection, expressing their "passionate, though often amorphous, criticism of American life not through realistic portraiture but through fable, picaresque, prophecy, and nostalgia." [18] Those like Styron who reject these strategies still must have some kind of placement or setting in the world of practical affairs. The choices are "to go abroad, go into the past, or go into those few pockets of elemental emotional life left in this country." [19] Thus, instead of dealing in minute detail with the "manners" of contemporary American life, the novelist's tendency is to project a moral critique of what is taken to be the *essential* quality of American culture. This, says Irving Howe, is the "post-modern" fiction, and it is clear that Styron's novel is very much a part of this experiment.

Indeed, his social concerns in *Set This House on Fire* prompt Styron to take up a "prophetic," even an apocalyptic, tone — which is most especially apparent in the heightened, almost hysterical, quality of those sections in which we hear the "voice" of Cass Kinsolving. And the apocalypticism even determines characterization. The movie makers using Mason's rented palace are painted as grotesque, demonic figures, almost like creatures out of Hieronymus Bosch. They are caricatures and are meant to be. So, in part, is Mason Flagg. To think of Mason in this way, of course, is to see in the novel a tendency toward allegory — which, as Northrop Frye reminds us, is what we have "whenever it is clear that [the writer] is saying, 'by this I *also* mean that.'" [20] At such points a novelist is giving priority of emphasis to an idea or theme and finding a fiction which will illustrate it, rather than beginning with a story and allowing it simply to suggest certain themes.

Poppy, and Francesca even more so, obviously have the two-dimensional character of allegorical figures: their lack of individuality is a consequence of the mainly symbolic function they have been assigned.

[18] *Ibid.*, pp. 88–89.
[19] Stanley Kauffmann, quoted in Howe, *World More Attractive*, p. 91.
[20] Northrop Frye, *Anatomy of Criticism* (Princeton, 1957), p. 90.

But Mason is most especially the problem. Recalling that Cass's salvation comes by the murder of Flagg for a crime he did not even commit and by Luigi's perjury and tampering with evidence, Elmer Borklund declares that, though Cass learns to love himself, it is "at the cost of an oversimplification, a moral arrogance, which should disturb most readers." [21] This really means that at times in this novel the demands of "theme" and "fiction" strive openly against each other, as when Styron attempts to represent the effect on Cass of the discovery that his vengeance on Mason was unjustifiable. After all, this symbolic destruction of Mason freed Cass for his new life. But it was a real murder also; yet Styron can do little more than have Cass remorsefully acknowledge this — to dramatize the acknowledgment too powerfully would be to weaken the symbolic function of the act.

Why "allegorize" at all, then? As R. W. B. Lewis rightly insists, the modern experience epitomized by Nietzsche in the declaration "God is dead" has led to the "death" of man as well. Thus, in the words of Albert Camus, ". . . to see the sense of this life dissipated, to see our reason for existence disappear: that is what is insupportable." [22] In such a time, says Mr. Lewis, the literary artist has had to adopt the strategy of trying to find ground for living in life itself. But for many writers this ground for living cannot be the undifferentiated stuff of existence itself; it must include some pattern which gives coherence and purpose (however limited) to experience. Thus Faulkner said of Christianity, for example: "Its various allegories are the charts against which [man] measures himself and learns to know what he is." [23] And Lewis points out that, whereas in the classic literature of the twentieth century that unifying pattern was likely to be an aesthetic design, in recent fiction it is more likely to be a "human" theme, relating to life and death and the aspiring, sinful nature of man. The action embodying this theme will often in-

[21] Elmer Borklund, in *Commentary*, November, 1960, p. 454.
[22] Quoted in R. W. B. Lewis, *The Picaresque Saint* (Philadelphia, 1959), p. 17.
[23] Cowley, *Writers at Work*, p. 132.

clude a "conversion," a radical shift of allegiance and belief. And the basis for this renewed sense of life is love.[24]

I have said that *Set This House on Fire* represents a broadening of context for certain themes which in the earlier novel are mainly restricted to the fortunes of individuals and families, and also a movement through and beyond the tragic toward liberation and renewal. Whatever judgment falls on Cass, then, and whatever salvation he finds are meant to be applicable, generally, to our American social and cultural predicament. In this struggle to "get it all in," Styron could have written (and almost did write) several different novels.

The novel bestows contempt on those who uncritically accept the emerging values of mass society, the "general wasting away of quality . . . [and the] sleazy common prostration of the human spirit" (p. 116), but it does not seek to escape into nostalgia. Nor does it major in satire or shade off, by fantasy, into "black humor." But there are points at which one feels it could have gone in either of these directions. Again, it comes close to turning into another kind of novel in those sections concerning Mason Flagg's way of life. It does seem, as Marvin Mudrick suggests, that in Mason Flagg Styron has produced a character somewhat like the Marion Faye of Norman Mailer's novel *The Deer Park*, and that he has done this to "demonstrate that Mailer's notions are foolish and wicked." [25] But the values controlling the rejection of hipsterist techniques of transcendence and the beliefs which inform the redemptive movement of the plot threaten at times to turn the novel into parable. When Mason is thrown into the abyss, and when Cass hears from Luigi the words of justification, "*Revelations* is being fulfilled," one feels that the parabolic intention has nearly altogether gotten out of hand.

The novel Styron is trying to save is, first of all, a story of potentially tragic involvements. Its power depends on our ability to identify with Cass Kinsolving—with his zest for life, his capacity for love, his creative impulses, his curiosity and intelligence. We must be able to suffer with him the sense

[24] Lewis, *Picaresque Saint*, p. 28.
[25] Mudrick, "Mailer and Styron," p. 359.

of being trapped by his history and his culture and of being threatened by the loss of all stable meaning. We must be able to feel, in the quickening rhythms of narrative and dialogue, the intensity of his self-pity, his terror, and his rage.

But Styron has also taken on another, even more difficult, task than that of sustaining tragic intensity. For he brings his protagonist through, and he must therefore make this transcending of despair something cogent and convincing: he must specify the terms in which it is made possible. And though it is not rendered in explicitly religious terms, Styron's way of meeting this problem artistically is of considerable theological interest.

If we try to specify what would have averted the catastrophe in *Lie Down in Darkness* and what is the source of reconciliation in *Set This House on Fire*, we may be inclined to quote W. H. Auden's "We must love one another or die." But Styron is careful to make it clear, in both novels, that this would not be enough. Certainly, as Milton approaches his "moment," his only plea is — in the words of the hillbilly song which is made so much of at the beginning of the second chapter — "Take me back and try me one more time" (p. 40). On the night of her wedding Peyton confides to the old family physician, Dr. Holcomb, in drunken intimacy: "You know what the trouble is, Doc? . . . It's time and remembrance, that's what it is. It's people having a little . . . humility about not what happens now, at this moment, but all the things that went before." Her need, she says, is "just to be understood for what you are, neither to be loved to death nor despised just because you're young" (p. 304).

It becomes clear that a special kind of love is sought — not undiscriminating undisciplined sentiment ("potato-love," Saul Bellow's *Herzog* calls it), but love with the knowledge and the courage to make possible good judgment and the assumption of responsibility. Peyton needs what has traditionally been understood as a *father's* love. Milton's responsibility was to be a father — not the martinet who was Helen's father nor the kindly weakling who was his own father, but a man whose character combines love and strength so that he can dispense both justice and mercy. In both novels the reference to fatherhood is broadened to include Jefferson and Lincoln and various other, less-respected and more recent "fathers" of our country. And the need for a father is symbolized, finally, in the Negro "Redeemer," not only in his message, which includes a declaration of love, but even — ludicrous as it may seem — in his name. The love which could have averted the tragedy in *Lie Down in Darkness* depends for its existence and power, in other words, on "Daddy-faith."

There are somewhat stronger father figures in *Set This House on Fire*: Alfred Leverett, the psychiatrist Slotkin, Alonzo Cripps, perhaps. But if Peter is a brother to Cass, and if certain of love's graces are mediated to Cass through Poppy and Francesca, it is Luigi who is his "Daddy-faith." Luigi knows Cass in all his degradation. He understands and upholds justice. Yet he takes the risk of setting legalism aside, of exercising mercy, and declaring his friend forgiven. "You sin in this guilt of yours!" Cass remembers him shouting. "And suddenly," Cass recalls, "I ceased trembling and became calm as if like some small boy on the verge of a tantrum I had been halted, the childish fit arrested by some almighty parental voice" (p. 490).

Here, as before, Cass's experience follows a pattern that is unmistakably Christian. For Cass does not merely "choose being": instead, he is judged, forgiven, accepted, and thereby restored to newness of life. So perhaps God is not really "absent," in the way that Cass and Luigi suppose; perhaps the "Jailer" (who only seems a Jailer to those who are self-imprisoned) speaks through his representatives, through Cripps and Poppy and Luigi. Perhaps Cass has found Grace after all, but does not recognize it as such because he thinks Grace can come only directly and only through explicitly Christian and "spiritual" channels. Only later, perhaps, will he discover that he has been accepted and granted a new access to abundance of life through the power of Grace.

The Voices of Tragedy in the Novels of William Styron

Admittedly, Styron's work — particularly *Set This House on Fire* — is marked by numerous obtrusive dissonances: in tone, between the tragic and the satiric-grotesque; in mode, between mimesis and parable; in style, between authentic intensity, on the one hand, and self-pitying rhetoric or hysterical rant, on the other; in theme, between existentialist and Christian insights. And these may be, as Irving Howe suggests, the telltale signs of the novelist having willed "a subject onto a novel rather than allowing it to grow out of a sure sense of a particular moment and place."[26] We should also bear in mind, however, that similar signs of strain can be detected in much recent literature, and they may simply betoken the strain under which all of us live today, in a time that is in so many ways "between the times."

Richard Sewall says of literary tragedy: "It puts to the test of action all the formulations of philosophy and religion."[27] And it is, I believe, the high distinction of William Styron to have demonstrated that the art of fiction can, in our time, render a similar service. For he has sought to reinstate the tragic vision in an unheroic age, to project a radical critique of his culture in a period of painful transition, and to envisage redemptive possibilities in a time that is said to mark the death of God. In some respects he may have failed. But partial failure, when much is attempted, is surely ultimately more valuable than the small but "safe" success.

[26] Howe, *World More Attractive*, p. 93.
[27] Sewall, *Vision of Tragedy*, p. 7.

8

The Two Roles of Norman Mailer
DAVID HESLA

The hero of Norman Mailer's story "The Time of Her Time"[1] is a twenty-seven-year-old ex-bullfighter who knows enough about depth psychology to sort Reichian terminology from Freudian. He lives in Greenwich Village and earns a slim livelihood teaching the art he has learned in Mexico. The story he relates does not concern bullfighting, however, but the way he brings a frigid N.Y.U. co-ed to her first orgasm. His expertise is a composite of psychoanalytic insight and the stamina, grace, and courage of a *torero* at the height of his powers. He manipulates her as a skilled bullfighter would manipulate a strong but skittish animal. His name is Sergius O'Shaugnessy.

This is the name of the hero-narrator of *The Deer Park*,[2] too, and they have other things besides names in common. Both grew up in Catholic orphanages; both have romantic and danger-filled pasts, one as bullfighter, the other as Air Force pilot. The pilot is ambitious to become a writer, the bullfighter to produce a carefully documented study of sexual intercourse. Both are "great in the hay," to borrow the title of another of Mailer's stories. Also, both have a common lineage in the family of characters he has created, for they both derive from a short piece entitled "The Man who Studied Yoga."[3] One of the secondary characters there is a psychoanalyst named Dr. Sergius. Another is Jerry O'Shaugnessy, "trapper in Alaska, a chauffeur for gangsters, an officer in

[1] Printed in *Advertisements for Myself* (New York: G. P. Putnam's Sons, 1959), pp. 478–503.
[2] New York: G. P. Putnam's Sons, 1955.
[3] Printed in *Advertisements for Myself*, pp. 157–85.

the Foreign Legion, a labor organizer," a veteran of Spain and an outcast from the Communist Party. Sergius is an Eastern European name, Russian, perhaps; also Jewish, carrying with it the connotations of rabbinical learning, homelessness and alienation, the suffering servant, bondage to the moral good and social concern; it is the name for the intellectual, the contemplative mystic, the artist. O'Shaugnessy is an Irish name — *the* Irish name; the man himself an adventurer, morally reckless in a style possible only for a Catholic Antinomian who still lives in dread of guilt and judgment; a lover of drink and women; all feeling and heart, sentimental, compassionate (from *An American Dream*: "The Irish are the only men who know how to cry for the dirty polluted blood of all the world"[4]); it is the name for the activist, the politician.

The types are already adumbrated in *The Naked and Dead* in Joey Goldstein and Roy Gallagher. From his grandfather Joey learns why it is that the Jews suffer: "It is so we will last. . . . We are a harried people, beset by oppressors. We must always journey from disaster to disaster. . . . Yehudah Halevy said Israel is the heart of all nations. . . . And the heart is also the conscience, which suffers for the sins of the nations."[5] Roy Gallagher hangs around the Democratic Club in Boston, sits on the bank of the Charles River and feels the beauty of a spring night, realizes with relief that his wife understands him and still loves him.

They are there in *Barbary Shore*,[6] too, although mostly submerged under Marxist symbolism and rhetoric. Mikey Lovett, the narrator, is another aspiring writer and an amnesiac as well, whose scars indicate a violent and dangerous past. Lovett becomes the pupil of William McLeod, sometime hero in the Party and a veteran of Spain, who has abdicated from leftist politics in order to devote his time to developing the theory which must undergird the future of the people's

[4] *An American Dream* (New York: Dial Press, 1965), p. 264.
[5] *The Naked and the Dead* (New York: Random House ["The Modern Library"], n.d.), p. 483. The novel was originally published by Rinehart & Co., in 1948.
[6] New York: Rinehart & Co., 1951.

revolution. In a confused ending, McLeod is killed by an F.B.I. agent, but Lovett escapes to carry on the revolution according to the wisdom of McLeod and with the vigor of his own youth.

This is the type of the hero of Mailer's fiction. He is a synthesis of intellectuality and sexuality, mind and body, sentiment and courage, experience and vitality, and also of the traditions and cultures which make up the American Style. Through the first three novels he is growing, adding knowledge to experience, and system to intuition. He is acquiring a history, too, and a greater scope and capacity. In Mailer's latest novel *An American Dream* he emerges in the ripeness of his years as Stephen Richards Rojack, Harvard graduate, war hero (D.S.C.), successful politician, socialite, television personality, and intellectual—as professor of existential psychology "with the not inconsiderable thesis that magic, dread, and the perception of death [are] the roots of motivation."[7] The traditional qualities are still there—the Irish in Stephen, the Jewish-East European in Rojack; but Mailer has filled out his American hero by giving him a middle name, Richards, WASP all the way back to Plymouth Rock.

Mailer's ideal hero is the whole man, as much at home in a brawl as in bed, as much alive to an idea as to the smells given off by life and death. But versatility is not enough. Mailer's heroes are committed to the two further demands of integrity and transcendence. In Mailer's world, the only significant act is one in which a man takes the enormous risk of doing or being what he knows he must if he is to obey the self-imposed imperative of transcendence. Some of the major patterns of challenge and triumph or defeat are set out in *The Naked and the Dead*: the Mexican scout Martinez is threatened by his own cowardice, but he conquers his fear; Lt. Hearn is threatened by social and political forces larger than himself, embodied in General Cummings, but when the test comes Hearn capitulates; Sgt. Croft has already

[7] *An American Dream*, p. 8. This essay was completed prior to the publication of *Why Are We in Vietnam?* (New York: G. P. Putnam's Sons, 1967).

conquered himself and his small society — the platoon — so he sets out to conquer Mt. Anaka. In *Barbary Shore*, McLeod is accused of having stolen a "little object" from a governmental agency and is promised leniency if he will surrender it. As the novel progresses, the "little object" becomes a symbol of integrity, and, while McLeod tells his interrogator that he will not give it up, he tells someone else that he never had it.

An identical pattern is present in *The Deer Park*, where Charles Francis Eitel is urged to report to a Congressional committee the names and activities of his leftist friends. If he cooperates with the committee, he will once again be permitted to make motion pictures. His temptation is rather obviously suggested by his initials and last name — "See if I tell." He does, of course, to the disgust and disillusionment of his protegé O'Shaugnessy. In contrast with Eitel, Marion Faye confronts his fear of being killed and does what he must to conquer that fear. Finally, in *An American Dream*, the themes of integrity and transcendence become all-dominating. To become whole and vital, Rojack must kill the person who is killing him, and to do that he must overcome the cowardice he first experienced on the occasion which earned him the D.S.C. Moreover, the political and social forces which had proved the ruin of Hearn and Eitel now take on supernatural dimensions, becoming in the person of Kelly magical and even ontological powers.

The same concern for the integration of thought and feeling influences Mailer's style when he writes non-fiction, for he argues his opinions with as much passion as he tells his stories. In the Preface to "The Political Economy of Time"[8] he asserts that science was originally founded on metaphor, and that, when experiment displaced metaphor, science itself sustained a loss. In the essay itself (it is really an interview), Mailer speculates on matters psychological, existential, and metaphysical, but always on the basis of a metaphor, and in highly figurative language.

[8] Printed in *Cannibals and Christians* (New York: Dial Press, 1966), pp. 312–76.

The Two Roles of Norman Mailer

To integrate intellect and sensibility; to exhibit in art the man of integrity; to insist for himself and for an entire nation that the cleavages and weaknesses in the life of the individual and in the life of the state must be transcended — this, it now appears, is the task Norman Mailer has set himself. It is an enormous task, deserving a lifetime of work, and not yet permitting formal evaluation. But eleven years after the publication of *The Naked and the Dead*, in a review of *Advertisements for Myself*, Alfred Kazin had to ask, "How good is Norman Mailer?"[9] Now, after two more volumes of miscellaneous writings and the appearance of his fourth novel, the answer seems to be as elusive as when Kazin first asked the question. Mailer's talent as a writer is considerable, and yet his latest novel had what only charity could call a mixed reception. At least one of his essays, "The White Negro," has provoked a great deal of controversy, but his status as a thinker is even more uncertain than his achievement as a novelist. These are the two roles Mailer has played in his career, and, if we are to find out how good he is, we shall have to consider him in relation to the duality of his elected vocation. Let us begin with Mailer in his role as thinker.

In his essay "The White Negro" Mailer describes the origin, aims, and methods of the American existentialist — the man whom Mailer calls "the hipster."[10] The hipster's style of life is designed to take account of the fact of death. Death can take one of three forms: instant death in an atomic holocaust; a relatively quick death at the hands of a paranoid State; or a slow death brought on by stifling one's creative and rebellious instincts and conforming to the codes, norms, and values of American society. The last mode of death is Mailer's principal concern, for it is the greatest despair of hipsterism.

[9] The review is reprinted in Kazin's *Contemporaries* (Boston: Little, Brown & Co., 1962), pp. 246–50.

[10] "The White Negro: Some Superficial Reflections on the Hipster" was written in 1957 and printed in *Advertisements for Myself*, pp. 337–58.

In the hipster's view of human existence, man is understood as a collection of possibilities, "some more possible than others," and his task is "to open the limits of the possible" for himself. To fail in this is to retreat toward death, for the hipster views existence dialectically and sees "every man and woman as moving individually through each moment of life forward into growth or backward into death." [11] The possible in Mailer's argument is more or less identical with the instinctual, so the problems the hipster encounters in amplifying the scope of his possibilities are describable in psychoanalytical terms. Like the psychopath, the hipster is encumbered with the traditional mores of society; but worse, he is equipped with "inefficient and antiquated nervous circuits of the past" which strangle his potentiality for responding to new possibilities for growth. As the psychopath is trying to create a new nervous system for himself, so too is the hipster: each trying to change his habits in order to be able to live in the present. To change these habits, it is necessary to return to the time of their origination and start afresh, thereby passing "by symbolic substitute the locks of incest." The purpose of this return, according to Mailer, is to permit one to "lessen the tension of those infantile desires," so that he may "remake a bit of his nervous system."

The psychopath (and presumably his brother the hipster) will not have recourse to the ordinary therapeutic processes, however, for he knows instinctively that "to express a forbidden impulse actively is far more beneficial to him than merely to confess the desire in the safety of a doctor's room." Hence he must master his repressed instinctual desires not by talking about them and understanding them, but by living them. So he seeks out those situations that bring his senses alive, that enable him to know what his habits are and how he can change them. In the extreme case, this means that the psychopath must commit murder. "The psychopath murders — if he has the courage — out of the necessity to purge his violence, for if he cannot empty his hatred then he cannot love, his

[11] *Advertisements for Myself*, p. 343.

being is frozen with implacable self-hatred for his cowardice."[12]

Murder is not necessarily an evil or immoral act from the point of view of the psychopathic element of Hip, for a man's nature and actions cannot be judged by a set of standards handed down from the past and conceived prior to the experience or act of murder. Values such as truth and morality are wholly relative, for these are neither given by the tradition nor fixed in the nature of man or the universe, but are dependent upon the possibilities available to a person at any given time. "Character being thus seen as perpetually ambivalent and dynamic enters then into an absolute relativity where there are no truths other than the isolated truths of what each observer feels at each instant of his existence." The same is true of morals: "The only Hip morality . . . is to do what one feels whenever and wherever it is possible and . . . to be engaged in the one primal battle: to open the limits of the possible for oneself, for oneself alone, because that is one's need." Hip, says Mailer, would return us to ourselves "at no matter what price in individual violence"; and since it is social restraints and categories which stand between us and ourselves, the "nihilism of hip proposes as its final tendency that every social restraint and category be removed."[13]

As Mailer tends to equate man's possibilities with his instincts, so he tends to reduce man's instincts to his sexual drives, and the satisfaction of the drives is the goal of the psychopath's existence (and so of the hipster's too), and is as well the means for enlarging his possibilities, and the touchstone for determining the quality of his life. At bottom, says Mailer, the psychopath seeks love.

> Not love as the search for a mate, but love as the search for an orgasm more apocalyptic than the one which preceded it. Orgasm is his therapy — he knows at the seed of his being that good orgasm opens his possibilities and bad orgasm imprisons him.[14]

[12] *Ibid.*, p. 347. [13] *Ibid.*, p. 354. [14] *Ibid.*, p. 347.

Thus the possibilities for good orgasm, when properly exploited, lead to better orgasm, and better orgasm points beyond itself to a better yet. For the Hip argument would claim that "even in an orgasm which is *the most* there is always the vision of an outer wider wilder orgasm which is even more *with it.*"[15] Since the quality of orgasm is a function of the scope or range of possibilities (or instincts) available, and since the enlargement of his possibilities is the business of the hipster, it follows that the hipster can use the quality of the orgasm as a touchstone for judging the success of his efforts to increase his own possibilities: "One's orgasm," says Mailer, in a footnote to the essay, "is the clue to how well one is living."[16]

Hipsterism, then, is America's version of Continental existentialism. Confronted by the fact of death, the Hipster responds with a life lived out of his feelings and for the sake of his feelings and an ever increasing range of feelings. But Hipsterism is more than just a rebellion against the repressive sexual standards of society, more than just an ethic. It is essentially a religious outlook. Mailer says, "To be a real existentialist (Sartre admittedly to the contrary) one must be religious, one must have one's sense of the 'purpose' — whatever the purpose may be — but a life which is directed by one's faith in the necessity of action is a life committed to the notion that the sub-stratum of existence is the search, the end meaningful but mysterious. . . ."[17] The atheist (Mailer no doubt has Sartre in mind) is on the side of rational and undialectical life and conceives of death as emptiness. The existentialist-Hipster-mystic is no less conscious of the fact of death; yet he values his feelings more than his reason. He counters the atheist's rational arguments with the "intensity of his private vision," and what he feels in his vision is so real that it cannot be overcome by logic.

A year after writing "The White Negro," Mailer returned to the quasi-theological theme he had posed there, and, in

[15] "Mailer's Reply," in *Advertisements for Myself*, p. 369.
[16] "Hipster and Beatnik: A Footnote to 'The White Negro'" in *Advertisements for Myself*, p. 373.
[17] *Advertisements for Myself*, p. 341.

an interview with Richard G. Stern, he said, "I think there is one single burning pinpoint of the vision in Hip: it's that God is in danger of dying." Mailer's theological speculations are worth quoting at length.

. . . God is in danger of dying. In my very limited knowledge of theology, this never really has been expressed before. I believe Hip conceives of Man's fate being tied up with God's fate. God is no longer all-powerful. . . . The moral consequences of this are not only staggering, but they're thrilling; because moral experience is intensified rather than diminished.

. . . He is not all-powerful; He exists as a warring element in a divided universe, and we are a part of — perhaps the most important part — of His great expression, His enormous destiny; perhaps He is trying to impose upon the universe His conception of being against other conceptions of being very much opposed to His. Maybe we are in a sense the seed, the seed-carriers, the voyagers, the explorers, the embodiment of that embattled vision; maybe we are engaged in a heroic activity, and not a mean one.

. . . [This idea of God] is far more noble in its conception, far more arduous as a religious conception than the notion of the all-powerful God who takes care of us.

Stern: And do you take to this conception for its perilous nobility, or do you take to it because you believe in it?

Mailer: I believe in it.[18]

He believed in it sufficiently to return to the same theme in 1962 and 1963, in a series of commentaries on Martin Buber's *Tales of the Hasidim*. There he repeats his notion that God is himself an existentialist but adds the idea that God is in conflict with the Devil. He writes, "If God is not all-powerful but existential, discovering the possibilities and limitation of His creative powers in the form of the history which is made by

[18] Richard G. Stern, "Hip, Hell, and the Navigator: An Interview with Norman Mailer" in *Advertisements for Myself*, pp. 380–81.

His creatures, then one must postulate an existential equal to God, an antagonist, the Devil, a principle of Evil whose signature was the concentration camps, whose joy is to waste substance, whose intent is to prevent God's conception of Being from reaching its mysterious goal."[19]

Besides these themes, speculations, and assertions, there are a few other things — not so much ideas as preoccupations — which Mailer makes much of: the difficulty of being a writer, the shoddiness of American architecture, the morally subversive power of the mass media, the notion that cancer is the result of psychological repression, the nature of the national subconsciousness, the importance of the hero. Norman Mailer has in fact a lot of opinions. As Gore Vidal wrote in an excellent review of *Advertisements*, "Mailer is forever shouting at us that he is about to tell us something we must know or has just told us something revelatory and we failed to hear him or that he will, God grant his poor abused brain and body just one more chance, get through to us so that we will *know*."[20] Taken altogether, the things Mailer is telling us *so we can know* make up a most strange body of ideas. For, as Mailer holds that God is in danger of dying, he is a timid disciple of Nietzsche; as he supports the idea of the teleological suspension of the ethical and affirms the primacy of subjectivity over objectivity, he is a Kierkegaardian; as he maintains the existence of two more or less equally powerful ontic forces, God and the Devil, he is a Manichean; as he holds that man is a project, he is a Sartrean; as he holds that the world has effects upon God, he is a Patripassian or Whiteheadian or Buberian; and as he affirms God, freedom, and the immortality of the soul (as he seems to do in "The Political Economy of Time"), he is an old fuddy-duddy of a nineteenth-century rationalist Christian.

When, in short, Mailer tries to think, he typically ends up in logical or terminological confusion. Sometimes he simply

[19] "Responses and Reactions III," *The Presidential Papers* (New York: G. P. Putnam's Sons, 1963), p. 193.

[20] The review, which first appeared in *The Nation* (January 2, 1960), is reprinted in Vidal's *Rocking the Boat* (Boston: Little, Brown & Co., 1962), pp. 161–77; the quotation is found on p. 171.

contradicts himself, sometimes he misuses technical or semi-technical terms (as when he speaks of a "Kierkegaardian nation"), and sometimes he uses terms which simply make no sense to anyone but himself.

For example, Mailer likes to think of himself as an existentialist. Of *The Presidential Papers* he claims, "This book has an existential grasp of the nature of reality." [21] No word in our contemporary jargon is more variously interpreted, of course, but there are certain constants we can expect in its disciplined use. One of these is the unicity of *Dasein* or the *pour soi* or the self; another is the radical freedom which the self has or is; and a third is the imperative of transcendence. Various philosophers describe these factors in various ways, the most extreme account being perhaps Sartre's, who expressed his understanding of existentialism in the formula "Existence precedes essence." At any rate, the existentialists tend to agree in insisting that there are no values which are self-sustaining and universally valid and which therefore cannot be transcended. Mailer wants to approve the notion that man is free, and his hipster is an existentialist insofar as he rejects all a priori laws and norms. The hero, says Mailer, is the "one kind of man who *never* develops by accident" but is "a consecutive set of brave and witty self-creations." [22] This is orthodox Sartreanism: the human reality is a project.

Mailer's hipster is clearly not an existentialist, however, for the hipster is not free. He is driven to murder by his pathological obsession, or he is driven to wider and wilder orgasm, because this opens the limits of his possibility, and one opens one's possibilities because that is one's *need*. But no self-respecting existentialist would be able to say that man is a creature of his needs, for man is perpetually self-transcendent; and to acknowledge the authority of various needs is to open the way to biological or — in Mailer's case — psychological and sexual essentialism. In fact, Mailer is hung up between the existentialism of Sartre and the essentialism of Wilhelm Reich. Thus his anthropology is confused: he doesn't know

[21] *Advertisements for Myself*, p. 5.
[22] *The Presidential Papers*, p. 6.

whether man is to be defined as essentially dependent or existentially transcendent. He has said both, and in "The White Negro" he says both at the same time.

Or consider the long and embarrassingly naive interview entitled "The Political Economy of Time," in which Mailer speculates upon — *inter alia* — Being, form, spirit, time, death, the Devil, and God. We are expected to take it seriously, but we could think of it as a parody of a Platonic dialogue, the characters being, say, Sycophantus and Opsimath. But we are meant to take it seriously. The issue is the nature of spirit:

> *Interviewer*: Is the tree also a spirit?
>
> *Mailer*: I have no idea. Maybe it is soul and spirit.
>
> . . . .
>
> *Mailer*: I feel new ideas emerging, but they make me uneasy. I remember I began to feel uneasy when I spoke of the amoeba as an army. An army after all is a spirit.
>
> *Interviewer*: An army is made up of men. Of a hundred thousand men. . . . Which by your count is one hundred thousand souls. Do all of these souls . . . make one spirit?
>
> *Mailer*: So far as they give themselves to an effort thrust on them by some larger spirit or soul, why yes, then that part of them which is obedient to the army obviously contributes to the *function* of the army. (*Happily*) The function is the center of the spirit. That may be a beginning. Suppose that souls possess a personal life and thus are unpredictable and full of turns, but a spirit is a function. It can only wax strong or weak.[23]

We are here privileged to witness the birth of an idea, the happy fruit of dialogical thought. Plato's *Phaedo*, Aristotle's *De Anima*, and Hegel's *Phenomenology of Spirit* never having existed for Mailer, they are easily transcended. And some eighteen pages later, after having touched on the issues of eternity, death, and metempsychosis, Mailer firmly establishes what he had earlier only tentatively suggested: "I've just come to the conclusion a spirit must be led by a soul. By

[23] *Cannibals and Christians*, pp. 336–37.

a soul which has lost eternity."[24] We relax; we are relieved. The prophet has spoken, revealing the mystery heretofore concealed from men. He has told us what we must *know*.

It is easy, of course, to make light of Mailer and his ideas, especially when one takes them out of context. There never has been a serious thinker who could not be transformed into a cretin or a maniac or simply a fatuous bore by a perversely judicious selection of quotations. But, this being granted, the point is that Mailer thinks in a vacuum. He thinks as if no one in the history of the world has ever thought before him. He will, to be sure, take particular words or ideas from other thinkers, but in his own elaboration of these concepts, he respects neither the tradition of their use nor even the ordinary rules of systematic thought. Apparently the only ideas he can feel and understand and use are those he himself has put forward — perhaps with a little help from an interlocutor — through his own idiosyncratic forms of expression. Even this would not be wholly reprehensible, had he any knack for success in the one task he cannot afford to botch — that of making himself understood. But, ignorant of the tradition and careless of logic and the meaning of words, he fails. A reader must have considerable sympathy with an interviewer when, fifty-seven pages into a dialogue and approaching the end of it all, he says to Mailer, "So I would ask you — what is form?" But Mailer, of course, has no such sympathy — he is stunned by the obtuseness of the questioner: "My God. I could have sworn I explained it a thousand times." He condescends to mortal weakness, however, and in his best gnostic style he elucidates: "Form in general — now I let you in on the secret — is the record of a war." Five pages later the interview expires of fatigue and incomprehensibility.

There is only one way to approach Mailer's novel of 1965, *An American Dream*, and that is with the assumption that it is a serious piece of work by a serious novelist. The reader

[24] *Ibid.*, p. 355.
[25] *Ibid.*, p. 370.

who refuses to make this assumption may not finish the book, or, if he does, he may conclude with Granville Hicks that Mailer has perpetrated a hoax, or with Elizabeth Hardwick that the novel is an intellectual and literary disaster. Certainly Mailer has put an enormous strain on even those readers who are favorably disposed toward him. Within the first sixty pages, the protagonist Stephen Richards Rojack has strangled his socialite wife Deborah, had intercourse with her maid, thrown Deborah out of the window of their tenth-story apartment to make her death appear to be suicide, and had intercourse with the maid again; all of it described in minutest detail. That the novel first appeared in eight installments in *Esquire* accounts in part for the sensationalism of the beginning ("How's *that* for getting their interest!"), but the plain reader may be excused if he thinks that this time Mailer has gone too far. He may be confirmed in his opinion when, later, in an after-hours bar, Rojack puts on a demonstration of his psychokinetic powers. His brain "had developed into a small manufactory of psychic particles, pellets, rockets the length of a pin. . . . I had even some artillery, a battery of bombs smaller than the seeds of caviar. . . ." He discharges some of this ordnance at a foe who had been laughing.

> His laughter stopped in the middle; he scowled as if four very bad eggs had been crushed on his head. . . . He looked about. He . . . located me as the probable source, and proceeded to kick an imaginary foot deep into my crotch. My shield went down to block it. Blocked! "Your foot hurts," said my mind to him, and he looked depressed. After a while he started to rub the toe of that shoe against his calf.[26]

Even this much a patient and broadminded reader might accept, on the ground that it is essential to the design of the novel; but then he is confronted with the resolution of Deborah's murder. Just as the police are beginning to put together a case against Rojack, they decide Deborah's death was a suicide and let him go. Pressure has been brought to

[26] *An American Dream*, p. 98.

bear, for it turns out that she was a secret agent, and a murder trial would bring to light secrets and mysteries better left unpublicized. With this, it appears that Mailer's novel is not only pornographic and incredible but simply and blatantly immoral.

These are the grosser faults of the novel, but there are others. The writing is no more careful than it ever has been. We are told that, when angry with Rojack, Deborah mistreated him badly, fought a vicious campaign against him, "hook and eye, tooth and talon." Hook and eye? Or Cherry is singing: "On [the words] *sleepy garden walls* she struck five perfect notes, five, like the five bells of an angel come to the wake of a bomb. . . ."[27] As happens so often in Mailer's writing, the rhythm is fine, but the sense is specious, for the simile tells us absolutely nothing. Or one might object to Mailer's obsession with olfactory sensations — the smells of sex, vomit, of the guts of an old man who had died of a burst appendix and peritoneal gangrene. Or one might object to still another assertion of his theory that cancer is a symptom of neurotic repression. There is, in short, so much that is meretricious and obscurantist in the novel that one's inclination is to respond only with irritation and impatience.

Yet I remain convinced that *An American Dream* warrants a closer reading than it has generally received. Begin with the obvious. Mailer has always written well about sex, and so he continues to do in this book. In this connection I would cite, for example, the description of Rojack's first encounter with Cherry, the singer: here is a handling of erotic material characterized not only by great power but even by a quality of tenderness which had surely been missing from Mailer's earlier work. (I must add, however, that Mailer's carelessness or perverseness mars even this fine incident, for it concludes, "I slipped into sleep like a boat garnering its dock. . . ."[28] A boat can do many things with a dock, but one thing it cannot do is garner it.) Or consider two of the secondary characters, Roberts the cop and Shago Martin the singer,

[27] *Ibid.*, p. 99.
[28] *Ibid.*, p. 129.

both expertly done. In just a few lines scattered through the book Mailer gives us not just the professional skill of the cop but his humanity as well, his tired idealism, a glimpse of the spiritual expense of a daily routine that takes him into the sordid, the violent, the dishonest. The scene involving Shago, Cherry, and Rojack is to my mind easily the most distinct and memorable in the entire book, and it is largely due to the vitality and precision of Shago's speech.

Perhaps most impressive, though, is the considerable advance in narrative skill which the novel reflects. In both *Barbary Shore* and *The Deer Park* a first-person mode of narration led Mailer into creating highly improbable situations for his narrators. In the latter, whole chapters, and those some of the best, simply disregard the narrative convention established at the beginning of the novel. Now, however, Mailer has succeeded in designing a story which is at least consistently congruent with the character of the narrator. Rojack is equipped by temperament and training to interpret the events which happen to him: his linguistic style and the capacity and quality of his imagination and sensibility are essential to the version of reality which the novel presents. From this point of view, *An American Dream* is a technical success, where both the earlier novels were failures.

Finally, the book is, in my reading of it, the most ambitious and complicated project Mailer has yet attempted, for he has added to his usual naturalism a symbolic dimension of major significance. In constructing his major characters, Mailer seems to have drawn on Talmudic and Cabalistic lore and has so enlarged the evil personages with ancient meanings as to make the novel a parable of the conflict between good and evil. Deborah, Rojack's wife, appears to be Mailer's version of Lilith. According to Jewish tradition, Lilith was a demon and the first wife of Adam. He lived and cohabited with her for 130 years, and during this time had no desire for Eve. After he purified himself, however, he mated with Eve and she gave birth to Seth. It is not until Rojack has "purified" himself of Deborah that he can meet and love his Eve, Cherry.

While it is difficult to know how far to pursue this line of interpretation, other passages in the novel tend to corroborate it. Deborah's father Barney Oswald Kelly is specifically related to the Devil. In the scene in which Rojack encounters Kelly, the former begins to lose his mind: "I slipped off the lip of all sanity into a pit of electronic sirens and musical lyrics dictated by X-ray machines for a gout of the stench which comes from devotion to the goat came up from him and went over to me." [29] At the end of the seventh chapter, Rojack corrects Shago Martin's assertion that, in refusing to sing for Deborah, Shago had spat in the face of the Devil. "He was wrong," says Rojack, "it was the devil's daughter." Again, in the same encounter between Kelly and Rojack, Kelly brings up one of Rojack's ideas, that God is engaged in a war with the Devil and that there is a chance that God may lose. In this battle, Kelly says, the Church is on the side of the Devil; and when he vexes his Jesuit friends with this idea, and they then ask why he gives so much money to the Church, he replies to them, "Well, for all we know, I am a solicitor for the Devil." We are also told that Kelly's legal wife Leonora did not conceive, so he one night besought Satan to grant him a child, and the fruit was Deborah.

Kelly is not the Devil himself, but he possesses the attributes of a *śêdu,* that class of demons who are like men in that they eat and drink, multiply, and die; but who are more than human, since they can traverse the world, as Kelly demonstrates when, by a telephone call, he puts an end to the investigation of Deborah's death; and the *śêdu* have foreknowledge, as Kelly had when he amassed his fortune on the stock market. Or Kelly may be an incarnation of one of the potent lieutenants of the Devil — Azael, Azazel, or even Samael. This last is husband to the Prostituted Woman, who was the serpent in the Garden of Eden. Ruta, and Deborah's apartment, which had "the specific density of a jungle conceived by Rousseau," come to mind. (Unfortunately, Mailer's taste and ingenuity fail him here, as so often before, and he must play games with Kelly's name as he did with Eitel's.

[29] *Ibid.*, p. 253.

Kelly's initials are BOK, homophonic with the German *Bock*, i.e., goat, a symbol of the Devil.)

Ancient lore has a high regard for symmetry, so there are male demons who destroy women. Shago Martin killed the most beautiful idea Cherry ever had; and she says that, when living with him, she felt as if she were living with a creature, "And the Devil had a pipeline into that creature and took all the hate in the country and piped it into him."[30] It is written that Samael, the Venom of the Lord, lay with Eve and corrupted her.

The Cabalistic symbolism overlies another group of Mailer's ideas. Some of his theories about psychoanalysis receive their first important expression in this novel. In "The White Negro," Mailer argues that the hipster wants to change outmoded habits which prohibit his full involvement in the present, and that, to do so, he has to pass "by symbolic substitute the locks of incest." This is precisely what Rojack does, not once but three times. Kelly is the Laertian figure in Rojack's life; at one time or another, he has been "married" to each of the three women with whom Rojack has sexual intercourse. Of the three, the brunette is psychologically castrating him, and the redhead is sterile; only the blonde, Cherry, is capable of loving and being loved. Moreover, in murdering Deborah Rojack is following the therapeutic program set out in "The White Negro," for the hipster knows that he cannot change or transcend himself simply by talking out his repressed impulses in the safety of a psychoanalyst's office but must in fact act them out. So, in the first place, Rojack murders in order to purge himself of the hatred that prohibits his loving anyone, including himself; in the second place, he murders in order to meet and overcome the fear of death and evil which had entered into him when he could not kill the last German soldier, and which haunts him still in the moon and in the eyes of Deborah.

But to say that *An American Dream* is ambitious and complicated is not to say that it is an artistic success; indeed, it must finally be labeled a failure. There are two main reasons

[30] *Ibid.*, p. 197.

for the failure, neither unfamiliar to readers of Mailer's earlier work, particularly *Barbary Shore*, where the same two problems occur. First, the symbolic and intellectual superstructure of the novel is ineptly handled. Not all of it: connecting Deborah with Lilith (if that is what he has done) and with Diana, the goddess of the hunt, of the moon, and of chastity (which is what he certainly has done) is a deft stroke: for Deborah is killing him sexually and spiritually, as the moon coaxes him to jump from the balcony of his friend's apartment. Thus to destroy Deborah is to destroy death: of course, it is also to destroy his wife, and while the first would presumably be permissible in American society, the second is most emphatically not. This is the problem with the symbolic superstructure: it is not integrated with the novel's foundation — the "realistic" account of a man who murders his wife. The critics who have objected to Rojack's getting away with the murder have not paid attention to Deborah's symbolic dimension and therefore see the novel as grossly immoral, and on such a reading it is. But though the suspension of ethical categories constitutes part of the obscurantism in the novel, there is an additional difficulty — namely, Mailer's quixotic notion that you can kill death as you can kill a person.

Still other ideas are brought into play which do not cohere with the basic tone and quality of the novel. Since about 1955 Wilhelm Reich's theories have played an increasingly important role in Mailer's work, and in *An American Dream* the Reichian influence is discernible in events and ideas such as vomiting, psycho-kinetic powers, character armor (which Mailer insists on inflating into "armature"), and the doctrine of orgasmic potency. Cherry is yet another of the women whose psychic maidenhead (in Reich's terminology, the seventh or pelvic armor segment) has been invulnerable to all but a Mailer hero. Whether or not these ideas are scientifically true is less important than whether they are artistically useful. Properly handled, some no doubt could be used: but the scene in which Rojack shoots people with his psychic bullets is simply ludicrous. That kind of mana does not make Rojack better, bigger, more interesting, or more believable in the design of the novel.

The second reason for the novel's failure is that the last quarter of it — the long scene in Kelly's apartment — is not integrated with the rest. What was supposed to have been the culminating episode in Rojack's encounter with evil becomes instead something of an anticlimax. In fact, the episode comes dangerously close to comedy — there is always something funny about compulsive behavior — when Rojack decides he must walk the parapet around Kelly's balcony; and then walk it again. So if twice, why not thrice? Thus we are left with the image of Rojack spending his life teetering around the rim — ropewalker, clown.

Then there is Cherry's death — presumably a crucial event in the total action. Why did she die? The obvious answer is that she was beaten to death by one of Shago's buddies. But why did he beat her to death? If we take seriously the power of magic, we might suppose that Cherry's death was caused by Deborah, either immediately or through the help of Kelly, her father. Or perhaps she died because Rojack himself failed her by not walking around the parapet a second time, or because Shago's friend made a mistake. If it is the first, *An American Dream* is a novel about the supernatural, similar to the fables of Charles Williams; if the second, then we have something vaguely existentialist; if the third, we have perhaps that meaningless world found in the fiction of Hardy or Hemingway. The fact is that Mailer never makes up his mind; so the novel ends in confusion and ambiguity.

An American Dream is weak in the same way that Mailer's second and third novels are weak — not so much in the "writing" or rhetoric as in the craft or construction. I venture the further remark that craft fails at just that point in his work where invention must take over from experience. Of the four novels, *Barbary Shore* is the most fully invented, and its characters are fuzzy and unmemorable, the plot confused, the rhetoric burdensome. *The Deer Park* was written after he had spent some time in Hollywood and its environs: it draws heavily on that experience and is a relatively coherent piece of work. *The Naked and the Dead* is a very good novel by just about any standard one chooses: it is complex and complete, powerful and proportioned, and its writing entailed almost no invention. It has been said that Mailer didn't even bother to invent names for some of the personages. Characters and incidents are developments of persons he must have lived with and events he must have experienced during World War II, and he simply appropriated them for his fictional purposes.

For more than ten years, Mailer has been talking about "the big novel" which will do something that books such as Bellow's *Herzog* and Mary McCarthy's *The Group* failed to do — "seize the temper of our time and turn it," or which will become a "Being, a psychological reality which lives afterward in our brain, touches our motives, affects the history we in turn will make." Mary McCarthy failed to do this, says Mailer, because "she is simply not a good enough woman to write a major novel; . . . she has failed from the center out." [31] Great literature issues, in Mailer's opinion, from great souls, and the writer's first task is to keep himself fit.

> By the time I'm done with writing I care about I usually have worked on it through the full gamut of consciousness. If you keep yourself in this kind of shape, the craft will take care of itself. Craft is very little finally. But if you're continually worrying about whether you're growing or deteriorating as a man, whether your integrity is turning soft or firming itself, why then it's in that slow war, that rearguard battle you fight against a diminishing talent that you stay in shape as a writer and have a consciousness. You develop a consciousness as you grow older which enables you to write about anything, in effect, and write about it well. That is, provided you keep your consciousness in shape and don't relax into the flabby styles of thought which surround one everywhere. The moment you borrow other writer's styles of thought, you need craft to shore up the walls. But if what you write

[31] *Cannibals and Christians*, pp. 138–39.

is a reflection of your own consciousness, then even journalism can become interesting.[32]

This Longinian theory of art — which Mailer would assuredly want to call "existential" — no doubt demands a great deal of the artist; but its demands may not, finally, be stringent enough. For the big novel requires what Mailer lacks: patience, care, invention, and craft.

Norman Mailer, in fact, has the mind neither of a systematic thinker nor of an artist, but rather of a newspaper reporter. I do not say this in a pejorative way, for the talents that make an excellent reporter are not only valuable in themselves but are also essential to the realistic novelist as well — an acute sensory apparatus, an inquiring mind, a lively style, and a commitment to the facts. When Mailer writes out of his immediate experience, or when he is able to magnify and ornament and interpret that experience, he is capable of making something valid and honest and important. In passage after passage of the autobiographical sections of *Advertisements*, he shows us what it costs — at least what it has cost him — to be a writer in America. His essays on the Democratic Convention of 1960 and the Republican Convention of 1964 are superb, in the way they capture the hope and anxiety, the color and import, of those events. His portraits of Kennedy, Eisenhower, Goldwater, and other public figures are often merciless but never vicious. His language, restrained by the fact, is as exciting as his best fiction:

When he was done [nominating Goldwater], they blew Dirksen down, the high screams of New Year's Eve went off, a din of screamers, rattles, and toots, a clash of bands, a dazzle of posters in phosphorescent yellow and orange and gold, the mad prance of the state standards, wild triumphant pokes and jiggles, war spears, crusader's lances, an animal growl of joy, rebel cries, eyes burning, a mad nut in each square jaw, *Viva-Olé*, *Viva-Olé*, bugle blasts and rallying cries, the call of heralds, and a fall from the rafters of a long golden rain, pieces of gold foil

[32] *Ibid.*, pp. 218–19.

one inch square, hundreds of thousands of such pieces in an endless gentle shimmer of descent. They had put a spot on the fall — it was as if sunlight had entered every drop of a fine sweet rain.

And then the interpretive elaboration:

And the sounds of the band went up to meet the rain. There was an unmistakable air of beauty, as if a rainbow had come to a field of war, or Goths around a fire saw visions in a cave. [Contrast this with "an angel come to the wake of a bomb."] The heart of the beast had loosed a primitive call. Civilization was worn thin in the center and to the Left the black man raised his primitive cry; now to the far Right were the maniacal blue eyes of the other primitive. The jungles and the forests were readying for war. It was certain beyond certainty now that America was off on a ride which would end — was it God or the Devil knew where.[33]

The paragraph illustrates Mailer's procedure: it begins with the historical fact and ends with God and the Devil. Yet the reporter and imaginative historian never leaves the empirical realm of concrete, public history; the work is brilliant. So is "Ten Thousand Words a Minute," Mailer's report on the Patterson-Liston fight.[34] Here, too, his animus toward the popular press and his flights of Manichean fancy (Patterson represents Good, Liston Evil) are kept in line by his loyalty to history, to "what happened there and then."

When Mailer tells us what he has seen and what it means to him; when he tells us about those things he has gut-knowledge of; when he contrives, either as reporter or as novelist, to establish himself as a glass of vision upon life as he has lived it; when his intuition and sensibility are free of theory and dogma and he is writing spontaneously — then he can be splendid. But when the Mosaic delusion is upon him, when he writes with the purpose of leading America into the promised

[33] *Ibid.*, p. 34.
[34] Printed in *The Presidential Papers*, pp. 213–67.

land of vitality, integrity, liberty, and creativity, when, as Vidal has said, he is trying to tell us something we have to know in order to be saved — in short, when he starts to think, declare, and prophesy — then thought, language, vision, and art collapse into disorder and nonsense.

At the end of *An American Dream*, Rojack is broken in the spiritual man, nearly mad. He sets off for Las Vegas, stops by a doctor-friend's home in Missouri, and observes an autopsy on an old man who had been dying of cancer but the immediate cause of whose death had been a ruptured appendix and peritoneal gangrene. The stench from the cadaver's opened belly is nauseating; madness is in it; and it follows Rojack to Las Vegas. There he parlays his stake into enough cash to finance a vacation. The last sentence reads, "But in the morning, I was something like sane again, and packed the car, and started on the long trip to Guatemala and Yucatan."

In a somewhat similar way another young hero, just eighty years earlier, was proposing to deal with the nightmare of death and madness, the stink of rot and disease, which is reality in America: "But I reckon I got to light out for the Territory ahead of the rest, because Aunt Sally she's going to adopt and sivilize me and I can't stand it. I been there before." It is typical of Innocence, when it has confronted the world and been shocked and disillusioned, to flee to the Territory, to Guatemala, to the primitive sources of nourishment and health, to the breast of Mother Nature. And Rojack and his creator are Innocents. There has always been something boyish and ingenuous about Mailer's rebellions and attitudinizings and enthusiasms: he is now as delighted with his new toy, Abstract Ideas, as he was earlier excited about Hip; before that, Sex; before that, Politics; and before that, War.

These vagaries of value and belief, while they ill-become the prophet, who is nothing if not monomaniacal, are yet perfectly congruous with Mailer's temperament; for, given the option, he will vote the straight Dionysian ticket every time:

vitality, not form; liberty, not justice; character, not plot, and style in favor of both; the individual talent, not tradition; the future, not the past; passion, not reason; disruption, not continuity. Commited to integrity and transcendence, the Dionysian self declares itself free from the laws of thought, art, and action. Observing and obeying no law, it breaks none and declares itself innocent. But the price of innocence is isolation; innocence has no sources of strength apart from itself. So when, in its discreteness and particularity, innocence is tested by the exigencies of art and life — by ambiguity, failure, and death — and learns that it is inadequate to the self-imposed task of transcendence, innocence has no alternative but to admit defeat or to flee out of reality into the realm of fancy — from now to then, either past or future; from here to some unsullied otherwhere, the Edens and Utopias of the adolescence of the race.

If there is one point, however, on which both the religious imagination and the literary imagination of our time are in some sort of agreement, it is that innocence as a way of life or even as a moral norm is no longer possible or desirable. Rudolf Bultmann's program for demythologization, Dietrich Bonhoeffer's declaration that the world has "come of age," and Paul Tillich's systematic theology are all saying in effect that the day of our adolescent alienation and disillusionment is past. They are telling us that we wrestle not against principalities, against powers, against the rulers of the darkness of this world, against spiritual wickedness in high places, but that we wrestle against flesh and blood. The main thrust of our recent theology has been to exterminate the last vestiges of gnosticism — the very system of thought which Mailer in his naiveté is now urging upon us under the name of Hipsterism and existential politics. And against him it must be said that now, in the seventh decade of the twentieth century, innocence is impossible: lighting out to the Territory is now simply evasion.

It is not accidental, therefore, that in much recent fiction the hero is found, at the end, standing in the place his experience has taught him to be his own. Nor does it seem to me merely accidental that some of these heroes are Jews or teachers, men of tradition and learning, who wear history and failure like a second skin, no more to be escaped than the first. The destiny is inadequacy, and after such knowledge as theirs, there is no forgiveness, at least not in any easy sense, certainly not through the mediating offices of a blue-eyed blonde. Salvation is to be found neither in a private act of love nor in a public act of rebellion; hence, in the novels of Saul Bellow and Bernard Malamud and John Updike the promise of fulfillment in love typically gives way to the present demand of responsibility, and the hopes which in a more youthful age rested upon rebellion are here abandoned for the immediate task of perseverance.

Predictably, Mailer has no time for the Caldwells and Herzogs and Levins of current American fiction, for he finds them pusillanimous and contemptible. He makes this clear in a paragraph in his address to the American Literature section of the Modern Language Association:

> Frank Cowperwood once amassed an empire. Herzog, his bastard great-nephew, diddled in the ruins of an intellectual warehouse. Where once the realistic novel cut a swath across the face of society, now its reality was concentrated into moral seriousness. Where the original heroes of naturalism had been active, bold, self-centered, close to tragic, and up to their nostrils in their exertions to advance their own life and force the webs of society, so the hero of moral earnestness, the hero Herzog and the hero Levin in Malamud's *A New Life*, are men who represent the contrary — passive, timid, other-directed, pathetic, up to the nostrils in anguish: the world is stronger than they are; suicide calls.[35]

And, of course, suicide does call. So do insanity, "the Territory," and the jungles of Guatemala. But giving way to these temptations is always a stratagem of evasion — prompted by an innocence that cannot bear to live with the knowledge that

[35] *Cannibals and Christians*, p. 100.

the world is imperfect. When the innocent learns that the game he has been playing is for keeps, that it will cost him his integrity (no Pamela ever took better care of her virginity than the American adolescent hero takes of his integrity), then, in a pout, he picks up his marbles and goes home — that is, to the Territory, or to his little sister Phoebe, or, in the case of Rojack, Mailer's all-American boy, to his mistress Cherry, or, at the last, to Guatemala. The one who resists the temptation to escape, however, is the one who knows that flight is futile, that you cannot run away from history.

In Rojack's theology, God is not love, but courage, and love comes as a reward for being brave. He delivers himself of this opinion as he is on his way to do single combat with Barney Kelly and to earn Cherry's love by feats of derring-do. If we are reminded of Tom Sawyer and Injun Joe and Becky, it is because the theme and the values of the two plots are so similar. They are not, however, the theme and values of maturity. No doubt it takes courage to kill one's wife, face down the Mafia, or walk a parapet thirty stories above the street; but it is a melodramatic and irrelevant sort of courage. The kind that is needed is, rather, the courage to love, when you know that love can be betrayed, or that your beloved can be carelessly destroyed: what is needed is the courage to think, when you know that thought is limited, incoherent, and enervating; and the courage to work, when you know that what you produce is transient and of little value; and then, when love and thought and work have all been swept away, what is needed is the courage to begin once again to love and think and labor. What is wanted, that is to say, is the courage of maturity, not the bravado of youth.

These are insights which Norman Mailer has not yet realized. Given the wrongheadedness with which he has deserted his natural métier (the lively reportage of the private anguish and the public occasion), it is no wonder that his fiction is so cluttered with the metaphor of melodrama and that his thought so quickly collapses into jargon and jingoism when he tries to engage the Big Questions. At this mid-point in his career, he leaves the impression of an enormously talented man who has been careless of intellectual and artistic discipline, so careless indeed that he is perilously close to becoming merely a personality (in the ad-man's sense of the term), an interesting eccentric, a "case." He is still, as we say, one of our "younger writers," so there is still time; but it is fast running out.

9

Epilogue: *Faith and the Literary Imagination—*
The Vocation of Poetry
HENRY RAGO

For the subject so calmly proposed by my title, there are many
possible places to start, none of them very comfortable. Even
if I narrow the meaning of the literary imagination to its function in poetry—as I must do immediately, for that is the
question of which I am less ignorant than of others—I must
give some responsible account of the way in which I locate the
poetry I am talking about. I must choose the poetry; and in
the choosing I am in danger of prepossessing the very question of its relation to religion. One way of avoiding that danger is to say that we shall put aside any question of "kind"
or subject or tendency; we shall simply take poetry where
we find it. And where do we find it? An unmistakable place,
I think, is in the truly contemporary; for that is the only poetry
we are sure of finding for ourselves. It is the only poetry that
happens to us; for in its experience we stand at the farthest
point to which language has come, and see the extension of
language beyond that point as an occurrence: live, instanta-
neous, unrenewable, unique. The experience of all other
poetry requires a patient work of recovery—we must be histo-
rians as well as critics—in order to locate the point at which
the language found itself at the time and to imagine the poem
as an event in that language.

By contemporary poetry, I do not mean merely twentieth-
century poetry, or "modern" poetry, or "recent" poetry—
even poetry as recent as a manuscript that came to my desk
this morning. We now stand in the last third of the twentieth
century. The literary histories that our grandchildren will

239

read will probably identify Yeats as an early twentieth-century poet. As for "modern" poetry: we should have to agree on what it is and where it begins. The question of modernity is a rich one; it draws us into the preceding century and into other countries, surely into France; and it has us busy defining qualities that are subtle and already surcharged with energies taking us beyond merely literary considerations into the philosophical and even the theological. But inviting as those explorations are, they do not give us the present moment, *as* present, the moment we know only in the most precise meaning of the word "contemporary," as an indivisible point in which faith and the literary imagination are to be seen together if their relationship is to be seen at all. The word "recent" is even less satisfactory than either of these alternatives: it suggests something less disciplined and rigorous than an orderly research into the idea of modernity, and something less thorough and systematic than an historical reckoning with twentieth-century poetry. Worse: that "recent" packet of manuscript I opened this morning may be so far from a wholly new making of experience into language, and of language into experience — that the fact of its composition in the twentieth-century would be merely coincidence and thus without significance for the historian; and it might very well be — the possibilities are not strained — somewhat less modern than the poetry Rimbaud or Mallarmé wrote in the nineteenth century.

Correspondingly, if our full task is to discern the relationship of this poetry to religion, I do not think that the question of locating the religion we are to talk about is any less difficult. I am not thinking of the obvious question of what particular belief we are considering; I assume that we are safely beyond the danger of taking a doctrinaire or parochial approach. But I have in mind the larger question, What is the essentially religious experience? We can easily imagine the great spectrum of possibilities that offer themselves, from the simplest experience of Wonder — the *thaumazein* — to its darker Hebrew expression of fear-and-trembling; from the sensing of the Numinous to the enacting of some relationship

to it; from the passion of excitement or even frenzy to the
action of some kind of oblation; from an increased sense of
one's being to a willingness to surrender that being, to be
changed; even — in some way — to die.

It is not necessary to put these gradations in order; it is
enough to indicate that they exist and that they challenge our
precision whenever we begin to suggest the religious experience. What interests us is the expression of this experience.
And the experience may occur simultaneously with the expression; may seem to be one with it; may indeed be one
with it. Thus what is contemporary as literature — I mean,
what is happening for the first time in literature — will also
be contemporary, happening for the first time, in theology.
The study of the present relations between theology and
literature means the study of that indivisible point — an *event*
here and now — in which we find theology inaccessible anywhere else or in any other "form," and in which we find literature unimaginable with any other *raison d'être* than the theology that energizes it. I suggest that the "field" conventionally called "theology and literature" might with more precision be called theology-in-literature *and* literature-in-
theology. Anything less than this inextricability would ask us
to imagine on the one hand theology in a pure state to which
we would bring for comparison and correction the refractions
and distortions seen in fiction or poetry, and, on the other
hand, a literature equally antiseptic, though the occasional
inquiries of the theologian might be tolerated with good nature and the confidence that nothing he does could have any
effect on literary values in their purest and clearest form.

The systematic theologian should not be shocked by these
observations. However he regards his function, he would be
the first to testify that the "given" in theology — at least as we
know it in the Judaeo-Christian tradition, but also, I incline
to think, in the other major traditions as well — is never pure
in the easy, rationalistic sense of that word. The sources for
the systematic theologian are images and signs; events and
visions; parables and hard sayings; a Life. Truth as he sees it
comes in the swaddling-clothes of the metaphor. The sacred

books are poetry immeasurably more mysterious in their analogical reflections, depth into depth, than the most recondite modern texts which the literary critic might set himself. And as for the Word itself, the same poet who gave new mystery to the reflections of Lancelot Andrewes on that "Word within a Word, unable to speak a word" tells us elsewhere:

There was a Birth, certainly.
We had evidence and no doubt. I had seen birth and death,
But had thought they were different; this Birth was
Hard and bitter agony for us, like Death, our death.

A theology attempting to speak that word, stammering into innumerable words that must be constantly redefined over the centuries, traced through their permutations, concealed and revealed in lives and acts and gestures, surely will understand poetry as "act" (I am thinking of Kenneth Burke's "symbolic action"), "language as gesture" (I think of the late R. P. Blackmur), surely will know that refraction *is* precision; will seek to read that language as yet another meeting with the urgencies of history, the language itself being the irreducible and untranslatable record of that meeting; will welcome the extension of the theological enterprise that that language means. I am speaking of theology, not of the faith that animates it. Theology, St. Thomas Aquinas told us long ago, is infinitely beyond philosophy; and faith is infinitely beyond both. In the man who would know in order to believe and would believe in order to know, the dialogue between self and soul is never done; that dialogue is theology, and it has no privileged language. Its language finally might be silence, or a going into the desert, or even a dying; its language thus might be a sign, indecipherable to others, in which the heart must try to read itself. When the language is that of the imagination, we can be grateful enough to read that language as it asks to be read: in the very density of the medium, without the violence of interpolation or reduction.

It is important also to assure the literary critic that this view of a theology inextricable from literary values and of a literature inextricable from theological values is not meant to suggest an undoing of the reading-lesson Ezra Pound gave us all with his pronouncement early in this century: "Literature is what is printed on the page." Mr. Eliot only a decade or so later in his running debates with Middleton Murry on the one hand and with I. A. Richards on the other made it permanently clear that poetry was not to be confused with religion, and vice versa; that poetry, despite Matthew Arnold's prophecies, was not a substitute for religion; and that in general it did not work very well for anything to be a substitute for anything else. At the same time, Mr. Eliot was occupied in turning out those severe and exact Elizabethan essays from which most of us learned, for the rest of our lives, how to look closely at the poem as poem. Mr. Richards had his own brilliant instruction to give us. There was the unremitting labor of F. R. Leavis and *Scrutiny*, with everything that the title implied. Mr. Empson's ambiguities both dazzled us and held us to that page that Mr. Pound was talking about. In this country there were new energies as widely varied in principle and inspiration as Yvor Winters and John Crowe Ransom, Kenneth Burke and Ronald Salmon Crane, Allen Tate and Robert Penn Warren, R. P. Blackmur and Cleanth Brooks.

When I speak of the necessity of reading the poem — or the prose fiction — in the exigencies of its medium, I mean just such tact with the filament of the structure and just such care for the life of the metaphor as these critics have demanded of us. That filament, that life, will not yield themselves to any handling less exquisite. I do not think then that I can exaggerate the delicacy we need, if exploring nothing but method in the poem, avoiding any direct concern with the "thematic," our interest is finally to see something of the theological ethos that that method suggests, both as a pressure upon it and as an implication of the poet's own technical procedures. An ethos will imply a method; a method will suggest an ethos and at the same time do something to affect that ethos; by confirming it or by reacting against it; by sensing, through the instrument of art, some newer and deeper implication hitherto unseen; by giving it a name or an image, and thus — in the shock of that recognition — will help to strengthen it or to destroy it. If the total culture helps to create the poem, the poem helps to create the total culture in which we live after the poem is written.

I have used the word "ethos" too simply. For there are at least two strains in it that must be distinguished. The poet's belief may be in opposition to the ethos in which he finds himself; both his belief and the total culture in which he must work, or more precisely the tautness between them, will have to be reckoned with in his method. Other distinctions try us: the belief may be the braving of disbelief in the same heart; an uncertain venturing in the narrow way that is left between the pristine faith one is vouchsafed only at moments and the clusmy knowledge one is constantly ordering and re-ordering. The tension between these elements in the poet, if sometimes in a triumph of simplicity beyond that tension, will be in the poem. I hear one of the great, lonely voices of our century breaking off from all the certainties, such as they were, of his earlier methods:

> That was a way of putting it — not very satisfactory:
> A periphrastic study in a worn-out poetical fashion,
> With words and meanings. The poetry does not matter.

And the meaning of all this, in what does matter, is:

> You are not here to verify,
> Instruct yourself, or inform curiosity
> Or carry report. You are here to kneel
> Where prayer has been valid.

I am interested to see that in trying to make these distinctions, all for the purpose of suggesting that the poem does not come with anything like Hegelian inevitability, I meet, sooner than I had planned, the phenomenon of the poet's quarrel with this poem. The context from which I have been quoting — the greatest long poem of our century — is clear enough with the spiritual urgencies that help Mr. Eliot to know that "the poetry does not matter." The same poet, long before he was prepared to make his way through the *Quartets*, told us in his prose that critics were wrong to assume that a poet wrote the poetry he wanted to write. This complexity is enough to counsel patience in the critic, whether "purely" literary or impurely theological, who might otherwise draw too simple a cause-and-effect diagram between the poet's belief and his poem; and even in putting the question in those terms, I neglect, simply to avoid parenthesis within parenthesis, the distinction between the faith that remains a mystery to oneself and the imperfect profession of it as "belief," no matter how diligent the mind or studious the will.

There is the poet's quarrel with his poem. There is also the poet's quarrel with poetry in general; and I am inclined more and more to say that the test of a genuine poet is his engagement in this quarrel. To write bad poetry is not, of course, to engage in this quarrel but to ignore it. When I explore these matters with students, I look, as you would expect from what I have already said, for the poem that suggests its own happening; the poem in which I can see also, perhaps, where the poem seems to break under its burden.

> Others because you did not keep
> That deep-sworn vow have been friends of mine;
> Yet always when I look death in the face,
> When I clamber to the heights of sleep,
> Or when I grow excited with wine,
> Suddenly I meet your face,

That is the entire text of Yeats's poem, "A Deep-Sworn Vow." It starts easily enough, in language indistinguishable from ordinary speech. The "Others" are not made clear, nor do we have any explicit context for the vow. "Friends of mine" not only is easy speech but has the suggestion of carelessness. Something seems to begin with "Yet always . . ." and the rest of that line takes us beyond the ordinary, the undefined, and the easily dismissed to at least the thought of the most telling moment of all, the moment of death. Mr. Tate has suggested that it is the function of poetry to recall us to that moment: to give us, he says, the image of man at the hour of death. We have, in any case, an intensity in this third line, the poem coming quietly and inevitably to it, and the rhythm is all that it should be; it has the ominous suggestion of a drumbeat. The moment in the next line is considerably less "crucial," though the suggestion of clambering to the heights carries over from the earlier line some uncertainty and danger. But whatever the resemblance, it is only resemblance — Donne tells Death in his sonnet that "rest and sleep" "but thy pictures be" — and so there is some diminuendo. I am sure of that diminuendo in the next line, which suggests neither the solemnity of death nor the reality of sleep; rather it suggests an illusory excitement, though touching for just that reason. The last line takes the poem back from this series of three less and less intense moments to the one intensity, the recollection that will not leave him. This is what brings the quiet little poem into existence at all; it is also what leaves it with nothing more to say.

I am sure that the Yeats of "That dolphin-torn, that gong-tormented sea," of "Lapis Lazuli," of "Sailing to Byzantium," of the poetry heavily bejeweled and gold-encrusted, splendid with that pride and sadness, or brooding upon ancestral country in

> The broken wall, the burning roof and tower
> And Agamemnon dead.

is more habitual to our imaginations. But I speak at this length of "A Deep-Sworn Vow" precisely because I see in it a transparency — the prefix in that word suggests a bolder phrase, a transcending of poetry — that I must look for elsewhere in Yeats only in single lines or isolated moments:

> All the Olympians, a thing never known again

or

> A sixty-year-old smiling public man

246

or

How could I praise that one?
When day begins to break
I count my good and bad,
Being wakeful for her sake
Remembering what she had,
What eagle look still shows,
While up from my heart's root
So great a sweetness flows
I shake from head to foot.

Those last two lines could almost be a banality if they had not been earned in the crucible of the poem — and in the crucible of all this poet's work, for he conceived his books as wholes, and the voice even in some small epigram in his *Last Poems* carries the authority of all that has gone before. It is not that we simply tolerate these lines as justified by the poem or by the context of the poet's *ouvrage*; I mean to say rather that such lines go beyond mere eloquence, they are among the most piercing moments in the poet's book, precisely because they suggest an abandonment of the poem, an exhaustion of its means.

Perhaps in all ages the struggle of a new poetry to exist — I do not say, to be recognized: that question does not interest us; I mean quite simply the struggle to come into being — must always be a struggle against what Paul Claudel called Literature, when he announced quite unambiguously, "Je déteste la littérature." Gide once complained that Claudel's mind "has no slopes," but Mr. Eliot's observation in his Norton lectures on *The Use of Poetry and the Use of Criticism* at Harvard in 1932 and 1933 was no more oblique. "Poetry," he said, "is not a career, but a mug's game." I see in the collocation of Claudel's disdain for Literature and Eliot's poet who "may have wasted his time and messed up his life for nothing" a narrowing of the poet's chances between a past, even a recent past, that is irrevocable, and his own poetry, which is by its nature unpredictable. If it could be predicted, it would not be his poetry, but Literature.

We ask of the poem that it happen each time in what is the present; which is to say simply that the new poem must happen, and there is no place for it to happen except outside, beyond, anything we had thought to be poetry. Whether we are talking of the School of Donne rising in the name of rough honesty against the suavities of their predecessors, or of Dryden leveling the middle style against what became the artificialities of Clevelandism, or of Wordsworth in the Preface to the *Lyrical Ballads* pleading anew the cause of common speech against the mere fomulas for elegance in lesser poets than Dryden or Pope, the principle each time is some new identification of the authentic. The true poet is willing to give up poetry in order to find poetry.

> I, too, dislike it: there are things that are important
> beyond all this fiddle.
> Reading it, however, with a perfect contempt for it,
> one discovers in
> it after all, a place for the genuine.

Marianne Moore's diffidence and her scruple are equally famous. The two taken together are what we mean by style. If poetry is at all possible it will be only because of the style that is the lady: the perseverance and probity that she herself is, "picking and choosing" (how many of her poems have to do with choosing!) among those "phenomena" that are "the raw material of poetry in all its rawness":

> . . . elephants pushing, a wild horse taking a roll, a
> tireless wolf under
> a tree, the immovable critic twitching his skin like
> a horse that feels a flea, the base-
> ball fan, the statistician —

Her requirements in that poem for poets who
> . . . can be
> 'literalists of
> the imagination' — above
> insolence and triviality and can present
> for inspection, 'imaginary gardens with real toads
> in them,'

will give us a poem astir with a kind of subtle reluctance that goes both ways: in the matter, and in the means. The complexity is resolved with grace — the more honorific word for the poet's perseverance — in such a title as "In This Age of Hard Trying, Nonchalance Is Good, and." The word "and" goes nonchalantly into the text of the poem. What the nonchalance costs we may guess from her praise of the sparrow-camel in the same volume, in a poem the title for which is adapted from Lyly's *Euphues*: "He 'Digesteth Harde Yron.'"

So Ezra Pound, beyond the furious lights and splendors of the *Cantos*, long after that early, beautiful *Cathay* in which, it seemed to his friend Eliot, he "invented Chinese poetry for our time," could sit down to Chinese poetry again in St. Elizabeth's Hospital, in that darkness, an old man who had come through many storms, and translate *The Classic Anthology Defined by Confucius*, not content this time to repeat the idiom and metric he had established in *Cathay* but determined to "make it new" once more, an arpeggio of translations that were at the same time correspondences to various moments in the history of our own literature, not excluding Uncle Remus or, for that matter, Pound himself. On the far side of all the choices that had been open to his virtuosity for more than four decades, he could render in these seven lines, gentle beyond all contrivance, a Chinese scholar looking back from his century to a less vulgar time:

> There was no fuss about the fall
> of the sash ends, there was just that much to spare
> and it fell, and ladies' hair
> curved, just curved and that was all
> > the like of which, today; is never met
> > And I therefore
> > express regret.

The effacement of the poem itself, in those rhymes that also "just fall," in those lines that measure themselves by the quietest breathing, is the exquisite paradigm of the esthetic and the morality meant by "no fuss." *The Cantos* are not without these arrivals beyond the effort of all poetry:

What thou lovest well remains,
the rest is dross

And if the sigh that is the last line of one of the great *Pisan Cantos* is not for the lute that Confucius plucked, it transcends eloquence and is a judgment on virtuosity:

Oh let an old man rest.

Is this what we hear, this speech beyond music — and what *else* do we hear — in "Marina," that most beautiful of Eliot's minor poems? I must give the whole of it, including the epigraph from Seneca: *Quis hic locus, quae regio, quae mundi plaga?*

What sea what shores what grey rocks and what islands
What water lapping the bow
And scent of pine and the woodthrush singing through
the fog
What images return
O my daughter.

Those who sharpen the tooth of the dog, meaning
Death
Those who glitter with the glory of the humming-
bird, meaning
Death
Those who sit in the style of contentment, meaning
Death
Those who suffer the ecstasy of the animals, meaning
Death

Are become unsubstantial, reduced by a wind,
A breath of pine, and the woodsong fog
By this grace dissolved in place

What is this face, less clear and clearer
The pulse in the arm, less strong and stronger —
Given or lent? more distant than stars and nearer than
the eye

Whispers and small laughter between leaves and
hurrying feet

Under sleep, where all the waters meet.

Bowsprit cracked with ice and paint cracked with heat.
I made this, I have forgotten
And remember.
The rigging weak and the canvas rotten
Between one June and another September.
Made this unknowing, half conscious, unknown, my own.
The garboard strake leaks, the seams need caulking.
This form, this face, this life
Living to live in a world of time beyond me; let me
Resign my life for this life, my speech for that unspoken,
The awakened, lips parted, the hope, the new ships.

What seas what shores what granite islands towards
    my timbers
And woodthrush calling through the fog
My daughter.

The poem, making its way through the broken music of its
lines, only half believing the promise it sees, and, for the rest,
still dumb with weariness, does resign its "life for this life,"
its "speech for that unspoken." It ends where it must end,
the imperative coming from beyond the poem; it ends in what
the poem dares aspire to but does not dare to claim; and the
abandonment is all the clearer for the return at the end to
the vision that had opened the poem. The first cry "O my
daughter" is modulated at the end to, simply, "My daughter":
enough a suggestion of acceptance to make a certain humble
resolution, enough a repetition to suggest that the dazed
wonderment continues beyond the poem. The writing flickers
with lights and darks; the mode is deliberate. In a poem that
stammers into the hardly sayable (the same poet much later,
in "The Dry Salvages," will strain in a sestina, of all forms, for
"the hardly, barely prayable Prayer of the one Annuncia-
tion"), speaks in fragments, and shatters before the unsay-
able, the *chiaroscuro* is almost inevitable. We cannot help
recalling that Mr. Eliot honored Arnaut Daniel, "master of
the obscure style," and that this poet was quite possibly

among the shadowy identities encountered in the phantom
of "some dead master"

In the uncertain hour before the morning
Near the ending of the interminable night
At the recurrent end of the unending

After the dark dove with the flickering tongue
Had passed below the horizon of his homing. . . .

It may be that the reaching of a poem toward all the others
that are to come in one poet's work — a motion we can observe in its full contour when the poet's life-work is done — is
one more function of the restlessness we see instead of what
several generations had imagined as the well-made poem,
the poem complete in itself, the poem well-behaved. Paul
Claudel, whose kind of poem Stanislas Fumet described as
"un animal qui marche," has told us that a poet is born into
the world to say one thing, and that it takes all his books to
say it.

There is still another series of transformations that await
us. We need only look into the very material of the poem
and ask whether we ever could have imagined the words
themselves as inert, as neutral and constant signs, without a
force of their own to draw the poet into their depths, always
a little beyond any intentions he could have made explicit
to himself. To be a poet at all is to be present to the ontology
that is hidden in words. And what shall we say of metaphor?
We might begin with the definitions we were taught as children, seeing it as a mere figure of speech rather than as speech
itself, as a depth of speech that is otherwise impossible. But
we have known for a long time from the brilliant explorations of such critics as Kenneth Burke, William Empson,
Maud Bodkin, and Northrop Frye what delicate meanings
hover in the *choice* of the metaphor, what webs might be
traced among the metaphors in one writer's work, and what
proliferations there are in the unspoken depths of the image.
Quite beyond all this there has been in our time — in European poetry and in our own; I do not know other poetries well
enough to speak of them — a forcing of new secrets from the

metaphor, by whatever means of deepening or compacting or violation. The ambitions of Mallarmé were explicit. They had nothing to do with the one thing that Claudel's poet takes all his life and all his books to write; they looked to the Great Work for which the universe itself was destined: "Tout, au monde, existe pour aboutir à un livre." The symbol in Mallarmé is no longer a sign to be understood in relation to something outside itself; it is the destined reality. To be understood, it asks to be entered and lived in. We have in Proust the dream of that complete enclosure; we have in the Joyce of *Finnegans Wake* the full realization: the final "sentence," "A way a lone a last a loved a long the" leads to the first: "riverrun, past Eve and Adam's. . . ." I know little in contemporary poetry that does not reveal something of this inward transformation of the metaphor. Hart Crane, especially in his "Voyages," reveals much of it. Not only are the metaphors "telescoped," as he described them in a long letter to Harriet Monroe shortly after he had finished the poems; they move in a ritual of transformations, in which love and death and the sea are constantly metamorphosed into one another, in

The silken skilled transmemberment of song

and almost always there is a prayer in which he unites himself to these tides and transformations.

What does this progression of signs mean, from the most arbitrary marks of the mathematician, through words, through "figures of speech," through the ambiguities of metaphor until we are beyond any allegorical tracing? I imagine a spectrum from what might seem to be the complete separation between sign and signified in the conventions of the mathematician — though even here I hesitate to grant, except for a moment's simplification, a disontologized mathematics — to a greater and greater convergence of the related terms, to something like identification. Does the motion toward otherness end in Mallarmé's symbol? in Hart Crane's sea? I think it important to know, in reading "Voyages," that Hart Crane's life ended in the sea, that he leapt from a ship into the very waters that "wind the hours" in those poems. I can return to those poems and find in them, as I do in much modern symbolism, an effort in the words not only to say something but more than that to *do* something, even to *turn into* something.

Beyond the symbol, there is another kind of sign, which asks for even a more complete offering of oneself: it is there for those who give themselves to it; I mean the sign that is called a sacrament. Is there in symbolism a longing for the poem to be more than a poem, and for the symbol to be a sacrament? My friend Caroline Gordon, the distinguished novelist, who with Allen Tate, her husband at that time, saw more of Hart Crane than most of his other contemporaries did, tells me that toward the end Crane would say to her he longed "to taste blood."

We know that to Yeats the symbol meant more than poetry but something *quite* different from sacrament. Understood and manipulated it could give us magic, and a control upon history. Jean Cocteau also was interested in magic, despite the prayer that ends *Orphée*: "Parce que j'adorais la poésie, et la poésie c'était Vous." His symbols have hard surfaces; his characters enter mirrors; and mirrors are not the sea. Magic is an arrest of the transformations we have been seeing; it is an attempt of the poet to *contain* the symbol.

I have suggested a design; and so it might be well to complete it. I think that one more kind of sign is possible, beyond the sacrament. If there is to be the complete transformation of one's life into a sign, the *becoming* a sign, what else remains but that disappearance into the mystery, which is called martyrdom? It is the theological *télos* in my subject that takes me so far beyond my competence to speak; and if my reader feels as uneasy with such matters as I feel unprepared, we can draw back quickly from that ground. It is enough to say that we teach even the young to make their lives "significant." The light in that unassuming word comes from this most minute, indivisible point of our design, this needle's-eye, where the whole meaning is in the Wholly Other.

I have already implied that these transcendental urgencies need not always be benign forces, nor the poet's invocation of them wise or fortunate. I have already suggested the *détraquement* into magic, the confusion of death with love, and the possible mistaking of the surrender that is suicide for the perseverance that is martyrdom. I should not presume to teach what the poem itself can teach so well, or more precisely, what we must learn elsewhere to learn from the poem: in the work, another word for which is travail; in the patience, which comes from the same Latin word that gives us the word "passion"; in the willingness to labor within the sign — and a dim sign — without demanding to *see* a sign; in the living in time, without the *hubris* that demands the new forms of Gnosticism that are all about us, in art, in conduct, and even in politics. I mean, finally, that we can learn within the poem "to care and not to care."

If I am to conclude with any aspirations, I choose to offer them within the discipline of the sign. I end with three poems of my own — or two poems and part of a third — in which there may be heard some echoes, or prefigurings, or possibly, farther reaches of the questions that have occupied us.

The first, "The Knowledge of Light," is the middle poem of the trilogy that opens my book, *A Sky of Late Summer*:

I

The willow shining
From the quick rain,
Leaf, cloud, early star
Are shaken light in this water:
The tremolo of their brightness: light
Sung back in light.

II

The deep shines with the deep.
A deeper sky utters the sky.
These words waver
Between sky and sky.

III

A tree laced of many rivers
Flows into a wide slow darkness
And below the darkness, flowers again
To many rivers, that are a tree.

IV

Wrung from silence
Sung in lightning
From stone sprung
The quickening signs
Lines quivered
Numbers flew

Darkness beheld
Darkness and told
Each in each
The depths not darkness.

V

To know
Meaning to celebrate:
Meaning
To become "in some way"
Another; to come
To a becoming:
To have come well.

VI

Earth wakens to the word it wakens.

These dancers turn half-dreaming
Each to the other, glide
Each from a pool of light on either side
Below the dark wings
And flutter slowly, come slowly
Or drift farther again,

Turn to the single note, lifted,
And leap, their whirling lines
Astonished into one lucidity:
Multiples of the arc.

Shapes of the heart!

VII

The year waits at the depth of summer.
The air, the island, and the water
Are drawn to evening. The long month
Is lost in the long evening.

If words could hold this world
They would bend themselves to one
Transparency; if this
Depth of the year, arch of the hour
Came perfect to
The curving of one word
The sound would widen, quietly as from crystal,
Sphere into sphere: candor
Answering a child's candor
Beyond the child's question.

The second effort to take these reflections beyond the
merely discursive is a poem called "Praise of Comedy: A Discourse." I hope that a further irony in its title is that its subject is not a literary genre but a plane of understanding:

My poem within a poem (for the bright riddle,
For the thread of song,
For the clear pool in a forest of disguises)
Speaks neither wisdom nor
"The love of wisdom"
But the dazzled learning
How wisdom might be loved.

The thunderous king
Commands the words to be commanded,
Orders the ordering of words

To measure love.
I praise that measure
He will traverse his kingdom
And his lost name to find
When he becomes
His Fool, gone
To bed at noon.

I praise the cage
Dreamed at last for the two birds
Where the world's gossip flows,
And one may know
A spy's pinprick
Of what God knows.
My praise is for
The measure of this knowing
That kneels and asks forgiveness
Answered by love
That asks a blessing.

I ask the comic muse
To light these words, granting
The self transparent with idea
In an enchantment; not
That swollen heaviness contending
Even with the stage. On either stage
The cost is a whole life: I praise
Beginning with that cost: the quick praise,
Tapers and revels
Quick with it.

So comedy, dancing, is
Dance, is
How many lights, brightening into
Pure lyric. Plato,
Writing philosophy, divined
Its muse is comic: the argument
Danced: gay dialectic! ages from

Philosophy rendered tragic, the German
Dialektik: dense
History
Quarreling into form.

I celebrate the celebration
The absent Duke
Somehow presiding: the crossed and teased
Loves learning
Behavior in that knowledge,
Brought to a sweet
Mischief in that
Benevolence.

We choose, or long to choose.
For tragedy is no choice:
It chooses us; we are already
Chosen. Only
That clearest music
Remote and immediate
Waits for consent
(Come, in your dazzle of tears!)
All else lost
In whatever is:
Voices
And civil instrument
Singing that choice.

The third amplification is from "The Promising," the final
poem in *A Sky of Late Summer*. Of it I include here only the
last two sections. Those who read this excerpt may know why
on this occasion also — and perhaps especially — I end with it,
leaving all else to the poem:

VI

"Born to say one thing,"
All the books for the one word:
The metaphor not means but end,
Not the technique

But the vocation, the destiny.
Let it be
One metaphor, deeper each time
With the life that fills it;
Let the meaning come from the abundance,
Not from the brilliance, not from some new rhetoric
Pretending to hate rhetoric
But from the overflow of meaning
Demanding even as the poem is heard
The next poem, and the next,
That are one poem.

Let it be: the poet bearing
What he was born for,
And among the words
Not meant to efface themselves in meaning,
Among the words
Wrenched into pedantry or fixed
In thin wit,
Among words traded and the small betrayals,
And there, island or city,
Where the words were all but extinguished,
Borne by that.

VII

The shore
Signs itself in silence.

If all has been for the poem
The poem has been
For the silence it comes from,
For the silence
It must create.

I have found,
Am found by
A shore of silence.

It yields these words.

It holds my word.

Biographical Notes

JERALD C. BRAUER was born in Wisconsin in 1921, graduated from Carthage College and Northwestern Lutheran Theological Seminary, and received his Ph.D. from the University of Chicago in 1948. He taught at Union Theological Seminary, 1948–50. He is professor of the History of Christianity and dean of the University of Chicago's Divinity School. His publications are in the area of English Puritanism, reformation, and religion in America.

NATHAN A. SCOTT, JR., is professor of theology and literature and chairman of the Theology and Literature Field in the Divinity School of the University of Chicago. He also serves as Canon Theologian of the Cathedral of St. James, Chicago. Among his books are *The Broken Center: Studies in the Theological Horizon of Modern Literature* (1966); *Samuel Beckett* (1965); *Albert Camus* (1962); and *Modern Literature and the Religious Frontier* (1958). He has edited *The New Orpheus: Essays Toward a Christian Poetic* (1964), *The Climate of Faith in Modern Literature* (1964), *The Tragic Vision and the Christian Faith* (1957), and numerous other volumes. He is Co-editor of *The Journal of Religion*.

GILES B. GUNN is an instructor in the Theology and Literature Field of the Divinity School of the University of Chicago. He is currently completing a book on F. O. Matthiessen which will be a development of his doctoral dissertation.

JOHN W. HUNT is professor of English at Earlham College. He is the author of *William Faulkner: Art in Theological Tension* (1965) and has contributed numerous essays to literary and theological journals. He is currently completing a book on contemporary British fiction.

JAMES T. LIVINGSTON is professor of English at Drury College.

PRESTON M. BROWNING, JR., teaches English and American literature at the University of Illinois, Chicago Circle. He is currently completing his doctoral dissertation on the novels of Flannery O'Connor.

MAYNARD KAUFMAN is a member of the faculty of the Department of Religion at Western Michigan University. He is at present completing his doctoral dissertation on James Joyce.

GUNNAR URANG is assistant professor of English at the College of Wooster. He is presently completing a book on three English fantasists — Charles Williams, C. S. Lewis, and J. R. R. Tolkien.

DAVID HESLA is assistant professor of the Humanities in the Graduate Institute of the Liberal Arts of Emory University, where his chief responsibility involves the direction of a new interdisciplinary doctoral program in Theology and Literature. His book on Samuel Beckett is soon to be published.

HENRY RAGO is professor of Theology and Literature at the University of Chicago: his primary attachment is to the College, but he is also a member of the Divinity School's Theology and Literature Field. Since 1955 he has served as Editor of *Poetry* Magazine. He is the author of *A Philosophy of Aesthetic Individualism* (1941) and of two volumes of poetry — *The Travelers* (1949) and *A Sky of Late Summer* (1963).

Acknowledgments

In the autumn of 1966 (November 28–30), the Divinity School of the University of Chicago presented the sixth in a series of seven Alumni Conferences commemorating its own centennial anniversary and the seventy-fifth anniversary of the University. This Conference embraced those who had taken graduate degrees in the Divinity School's Theology and Literature Field, as well as those presently teaching and studying in this Field, and most of the essays included in this volume were delivered (in condensed versions) on that occasion. Professor Rago's essay was given as one of two public lectures delivered in the course of the Conference, the other having been a brilliant and moving presentation by Amos N. Wilder (Hollis Professor of Divinity *Emeritus* of the Harvard Divinity School) under the title "Biblical Epos and Modern Narrative."

In this colloquium, Wayne Booth (professor of English, University of Chicago; and dean of the University's College) was the prepared discussant for John Hunt's paper; Giles Gunn for Gunnar Urang's; Arthur Heiserman (associate professor of English, University of Chicago) for David Hesla's; James E. Miller, Jr. (professor of English, University of Chicago) for Preston Browning's; Vernon J. Ruland, S.J. (lecturer in Theology and Culture, Bellarmine School of Theology, Loyola University) for Maynard Kaufman's; and John Loose (professor of Religion, Gettysburg College) for James Livingston's. And it is unfortunate that limitations of space make it impossible to include here the discussions prepared by these participants, for they played a large part in giving the whole event the liveliness and considerable interest that it had.

Much of the detailed planning for the Conference was in the capable hands of Miss Kathryn West, who was then administrative assistant to the dean of the Divinity School; and the grace attending Conference hospitality was largely an expression of her remarkable thoughtfulness.

Thanks are also due to Mrs. Sonya Illianova and Mrs. Toshi Takahashi, whose carefulness in the preparation of the final typescript very greatly lightened the editor's task. And I am grateful to my student, Edwin Curmie Price, for various kinds of help in seeing the book through the press.

Mr. Rago's essay has appeared in *Poetry* Magazine (vol. 110, no. 5, August 1967) and is here published with that journal's permission. The editor of *Critique* has graciously consented to our use here of Mr. Urang's essay on William Styron, which is a revision and a substantial enlargement of an article originally published in that journal (vol. 8, no. 2).

We are also indebted to the following publishers for permission to quote passages from their publications: Bobbs-Merrill Co. (William Styron, *Lie Down in Darkness*, Copyright 1951 by William Styron); Doubleday & Co. (J. F. Powers, *Morte D'Urban*, Copyright 1956, 1957, 1960 by James F. Powers); Faber & Faber, and Harcourt, Brace & World (T. S. Eliot, *Collected Poems 1909–1962* ["Marina" quoted in full; Copyright 1936 by Harcourt, Brace & World, and 1963, 1964 by T. S. Eliot]); Faber & Faber, and Harvard University Press (T. S. Eliot, *The Use of Poetry and the Use of Criticism*); Harvard University Press (Version of Tu Jen Shy's Poem 225 in Shih Ching, *The Classic Anthology Defined by Confucius*, translated by Ezra Pound); Liveright Publishing Corporation (*The Collected Poems of Hart Crane*, edited and with an introduction by Waldo Frank); Macmillan Co. (Marianne Moore, *Selected Poems*, Copyright 1935 by Marianne Moore, 1963 by Marianne Moore and T. S. Eliot; and William Butler Yeats, *Collected Poems* ["Deep-Sworn Vow," Copyright 1919 by Macmillan Co., renewed 1946 by Bertha Georgie Yeats; "Leda and the Swan," and "Among School Children," Copyright 1928 by Macmillan Co., renewed 1956 by Bertha Georgie Yeats; "Friends," Copyright

Acknowledgments

1912 by Macmillan Co., renewed 1940 by Bertha Georgie Yeats]); Macmillan & Co. Ltd., and Mr. M. B. Yeats (W. B. Yeats, *Collected Poems*); New Directions (Ezra Pound, *The Cantos*, Copyright 1948 by Ezra Pound); and Random House (William Styron, *Set This House on Fire*).

Index

Algren, Nelson, 29, 30
Andrewes, Lancelot, 242
Aquinas, Thomas, 158, 242
Aristotle, 222
Arnold, Matthew, 243
Auden, W. H., 189, 207

Baal-Shem-Tov, 47
Baldwin, James, 24
Balliett, Whitney, 92
Balthasar, Hans Urs von, 85
Barth, John, 24, 29, 90
Barth, Karl, 3, 13, 14
Baudelaire, Charles Pierre, 16
Baumbach, Jonathan, 68, 78, 195
Beckett, Samuel, 98
Bellow, Saul, 24, 27–57, 60, 87,
    88, 98, 207, 236
Bernanos, Georges, 57
Blackmur, Richard P., 27, 132,
    242, 243
Blake, William, 46
Blotner, Joseph, 114
Bodkin, Maud, 252
Bonhoeffer, Dietrich, 9–13, 235
Borklund, Elmer, 205
Braun, Herbert, 8
Brecht, Bertolt, 16
Brooks, Cleanth, 21, 243
Brown, Norman O., 166
Brustein, Robert, 92
Buber, Martin, 7, 15, 219
Buechner, Frederick, 24
Bultmann, Rudolf, 3, 8, 9, 13, 235
Burke, Kenneth, 22, 242, 243, 252
Burroughs, William, 24

Camus, Albert, 19, 33, 90, 98, 205
Canetti, Elias, 34

Claudel, Paul, 247, 252, 253
Cocteau, Jean, 254
Coffey, Warren, 134, 158 n.
Cooper, James Fenimore, 65
Cowley, Malcolm, 184 n., 205 n.
Cox, Harvey, 179 n., 180, 181
Crane, Hart, 253, 254
Crane, Ronald Salmon, 243
Cullmann, Oscar, 7–8

Dante, 19, 91
De Vries, Peter, 164
Donleavy, J. P., 90
Donne, John, 246, 248
Dos Passos, John, 34
Dostoievski, Fyodor Mikhailovich,
    16, 30, 39, 95, 98, 147, 160
Dowell, Bob, 157 n.
Dreiser, Theodore, 28, 29, 44
Dryden, John, 248
Durrell, Lawrence, 89, 98

Ebeling, Gerhard, 6, 9
Eckhart, Meister, 47
Edwards, Jonathan, 63
Eichrodt, Walther, 7, 9 n.
Eliade, Mircea, 113, 132 n.
Eliot, T. S., 16, 19, 20, 24, 28, 49,
    63, 185, 197, 243, 245, 247,
    249–51
Ellison, Ralph, 24, 29, 60
Empson, William, 243, 252
Erikson, Erik, 3

Farrell, James T., 29
Faulkner, William, 16, 25, 28–29,
    30, 37, 61, 88, 89, 183, 186, 202,
    205
Fergusson, Francis, 157

267

Fitzgerald, F. Scott, 28, 63, 88
French, Warren, 117, 121
Freud, Sigmund, 3, 186
Friedman, Bruce, 90
Frye, Northrop, 21–22, 204, 252
Fuchs, Ernst, 9

Galloway, David, 89
Geismar, Maxwell, 29
Gide, André, 247
Goethe, Johann Wolfgang von, 18
Gogarten, Friedrich, 9
Gold, Herbert, 24
Gold, Ivan, 88
Golding, William, 98
Gollwitzer, Helmut, 11 n.
Goncharov, Ivan Alexandrovich, 39
Gordon, Caroline, 254
Green, Martin, 130
Greenberg, Eliezer, 61 n.
Greene, Graham, 34, 57, 165
Gwynn, Frederick, 114

Hardwick, Elizabeth, 224
Hardy, Thomas, 230
Hare, R. M., 20–21
Hassan, Ihab, 65, 76 n., 110, 119, 120, 160 n.
Hawkes, John, 24, 29, 90, 134, 135 n., 160
Hawthorne, Nathaniel, 30, 61, 63, 65
Hazelton, Roger, 16 n., 200 n.
Hegel, Georg Friedrich Wilhelm, 222
Heim, Karl, 47 n.
Heller, Erich, 20 n.
Heller, Joseph, 88, 90–98, 110–12
Hemingway, Ernest, 28, 37, 65, 88, 89, 230
Henault, Marie J., 177
Herder, Johann Gottfried von, 18
Heschel, Abraham, 7
Hicks, Granville, 224
Hollander, John, 202 n.
Howe, Irving, 61 n., 203–4, 209
Hyman, Stanley Edgar, 139, 147

Ibsen, Henrik, 157

Jacobsen, Josephine, 127 n., 131 n.
James, Henry, 21, 61, 65
Joyce, James, 16, 28, 33, 34, 95, 163

Kafka, Franz, 16, 28, 30, 41, 95, 98
Kauffman, Stanley, 204 n.
Kazin, Alfred, 62 n., 64, 114, 215
Kesey, Ken, 60
Kierkegaard, Sören, 57, 193
Kirvan, John J., 181
Klein, Marcus, 30, 66 n., 72, 83 n.

Lao-tse, 47
Lawrence, D. H., 33
Leavis, F. R., 56, 243
Lévi-Strauss, Claude, 3
Levine, Paul, 119
Lewis, R. W. B., 64, 205, 206 n.
Luther, Martin, 46
Lyly, John, 249

McCarthy, Mary, 231
Mailer, Norman, 29, 206, 211–38
Malamud, Bernard, 24, 29, 59–85, 88, 98, 236
Mallarmé, Stéphane, 240, 253
Malraux, André, 33
Mann, Thomas, 16, 20, 28, 33, 55, 159
Marcel, Gabriel, 47
Marlowe, Christopher, 183
Marquand, John P., 29
Melville, Herman, 30, 63
Merleau-Ponty, Maurice, 3
Meyer, Donald, 3
Michalson, Carl, 5
Miller, James E., Jr., 116, 118, 129 n.
Miller, Samuel H., 46 n.
Milton, John, 2
Mizener, Arthur, 114
Monroe, Harriet, 253
Moore, L. Hugh, 183 n.
Moore, Marianne, 248
Morris, Wright, 60
Mudrick, Marvin, 187, 201 n., 206
Murry, John Middleton, 243
Musil, Robert, 33

Index

Nabokov, Vladimir, 23
Niebuhr, H. Richard, 13
Niebuhr, Reinhold, v, 13
Nietzsche, Friedrich, 205, 220

O'Connor, Mary Flannery, 25, 133–61
O'Connor, William Van, 176
O'Hara, John, 29, 30
Ong, Walter J., S.J., 36
Orwell, George, 29

Pascal, Blaise, 158
Peursen, Cornelis van, 5
Pirandello, Luigi, 27
Plato, 222
Poe, Edgar Allan, 98
Pope, Alexander, 248
Pound, Ezra, 28, 243, 249–50
Powers, J. F., 163–81
Preiss, Théo, 5 n.
Procksch, Otto, 7
Purdy, James, 24
Pynchon, Thomas, 29, 88, 90–91, 98–112

Rabelais, François, 91
Rad, Gerhard von, 7
Rago, Henry, 25
Rahner, Karl, 3
Ransom, John Crowe, 243
Reich, Wilhelm, 221, 229
Richards, I. A., 243
Rilke, Rainer Maria, 16, 28
Rimbaud, Arthur, 240
Roth, Philip, 24, 33, 88
Rowley, H. H., 197 n.
Rubin, Louis D., Jr., 88, 186

Salinger, J. D., 60, 113–32, 133
Santayana, George, 24
Sartre, Jean-Paul, 30, 90, 98, 221
Schlegel, A. W., 18
Schlegel, Friedrich, 18
Scott, Nathan A., Jr., 14 n., 88
Seneca, 250
Sewall, Richard, 183, 191 n., 209
Shakespeare, William, 19, 183
Shaw, Irwin, 30

Sirluck, Ernest, 2
Smith, Ronald Gregor, 4, 8, 14 n., 167, 179 n.
Stern, Richard, 24, 92, 219
Stevens, Wallace, 16, 20, 28
Styron, William, 24, 29, 98, 183–209
Svevo, Italo, 30, 39
Swados, Harvey, 24
Swift, Jonathan, 91

Tanner, Tony, 44–45
Tate, Allen, 243, 246, 254
Tennyson, Alfred, 19
Terence, 15
Tillich, Paul J., v, 3, 9, 13, 126, 129, 130, 235
Trilling, Lionel, 32, 56, 135
Twain, Mark, 30

Updike, John, 88, 133, 236

Vahanian, Gabriel, 165
Valéry, Paul, 20, 28
Vidal, Gore, 220
Voltaire, François Marie Arouet de, 91
Vonnegut, Kurt, 90

Wahl, Jean, 54
Warren, Robert Penn, 30, 33, 37, 43, 243
Weber, Max, 3
Weil, Simone, 47
Whitman, Walt, 27, 59, 60, 61, 63, 64, 85
Wiegand, William, 115, 116 n., 123
Williams, Charles, 230
Wittgenstein, Ludwig, 3, 106
Wolfe, Thomas, 28
Wolfert, Ira, 29
Woolf, Virginia, 36
Wordsworth, William, 248

Yeats, William Butler, 16, 240, 245, 246–47

Zerkovsky, V. V., 147 n., 160 n.